Towards Sustainable Land Use

ALIGNING BIODIVERSITY, CLIMATE AND FOOD POLICIES

OECD
BETTER POLICIES FOR BETTER LIVES

Please cite this publication as:
OECD (2020), *Towards Sustainable Land Use: Aligning Biodiversity, Climate and Food Policies*, OECD Publishing, Paris, *https://doi.org/10.1787/3809b6a1-en*.

ISBN 978-92-64-47801-5 (print)
ISBN 978-92-64-63882-2 (pdf)

Photo credits: Cover © Sunday Stock/Shutterstock.com.

Corrigenda to publications may be found on line at: *www.oecd.org/about/publishing/corrigenda.htm*.

Foreword

Land use is central to many of the environmental and socio-economic issues facing society today. The production of agricultural and forestry goods, which are fundamental to human well-being, has profound consequences for biodiversity and climate change. For example, the Global Assessment by IPBES estimates that 25% of animal and plant species are facing extinction, in part due to the loss and degradation of ecosystems, and the IPCC estimates that 23% of global anthropogenic emissions came from agriculture and land use between 2007 and 2016. Further, a rising global population and changes in consumption patterns towards more carbon-intensive diets are expected to place a growing strain on global land-use systems.

The twin challenges of reversing biodiversity declines and mitigating climate change, while producing sufficient food to ensure zero hunger, must be tackled together. Making land-use systems sustainable is central to achieving these – and other – Sustainable Development Goals.

This report, *Towards Sustainable Land use: Aligning biodiversity, climate and food policies*, provides good practice insights on how governments can transition to more sustainable land-use systems. It draws on experiences and insights across six case study countries, characterised by large agricultural and forestry sectors and associated greenhouse gas emissions, which in many cases also host globally important biodiversity. These countries are Brazil, France, Indonesia, Ireland, Mexico and New Zealand where emissions from agriculture ranged from 13-49% of their total greenhouse gas emissions (excluding land use, land-use change and forestry) in 2016. The report highlights how governments can facilitate the creation of coherent policies for sustainable land use at three important points in the governance process: relevant national strategies and action plans; institutional co-ordination; and the design and implementation of policy instruments (including comprehensive spatial planning).

We need to better understand and manage the synergies and trade-offs inherent in land-use systems, so they can deliver multiple benefits to society and nature. This report is for policy makers and practitioners operating in the land-use, biodiversity, climate and food nexus. I believe it provides valuable guidance on how to help address these challenging, yet crucially important, objectives.

Rodolfo Lacy

OECD Environment Director

Acknowledgements

This publication was prepared by the OECD Environment Directorate, under the leadership of Director Rodolfo Lacy and the subsidiary Climate, Biodiversity and Water Division led by Simon Buckle. The project managers are Katia Karousakis and Jane Ellis. The authors are William Symes, Katia Karousakis and Jane Ellis, with substantive input from Janek Toepper and David Gawith (both formerly ENV/CBW).

The work benefited from the presentations and discussion at the OECD workshop on Biodiversity, Climate Change and Agriculture: Towards Coherent Approaches, held on 25 October, 2017.

The authors would also like to thank the following OECD colleagues for their useful comments and suggestions during the drafting of this publication: Guillaume Gruére, Gwendolyn DeBoe, Santiago Gurrero, Ben Henderson, Jussi Lankoski, Morvarid Bagherzadeh, Urzula Ziebinska (TAD/ARP), Gregoire Garsous (TAD/EPI), Shunta Yamaguchi, Peter Borkey (ENV/EEI), Rob Youngman, Xavier Leflaive, Gerard Bonnis, Hélène Blake, Lisa Danielson, Edward Perry and Simon Buckle (ENV/CBW). Feedback and comments from delegates of the Working Parties on Climate, Investment and Development (WPCID) and Biodiversity, Water and Ecosystems (WPBWE) are gratefully acknowledged, as are comments from the Joint Working Parties on Agriculture and Environment (JWPAE) and Trade and Environment (JWPTE) Nassera Belkhiter, Elodie Prata-Leal and Innes Reale provided administrative support in the preparation of this publication.

The OECD gratefully acknowledges the financial support and detailed review from the Department of Agriculture, Food and the Marine and the Environment Protection Agency of Ireland. The authors would also like to thank the Ministère de la Transition Écologique et Solidaire of France for providing case study information. The views expressed herein can in no way be taken to reflect the official opinion of the Department of Agriculture, Food and the Marine and the Environment Protection Agency of Ireland or the Ministère de la Transition Écologique et Solidaire of France.

Table of contents

Tables

Figures

Boxes

List of Acronyms and Abbreviations

ABC	Agricultura de Baixa Emissão de Carbono (Low-carbon agriculture programme, Brazil)
AES	Agri-Environment Schemes (EU)
AFB	Agence Française pour la Biodiversité (Agency for Biodiversity, France)
AFOLU	Agriculture, Forestry and Other Land Use
ANC	Areas facing Natural Constraints scheme (EU)
BDGP	Beef Data and Genomics Programme (Ireland)
BECCS	Bio-Energy with Carbon Capture and Storage
BRG	Badan Restorasi Gambut (Peatland Restoration Agency, Indonesia)
BUR	Biennial Update Report
CAP	Common Agricultural Policy
CAR	Cadastro Ambiental Rural (Rural Environmental Registry, Brazil)
CBD	Convention on Biological Diversity
CCICCCH	Comisión de Coordinación Intersecretarial de Cambio Climático del Estado de Chiapas (Inter-institutional Co-ordination Commission on Climate Change of the State of Chiapas, Mexico)
CCI-LC	Climate Change Initiative-Land Cover
CCS	Carbon Capture and Storage
CIM	Comitê Interministerial sobre Mudança do Clima (Inter-ministerial Committee on Climate Change, Brazil)
CONABIO	Comisión Nacional para el Conocimiento y Uso de la Biodiversidad (National Commission for knowledge and use of biodiversity, Mexico)
CONAMA	Conselho Nacional do Meio Ambiente (National Environmental Council, Brazil)
CUSTF	Programa de Compensación por Cambio de Uso de Suelo en Terrenos Forestales (Land Use Change in Forest Lands compensation programme, Mexico)
DETER	Detecção de Desmatamento em Tempo Real (Real time deforestation detection, Brazil)
DGF	Dotation Globale de Fonctionnement (fiscal transfer system, France)
DoC	Department of Conservation (New Zealand)

EC	European Commission
EFESE	L'Évaluation Francaise des Écosystèmes et des Services Écosystémiques (French assessment of ecosystems and ecosystem services, France)
EIA	Environmental Impact Assessments
ES	Ecosystem Services
ETS	Emissions Trading Scheme
EUR	Euro
FLW	Food Loss and Waste
FOLU	Forestry and other Land Use
FSC	Forest Stewardship Council
GDP	Gross Domestic Product
GFR	Gross Farm Receipts
GHG	Greenhouse Gas
GIMGC	Comissão Interministerial de Mudança Global do Clima (Inter-ministerial Commission on Global Climate Change, Brazil)
GLAS	Green and Low carbon Agri-environment Scheme (EU)
GLOBIOM	Global Biosphere Management Model
GNFT	Groupe National des Forêts Tropicales (National Group on Tropical Forests, France)
HCV	High Conservation Value
IBSAP	Indonesian Biodiversity Strategy and Action Plan
ICMS-E	Imposto Sobre Circulação de Mercadorias e Serviços – Ecológico ('Ecological Value-Added Tax', Brazil)
IEA	International Energy Agency
IFT	Intergovernmental Fiscal Transfers
IPCC	Intergovernmental Panel on Climate Change
LCA	Life-Cycle Assessment
LEDS	Low Emission Development Strategy
LUCC	Land Use and Land Cover Change
LULUCF	Land Use, Land-Use Change and Forestry
MAA	Ministère de l'Agriculture et de l'Alimentation (Ministry of Agriculture and Nutrition, France)
MAES	Mapping and Assessment of Ecosystems and their Services (EU)
MFC	Mexico Forest Certification (MFC)
MPI	Ministry for Primary Industries
MRV	Monitoring, Reporting and Verification
MTES	Ministère de la Transition Écologique et Solidaire (Ministry for an ecological and solidarity transition, France)

MXN	Mexican Peso
NBS	National Biodiversity Strategy
NBSAP	National Biodiversity Strategy and Action Plan
NC	National Communication
NDP	National Development Plan (Ireland)
NRS	Natural Resources Sector (New Zealand)
NSO	National Strategic Outcome
OG	Origin Green (Ireland)
PA	Protected areas
PCET	Plan Climat-air-Énergie Territorial (Territorial climate-energy plan, France)
PECC	Programa Especial de Cambio Climático (General law on climate change, Mexico)
PEFC	Programme for the Endorsement of Forest Certification
PES	Payment for Ecosystem Services
PPA	Plano Plurianual (Multi-Year Development Plan, Brazil)
PRODES	Programa de Cálculo do Desflorestamento da Amazônia (Amazon Deforestation Monitoring Program, Brazil)
PSAH	Programa de Servicios Ambientales Hidrológicos (Payments for hydrological environmental services, Mexico)
PSE	Producer Support Estimate
RAN-GRK	Rencana Aksi Nasional Penurunan Emisi Gas Rumah Kaca (National Action Plan for Reducing Greenhouse Gas Emissions, Indonesia)
REDD+	Reducing Emissions from Deforestation and Forest Degradation and the role of conservation, sustainable management of forests and enhancement of forest carbon stocks in developing countries
REFIT	Renewable Energy Feed-in Tariff scheme (Ireland)
RPJMN	Rencana Pembangunan Jangka Menengah Nasional (National Medium Term Development Plan, Indonesia)
RSPO	Round Table on Sustainable Palm Oil
SAGARPA	Secretaría de Agricultura, Ganadería, Desarrollo Rural, Pesca y Alimentación (Ministry of Agriculture, Livestock, Rural Development, Fisheries and Food, Mexico)
SDGs	Sustainable Development Goals
SEA	Strategic Environmental Assessments
SEEA	System of Environmental-Economic Accounting
SGAE	Secrétariat Général des Affaires Européennes (General Secretariat of European Affairs, France)
SISNERLING	System of Integrated Environmental and Economic Accounting (Indonesia)
SMART	Specific, Measurable, Actionable, Realistic and Time-bound

SNBC	Stratégie Nationale Bas-Carbone (National Low-Carbon Strategy, France)
SNUC	Sistema Nacional de Unidades de Conservação (National System of Units of Conservation, Brazil)
SSP	Shared Socioeconomic Pathways
TORA	Tanah Objek Reforma Agraria (Programme of Agrarian Reform, Indonesia)
TVB	Trames Verts et Bleus (Green and Blue belt networks, France)
UNFCCC	United Nations Framework Convention on Climate Change
UNFF	United Nations Forum on Forests
USD	US Dollars
VAT	Value Added Tax
VNRs	Voluntary National Reviews
WAVES	Wealth Accounting and the Value of Ecosystem Services

Executive Summary

Land use is central to many of the environmental and socio-economic issues facing society. Globally, greenhouse gas emissions from the agricultural and land-use sectors account for 23% of anthropogenic emissions, and the loss and degradation of terrestrial ecosystems threatens 25% of animal and plant species with extinction. With global population projected to grow to nearly 10 billion people by 2050, food production will need to increase significantly. Additionally, global action on climate change will likely include substantial increases in energy production from biomass – further increasing the pressures on global land-use systems. Given the inter-connected nature of these biodiversity, climate, land and food-related challenges, co-ordination and coherence between different government policies affecting the land-use nexus is crucial.

This report examines on-going challenges for aligning land-use policy with biodiversity, climate and food objectives and the opportunities to enhance the sustainability of land-use systems. The report looks at six countries with relatively large agricultural and forestry sectors and associated greenhouse gas emissions, many of which also host globally important biodiversity. These countries are Brazil, France, Indonesia, Ireland, Mexico and New Zealand. The report first highlights some key data relevant to this nexus. It then examines opportunities and challenges in three areas: coherence across relevant national strategies and plans, institutional co-ordination, and policy instruments relevant to the land-use nexus.

Key Findings

Coherence across relevant national strategies and plans

Land use is considered separately in national plans such as those on development, climate, biodiversity, and agriculture across all case study countries. The prominence of land-use issues covered in different national strategies relevant to this nexus, and the degree of coherence between the strategies, varies substantially across countries. Overall, few of the national strategies and plans examined are specific enough to facilitate coherent action on this nexus by the various Ministries (and other stakeholders) involved. Moreover, although misalignments across national strategies exist, few national strategies explicitly acknowledge this.

Recommendations

- Prepare national strategies and plans in a consultative and co-ordinated manner, with engagement from all the relevant Ministries and other key stakeholders. This is essential to identify potential synergies and misalignments in the overarching objectives. A good practice example is the National Planning Framework for Ireland, the creation of which included a cross-departmental steering group and a national consultation process.
- Ensure strategies and action plans have targets that are specific, measurable, actionable, realistic, and time-bound (SMART). More specific and measurable targets, in particular, will improve the ability to assess the coherence between them. Further, developing indicators to monitor progress towards the targets would enhance transparency and accountability.

- Identify, assess and consider how to address any transboundary impacts associated with national strategies relevant to the land-use nexus (e.g. French plan to eliminate deforestation from supply chains).

Institutional co-ordination and coherence

Both weak institutional co-ordination and overly complex institutional arrangements contribute to policy misalignments. Relevant decision-making power in the land-use, nexus is split between different institutions of national governments, sub-national governments, and private actors, including those who produce, trade or retail nexus-relevant products in multiple countries. This split complicates the implementation of policies through poor horizontal and vertical co-ordination and differing institutional priorities and capacities. Several of the case study countries are working to improve co-ordination of relevant policies in the land-use nexus, in part by intensifying co-ordination of national and sub-national ministries.

Recommendations

- Strengthen institutional co-ordination between different ministries responsible for land-use issues related to climate, biodiversity, food, both horizontally (at national level) and vertically (between different levels of government). Leadership from the top (i.e. the office of the President, Prime Minister or cabinet) is crucial in developing consistent and co-ordinated policies for sustainable land use. National governments should clearly define the roles and mandates of different institutions as they relate to land use.
- Improve policy co-ordination mechanisms. Setting up a cross-cutting body, for example in response to the Sustainable Development Goals, long-term low-emission development strategies, or institutionalising co-ordination processes such as via inter-ministerial committees can help improve coherence (e.g. as between the French ministries of agriculture and food, and ministry for an ecological and solidarity transition).

Policy instruments relevant to the land-use nexus

The range of policy instruments utilised in the land-use nexus is broad and their interactions with each other and wider governance systems are multifaceted. Despite this variety, there are common themes. Firstly, the effective implementation of policy instruments for sustainable land use requires clearly defined and enforced land tenure. Secondly, across the case study countries, the negative externalities associated with certain types of land use remain largely unpriced or under-priced – meaning the benefits provided by ecosystems to society, except food production, are generally not reflected in land-use policy.

In contrast, government support for agricultural production is significant (with the exception of New Zealand). This support includes subsidies that can incentivise unsustainable practices and the expansion of agriculture. Thirdly, quantitative, national-level targets or policies for reducing land-use impacts associated with both food loss and waste and international trade in agricultural and forestry products are lacking (with the exception of France).

Recommendations

- Support and intensify land reform efforts (most notably in Brazil and Indonesia) to ensure security of tenure, especially for indigenous and other vulnerable communities, and sustainable, inclusive land use.
- Integrate spatial data into land-use decisions better (e.g. Indonesia's One Map). This aids the design and implementation of the broad mix of policy instruments required to manage land-use systems (e.g. protected areas, environmental impact assessments and spatial planning).

- Apply economic instruments, such as taxes and fees and charges, more broadly to price environmentally damaging practices. Economic instruments can enhance the effectiveness of existing regulatory approaches, by providing incentives to stakeholders to invest in more sustainable practices (e.g. pesticide taxes in Mexico and France).
- Reassess the balance of support between the relevant ecosystem services from land (e.g. food, carbon, biodiversity, water). A good first step is the reform of potentially market-distorting and environmentally harmful agricultural support, which New Zealand has implemented.
- Monitor and enforce regulations in a consistent and regular manner. Land-use policies can otherwise cease to function effectively and previous environmental gains can be reversed.

1 Towards sustainable land use: key issues, interactions and trade-offs in the land-use nexus

Understanding where and how the different elements of the land-use, biodiversity, climate and food nexus interact is key for policy alignment. This chapter examines the issues, interactions, trade-offs and synergies that need to be considered. It highlights the biophysical interactions and their implications, economic approaches to decision-making in the nexus and makes the case for policy coherence. The chapter also summarises the key findings of the report on how to promote coherence across national strategies and action plans, institutions and policy instruments.

Global land use is currently unsustainable. As global populations rise and economies develop, the demands placed on land-use systems will further increase. Consequently, providing sufficient food, mitigating greenhouse gas (GHG) emissions, storing carbon in ecosystems and addressing biodiversity loss is challenging. Historic land-use change globally, predominantly from the expansion and intensification of agriculture, has resulted in widespread declines in biodiversity, with around 25% of animal and plant species now threatened with extinction (Díaz et al., 2019[1]), the degradation of 74% of the world's terrestrial surface (IPBES, 2018[2]), and significant GHG emissions.

As the pressures on land-use systems increase, the need for transformative change to address unsustainable land-use practices is growing. There is a growing body of evidence on current and expected impacts of consumption patterns (see e.g. (Willett et al., 2019[3]) and (The Economics of Ecosystems and Biodiversity (TEEB), 2018[4])). Nevertheless, the understanding of what constitutes a sustainable land-use system and what institutions, strategies and policies are required to create it at global, national and regional levels, is still evolving.

Multiple interlinked challenges and the need for coherent and co-ordinated action

Governments are faced with multiple and overlapping challenges, including improving livelihoods, tackling climate change, mitigating biodiversity loss and addressing food insecurity, shortages and waste. To address these interconnected challenges, governments would benefit from national strategies and plans, institutions and policies that provide coherence between these areas. Looking across these three elements, this report assesses the interactions, potential synergies and trade-offs between climate mitigation, sustainable ecosystems management and food security in the land-use sector[1]. Drawing on experiences and insights across six countries, the report examines both supply-side and demand-side policies, and aims to identify best practices and options for aligning these issues in the land-use sector.

Land-use systems and management play a crucial role in achieving several of the Sustainable Development Goals (SDGs), including those on ending hunger (SDG 2), clean water (SDG 6), clean energy (SDG 7), climate action (SDG 13), and life on land (SDG 15). Effective land-use management is also critically important for meeting climate goals under the UNFCCC's Paris Agreement and the Aichi biodiversity targets under the Convention on Biological Diversity (CBD). GHG emissions from the land-use sector are significant, accounting for 17% of total anthropogenic GHG emissions in 2014 (Figure 1.1) (CAIT Climate Data Explorer, 2017[5]). Moreover, approximately 80% of all threatened terrestrial bird and mammal species are imperilled by agriculturally driven habitat loss (Tilman et al., 2017[6]). Agriculture is a major source of nitrous oxide emissions, which is a greenhouse gas and the dominant anthropogenic cause of ozone depletion (Ravishankara, Daniel and Portmann, 2009[7]). Agriculture also accounts for an estimated 70% of total freshwater withdrawal worldwide (OECD, 2018[8]) and is a significant source of phosphorous and nitrogen pollution.

More specifically, CO_2 emissions (and to a lesser extent N_2O) need to peak as soon as possible and then fall sharply to meet the Paris Agreement's goals. The Paris Agreement calls explicitly for all countries to "take action to conserve and enhance, as appropriate, sinks and reservoirs of greenhouse gases as referred to in Article 4, paragraph 1(d), of the Convention, including forests", and "take action to implement and support" REDD+. The Paris Agreement also recognises the importance of safeguarding food security, and the vulnerability of food production systems to climate change. Even when accounting for food security constraints, REDD+ and reforestation are potentially very important for mitigating CO_2 emissions from land use (Griscom et al., 2017[9]). Grassi et al. (2017[10]) show that full implementation of (Intended) Nationally Determined Contributions ((I)NDCs) submitted by countries for UNFCCC COP21 would turn land use from a global net anthropogenic source during 1990-2010 (1.3 +/- 1.1GtCO$_2$e/yr) to a net sink of carbon by 2030 (up to -1.1 +/- 0.5GtCO$_2$e/yr).

Reaching the long-term goals of the Paris Agreement is also likely to require the considerable use of biomass-based energy, as well as sequestration by land-based sinks. For example, the IEA project that biomass energy use would triple between 2015 and 2060, doubling its share of the total energy mix to reach 22% in a scenario that limits temperature increases to two degrees above pre-industrial levels (IEA, 2017[11]). The implications for land use are even more pronounced under the IPCC scenarios to keep global warming below 1.5 degrees, which estimate an additional 0-600 million ha of land will be required for bioenergy crops by 2050 relative to 2010 (IPCC, 2018[12]). The additional land for bioenergy crops is predicted to come from a reduction in pasture areas and represents a significant transformation of land-use systems. The extent to which these scenarios rely on bioenergy crops depends to some extent on the reliance on bio-energy with carbon capture and storage (BECCS) technology. But where increased use of bioenergy is required, it is likely to have significant implications for land use (Creutzig et al., 2014[13])[2], and the increased use of bioenergy may increase pressure on land, water, food systems, biodiversity and ecosystems. However, the IPCC notes "there is still low agreement on these interactions", and there are local niches where different objectives can be successfully balanced (de Coninck et al., 2018, p. 324[14]).

Figure 1.1. Greenhouse gas emissions by sector (2014)

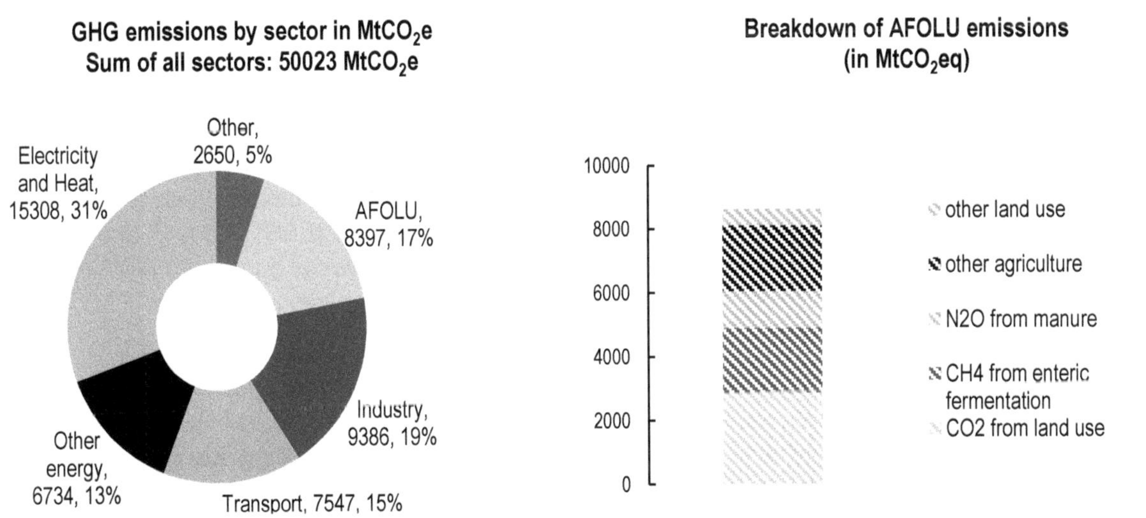

Source: CAIT (2017[5]), *Country Greenhouse Gas Emissions* (database), http://cait.wri.org/ and FAOSTAT (2018[15]), *Food and Agriculture data* (database), http://www.fao.org/faostat/ .

Land use, agriculture and forests are also key to meeting several of the Aichi Biodiversity Targets under the CBD and are also likely to remain important in the CBD's post-2020 biodiversity framework. Aichi Target 5 for example states: "By 2020, the rate of loss of all natural habitats, including forests, is at least halved and where feasible brought close to zero, and degradation and fragmentation is significantly reduced" and Target 7 is: "By 2020 areas under agriculture, aquaculture and forestry are managed sustainably, ensuring conservation of biodiversity".

More generally, ecosystems provide an array of goods and services that contribute to human well-being. Land-use decisions alter ecosystems, ranging from minor and reversible changes to complete and non-reversible transformation of natural and human-dominated landscapes (Adams, Pressey and Álvarez-Romero, 2016[16]). Ecosystems provide services such as food provisioning, forage, and bioenergy, and thus contribute to livelihoods. Ecosystems also provide services such as nutrient cycling, water quality, habitat provision for biodiversity, and carbon sequestration. These latter services provide benefits that are more difficult to quantify in monetary terms and therefore frequently underestimated, though the values can be very high. Climate change also affects ecosystems, in various ways, including geographic shifts, changing their composition, and disrupting functioning.

Policies to ensure sustainable land use, therefore, need to account for – and be synergistic with – other nationally and internationally agreed objectives in the areas of food security, climate, biodiversity and forests, amongst others, and contribute to national development goals. Climate change itself will have impacts on the ability of land to store carbon, the productivity of land (in particular, changing levels of water availability are expected to significantly impact on agricultural production) and on the resilience of ecosystems. And projected increasing levels of reactive nitrogen (compounds that support plant growth) will influence the storage of carbon by ecosystems.

Besides competition between different land uses, there may be conflicts between the policy goals of mitigating climate change and reducing biodiversity loss. Certain monoculture plantations, for example, have a greater carbon uptake per hectare than a mixed forest. However, planting monocultures can have negative local impacts, such as reducing biodiversity, or impacting the nitrogen cycle (Smith et al., 2014[17]). If plantations replace tropical forests, they can lead to significant carbon losses, particularly in the short term (e.g. from losses in soil carbon), though a significant fraction of the CO_2 emitted remains in the atmosphere for thousands of years (Archer et al., 2009[18]).

The trends in land-use change and emissions, and their underlying drivers, vary considerably across regions and countries (see Chapter 2). Demand for agricultural land (predominantly for food or livestock feed) places large pressure on forests, notably in developing countries. If demand for bioenergy also rises, this could further exacerbate competition for land. There was a net forest loss globally of seven million hectares per year in 2000-2010 (approximately the size of Belgium and Netherlands combined), and a net gain in agricultural lands of 6 million hectares per year (FAO, 2016[19]). Indeed, despite the continual intensification of agricultural production over the last several decades (FAO, 2011[20]), the majority of deforestation between 2000 and 2010 was driven by large-scale commercial agriculture (40% of the total) and subsistence agriculture (33% of the total) (OECD, 2016[21]). However, according to FAO (2018[22]), the rate of forest loss slowed between 2010-2015.

Almost all deforestation in 2000-2010 was in the tropics whereas forested areas in temperate regions actually increased (FAO, 2016[19]). The loss of tropical forest is significant, as these forests contain proportionally more biodiversity than temperate forest. For example, despite covering only 7% of the Earth's surface, tropical forests contain around 50% of all animal and plant species. In some countries (e.g. Korea, Portugal), both agricultural land and forests have shrunk since 2000. In contrast, some other countries (e.g. UK, Chile) have increased both agricultural and forested areas (FAO, 2016[19]; UCS, 2014[23]). Where countries have increased both agricultural land and forested areas, this is often the result of converting grassland or bare land, which could have negative consequences for biodiversity (Haščič and Mackie, 2018[24]).

The competition in land use between forest and agriculture will be exacerbated by the projected rise in world population to 9.7 billion people by 2050, the consequent increase in food demand and changing consumption patterns towards more carbon intensive diets (OECD, 2016[25]; United Nations, Department of Economic and Social Affairs, Population Division, 2019[26]). The OECD (2012[27]) projects a continued decline in the area of primary forests to 2050 (Figure 1.2), although the level of total forest area is expected to grow slightly.[3] A decline in primary forests would have adverse impacts on biodiversity, carbon storage, lead to significant emissions and negatively impact the welfare of local communities that depend on the forests for primary consumption and other resources.

Competition for land use will be intensified further if land is needed for the production of biofuel (e.g. for transport) or other biomass. The extent of such competition would vary considerably, depending on the type of bioenergy use assumed (IPCC, 2018[12]). Thus, bioenergy land use would be much higher if a large proportion is first-generation bioenergy (produced from crops), than if bioenergy was second generation (produced from agricultural residues and waste or forest residues) or third generation (from engineered energy crops such as algae).

Figure 1.2. Global forest area change baseline (2010-2050)

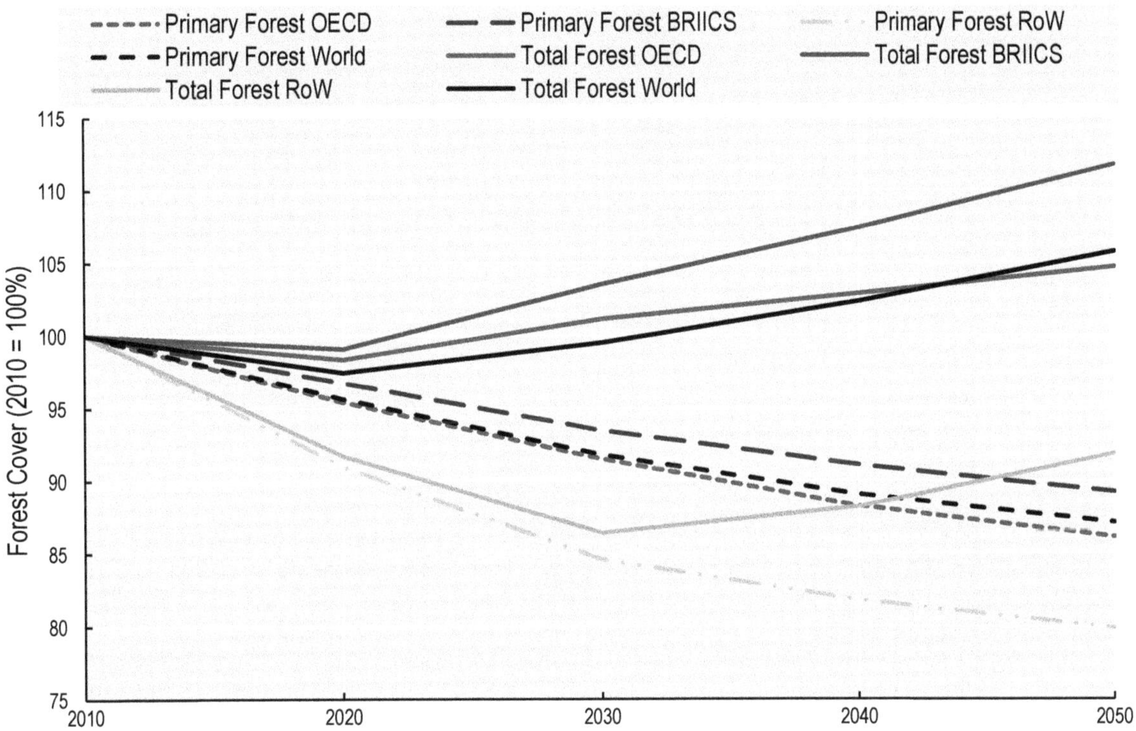

Source: OECD (2012[27]) *OECD Environmental Outlook to 2050*, http://dx.doi.org/10.1787/9789264122246-en.

Emissions from land use, land use change and forestry (LULUCF) play a much larger role in some countries than in others (see Chapter 2). LULUCF was responsible for a particularly large share of total national emissions in some countries, including Indonesia and Brazil.

In the OECD, agricultural production volume increased by an average of 1.6% per year between 1990-2010, while GHG emissions intensity of agriculture declined by an average of 2% per year over the same timeframe (OECD, 2014[28]). This was achieved by switching to cost-effective practices such as more efficient fertilisation and input that reduces nitrous oxide emissions. Technical solutions to address potential risks to agricultural yields from climate change exist, though further efforts will be needed at national, sector and farm level to ensure a productive and resilient agricultural sector (OECD, 2014[28]). Projections to 2050 under a business-as-usual scenario have been developed for terrestrial biodiversity, measured by Mean Species Abundance.[4] The projections suggest the decrease in mean species abundance will go from 34% in 2010 to 38%, 43% and 46% in 2050 under three different Shared Socioeconomic Pathways (SSP) scenarios (Figure 1.3).

Figure 1.3. Pressure on global diversity, under different scenarios, compared to natural conditions

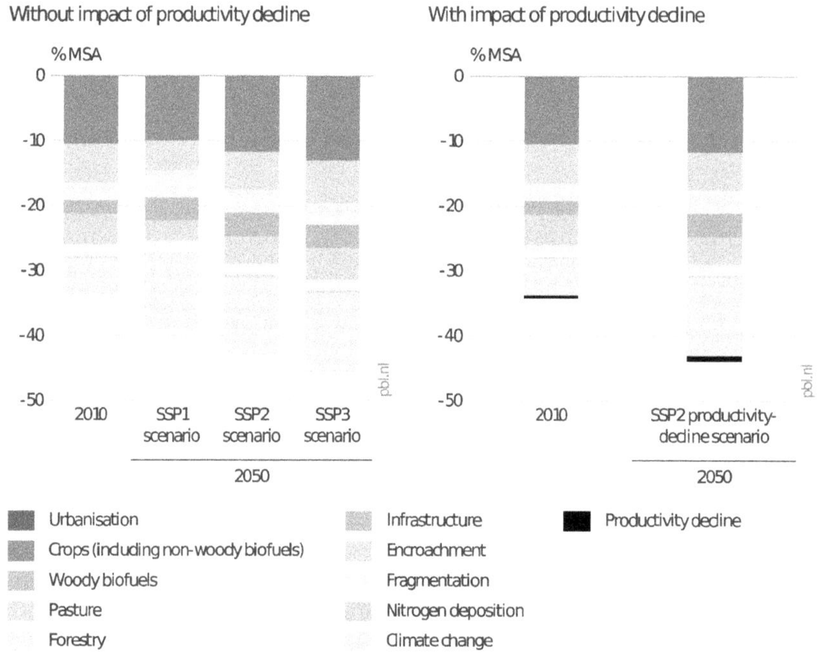

Source: Van der Esch et al (2017[29]), Exploring future changes in land use and land condition and the impacts on food, water, climate change and biodiversity: Scenarios for the Global Land Outlook, https://www.pbl.nl/sites/default/files/cms/publicaties/pbl-2017-exploring-future-changes-in-land-use-and-land-condition-2076b.pdf

Note: MSA is an indicator of naturalness or biodiversity intactness. It is defined as the mean abundance of original species relative to their abundance in undisturbed ecosystems. An MSA of 0% means a completely destroyed ecosystem, with no original species remaining.

Biophysical interactions and their implications

An evaluation of potential synergies and trade-offs between climate mitigation, ecosystems management and food security[5] in the land sector is crucial to ensure a coherent response and help policy-makers at both national and sub-national levels to make better-informed policy choices. A first step is to explicitly identify the biophysical interactions between different aspects of this nexus.

Recent literature (e.g. (Bustamante et al., 2014[30]; Power, 2010[31]; Munaretto and Witmer, 2017[32]; The Royal Society, 2007[33]; Cramer et al., 2017[34]; Delzeit et al., 2016[35]; ICSU, 2017[36])) has highlighted different strengths of biophysical synergies and trade-offs, as well as variation in the strength of these synergies and trade-offs in different contexts. Munaretto and Witmer (2017[32]) and the ICSU (2017[36]) assigned scores estimating the direction and strengths of various interactions, based on expert opinion. In some areas, there are no or only limited interactions. For example, a supply-side action such as improving agricultural resource efficiency is unlikely to impact a demand-side action such as reducing food waste. However, in other areas, interactions can be significant – and either positive or negative (see below and Table 1.1). The extent of such interaction can be influenced by site-specific issues, as well as by policies.

For the purposes of this analysis, these interactions are characterised as:

- Strong synergies. For example, maintaining or expanding native forest cover, in some regions[6], will maintain or increase carbon stocks and therefore mitigate GHG emissions, prevent a decline in soil quality (soil degradation), and will protect or enhance biodiversity and other ecosystem services provided by forests.
- Either synergies or trade-offs depending on how a particular issue is addressed.[7] For example, intensifying food production could either reinforce or impede GHG mitigation efforts. Intensifying

livestock farming can help to reduce GHG emissions from livestock by allowing for manure management systems to be put in place.[8] In contrast some measures to intensify food production could increase emissions of GHG, e.g. via a higher use of fertilisers and associated N_2O emissions, or increased energy-related GHG emissions from increased use of farming machinery.

Key synergies and trade-offs are presented in Table 1.1. This highlights that there are many win-win synergies in the land-use nexus (i.e. positive scores). It also highlights that in some areas, impacts can range from positive to negative (depending on how the action is carried out), or can just involve trade-off (i.e. negative scores).

Ranges from positive to negative impacts can occur, for example, in the context of efforts to meet the growing demand for food. If this is met via expansion of agricultural land via conversion from forests, this could lead to increased GHG emissions, increased soil degradation, and reduction in biodiversity. Alternatively, efforts could be made to meet increased food demand by intensifying agricultural production, i.e. to further decrease the yield gap. This gap can be considerable for production of key crops in some areas (Fischer, Byerlee and Esmeades, 2014[37]), and reducing the gap may reduce pressures on land conversion, thus leading to positive impacts on biodiversity (however there is still considerable debate on this point - see (Phalan et al., 2011[38])).

Considering the spatial dependence of impacts is key to ensure the delivery of win-wins. Delivering both climate mitigation and biodiversity presents a good example of the spatial dependence of impacts. The biodiversity value of habitat does not scale linearly with area, so large contiguous areas of habitat will deliver greater biodiversity benefits than an equivalent area contained in discontinuous fragments, due edge and other fragmentation effects (e.g. forests, savannah, wetlands) (Haddad et al., 2015[39]). However, carbon sequestration is generally aspatial, thus small patches of land managed for carbon sequestration (such as forest) can deliver similar carbon sequestration to a large contiguous area of the same extent and land cover type, but without providing the same biodiversity benefits (Nelson et al., 2008[40]). Hence, managing land to deliver biodiversity benefits will provide a co-benefit for GHG mitigation, but managing land for GHG mitigation may not provide biodiversity co-benefits (or those benefits will be limited) if the result is an increase in small fragmented areas of forest.

Table 1.1. Selected synergies and trade-offs in the land-use, biodiversity, climate and food nexus

	Affecting								
Affected	**GHG mitigation**	**Expand biofuel production**	**Prevent soil degradation**	**Maintain and expand forest cover**	**Prevent expansion of agricultural land**	**Improve agricultural resource efficiency**	**Intensify food production**	**Reduce food waste and food loss**	**Protect biodiversity and ecosystems[1]**
GHG mitigation		2/-1	2	3	2	2/-1	-2/1	2	2/3
Expand biofuel production	2/-1			1/-1	-1				-1
Prevent soil degradation	2	0/-1		2	2	1	-1/0		2
Maintain and expand forest cover	2	0/-2	2/-1		3		2		2
Prevent expansion of agricultural land	2/0	0/-2	2/-1	2/-1		1	2	1/2	2
Improve agricultural resource efficiency	2		2	2/0			-1/2	0/2	-1/1
Intensify food production		0/-1	-1			2/0			-1/1
Reduce food waste and food loss					1/2				2/3
Protect biodiversity and ecosystems	3/-1	-1	2	3	3	1	-2	1	

Note: The ICSU scoring system is as follows:

+ 3: Indivisible: one objective is inextricably linked to the achievement of another
+2: Reinforcing: one objective directly creates conditions that lead to the achievement of another objective
+1: Enabling: the pursuit of one objective enables the achievement of another objective
0: Consistent: no significant interaction, or interactions that are neither positive nor negative.
-1: Constraining: when the pursuit of one objective sets a condition or a constraint on the achievement of another.
-2: Counteracting: the pursuit of one objective counteracts another objective.
-3: Cancelling: progress in one goal makes it impossible to reach another goal.

The table was compiled using this seven-point ICSU scoring framework that identifies causal and functional relations between specific issues. Blank cells indicate no or limited interaction.

[1] This category considers actions to protect biodiversity and ecosystems that does not include the expansion and maintenance of forest cover

Source: Authors based on Munaretto and Witmer (2017[32]), *Water-land-energy-food-climate nexus: policies and policy coherence at European and international scales*, https://www.pbl.nl/sites/default/files/cms/publicaties/WP2_Deliverable%202.1_15nov17_FINAL.pdf and *ICSU* (2017[36]), *A Framework for Understanding Sustainable Development Goal Interactions*, https://sustainabledevelopment.un.org/?menu=1300..

The economics of optimal land use

There are strong economic, social and environmental rationales for optimising land use. Globally, ecosystems services were estimated at a value of USD 125-140 trillion (in 2011) (Costanza et al., 2014[41]), higher than the total estimate of GDP in that year. The potential costs of mismanagement in the land-use sector are therefore high. Land degradation[9] currently has negative impacts on the well-being of an estimated 3.2 billion people worldwide (IPBES, 2018[2]). The estimated global costs of land degradation vary widely.[10] When the costs associated with lost agricultural production, diminished livelihoods, and the lost value of ecosystem services (e.g. clean water and air, erosion prevention and nutrient cycling)[11] are included, degradation is estimated to cost up to USD 10.6 trillion every year (ELD Initiative, 2013[42]). This is equivalent to 17% of global gross domestic product.

Landscapes are not static, but rather dynamic systems with significant feedbacks between people and the environment. Therefore, land-use systems must deliver both socially-desirable and environmentally-sustainable outcomes. Understanding the best configuration of land use in a given landscape is challenging from both a technical and policy perspective. Land use should aim to maximise the delivery of ecosystem services, to ensure the maximum societal and environmental benefit is derived from a given landscape. However, trade-offs between the land-uses required to deliver different services mean decisions must be made regarding which services to prioritise in a landscape (IPBES, 2018[2]). For example, maximising food production can negatively impact habitats (and biodiversity), or maximising carbon sequestration can alter the availability of water. While maintaining and enhancing the flows of ecosystem services is important, understanding how to use land to maintain the natural capital stocks which underpin these flows is also crucial (Cowie et al., 2018[43]). Given the increasing impact of climate change on both environmental and human systems, what constitutes optimal land use in a given landscape will change over time, making adaptive management approaches essential for ensuring sustainability.

From an economic perspective, optimal land use entails maximising the net present value of social benefits at global, regional or local scales. However, in practice, measuring the net present value of global social benefits is challenging given the difficulties of comparing market values (e.g. food production) and non-market values (e.g. recreation, habitat provision). Further, the value of social benefits derived from land-use depend on the scale at which they are measured, so the land-use which corresponds to maximum social benefits at local scales may be different to the land-use required to maximize global-scale social benefits (and vice versa). There has been significant progress on incorporating non-market values into economic decision tools, such as cost benefit analysis (for full discussion see (OECD, 2018[44])). However, valuation of non-market goods remains challenging and economic models based on monetary values can fail to adequately account for the societal and cultural values of some ecosystem services.

To address the issue of comparability, multi-criteria decision analysis (MCDA) has been developed to allow the inclusion of data from various sources (e.g. economic, ecological, stakeholder opinions) into quantitative decision making models and has been used extensively for land use (Kaim, Cord and Volk, 2018[45]). MCDA techniques are more flexible that traditional economic decisions methods and can be used to identify win-wins in land use, where economic, social and environmental goals align (e.g. (Dwyer et al., 2009[46]) or where current land use plans could be improved (Kennedy et al., 2016[47]). But, understanding the desired outcomes for land use from social, economic and environmental perspectives (including ecosystem services and natural capital) and how they influence each other at national and local scales is a key prerequisite for using MCDA (Kaim, Cord and Volk, 2018[45]).

Many analyses estimate the environmental or human welfare impact of expected global land use and land cover change (e.g. (IPBES, 2018[2]). While useful for identifying opportunities for optimising land-use at a broad scale, these assessments often do not reflect the variety of land uses nor the local scale biophysical and economic conditions within countries, and thus likely do not reflect land-use realities at a local and landscape level. A comprehensive model is the Global Biosphere Management Model (GLOBIOM) (Havlik et al., 2014[48]), a partial equilibrium model that covers the agricultural and forestry sectors, including the bioenergy sector. Other tools are also evolving, such as InVEST (Integrated Valuation of Ecosystem Services and Trade-offs), from the Natural Capital Project, which enables assessment of trade-offs in ecosystem services at a more local scale.[12]

International trade

International trade in goods and services is of fundamental importance to land use, climate mitigation, ecosystems and food globally. At the macro level, international trade can, in theory, contribute to positive land-use outcomes through various mechanisms. By allowing the production of forest and agricultural products in the most suitable places, for instance, international trade could potentially increase global production efficiency. Through allocative efficiency, increased competition, and incentives for R&D, international trade can, in theory, contribute to reducing the net environmental impact of a given level of production (Blanco G. et al., 2014[49]), thereby enhancing resource efficiency and the transition to a circular economy. In addition, international trade plays an important role in global food security (Tallard, Liapis and Pilgrim, 2016[50]).

In practice, however, by shifting production sites and patterns, international trade can drive dynamics leading to adverse outcomes at the local level, for at least some dimensions of the land-use, biodiversity, climate and food nexus (henceforth referred to as the land-use nexus). Trade exerts land-use impacts in the case study countries by increasing international demand for land-related products such as agricultural commodities and forest products, which can be produced domestically. Supply-side responses to demand increases drive agricultural expansion (e.g. in Brazil, Indonesia) and agricultural intensification (e.g. in France, Mexico, New Zealand, Ireland). Effective policies for managing land-use domestically are need to prevent the supply side responses leading to increased GHG emissions, biodiversity loss and increased pollution. These impacts often originate from incorrectly priced externalities, undermining the maximisation of global social benefits. These shifts in the production of agricultural goods as a consequence of international trade have resulted in some of the burden of the environmental impacts of production moving from the developed world to the developing world (Krausmann and Langthaler, 2019[51]).

Unless carefully managed at the domestic level, the inherent trade-offs between domestic polices for controlling environmental impacts and the promotion of products for export can result in policy misalignments. Further, exclusive reliance on the internationally agreed method of counting GHG emissions at the point of production (rather than consumption) can mask climate impacts of production systems and consumption choices that are inefficient from a GHG emissions perspective, in particular from induced land-use change. For instance, because emissions embodied in imported intermediate inputs (such as animal feed) are not associated with final outputs (such as beef or dairy), production systems with significant upstream emissions can appear less emissions-intensive than they indeed are (see also Box 2.1).[13] At the same time, awareness of consuming countries' responsibility for nexus outcomes in producing countries, and their impacts abroad that their consumption and policy choices can have, is growing. This is particularly true for national policies relating to global goods such as climate mitigation and biodiversity protection.

The need for coherent frameworks

Coherent land-use frameworks are key for informing the decisions made by governments, corporations and society. Setting up coherent frameworks can be facilitated at key entry points in the decision-making process. One is via the establishment of national strategies or plans, which aim to provide a shared vision and objectives of where a country wishes to transition towards. The institutional framework within a country, and the degree of oversight, collaboration and interaction in policy areas or sectors that have impacts on each other, will also likely impact on how decisions are made. These two elements, national strategies and institutional co-ordination, will ultimately also impact on the policy-making process and the resulting policy instruments that are adopted, or how existing policy instruments are revised, to take account of trade-offs and so as to maximise synergies.

Policies relating to land use, biodiversity, climate and food can impact multiple other areas such as economic development, health, poverty eradication and trade. Many countries have explicitly recognised these interlinkages, e.g. in the "voluntary national reviews" (VNRs) (UNDESA, 2017[52]) prepared to review progress to the SDGs, and are increasing institutional co-ordination as a result. Many countries' VNRs also recognise the institutional, financial, environmental and other challenges in meeting these challenges.

Multiple types of policies can be used to improve environmental outcomes and policy alignment in the land use nexus. Details of policy design and implementation can exacerbate or mitigate biophysical trade-offs. For example, a country may have in place both incentives for food production from specific crops, and incentives to maintain or expand forestry. The impact of these incentives will depend on their relative level, coverage and ease of access.

Trade-offs and synergies in the land-use nexus are, however, broader than biophysical ones. Indeed, there are synergies and trade-offs at and across varying dimensions, including:

- At the level of an individual farm. For example, increased use of agroforestry systems (when trees are planted in combination with crops) can improve resilience to climate impacts such as drought or extreme heat because of the shade provided by the trees. However, this shade can also reduce crop yields.
- Between different spatial scales (including sub-national and transboundary impacts). For example, increased consumption of water for agriculture upstream can increase upstream agricultural yields, but reduce water availability and agricultural yields downstream.
- Over time. For example, leaving crop residues onsite will reduce the potential for bioenergy production in the short term, but can avoid a reduction in soil fertility in the longer-term.
- Between different groups of stakeholders. For example, if intensifying food production leads to increased nitrate pollution in surface water, then this could negatively affect water quality for downstream populations and ecosystems. However, by increasing food production levels and limiting pressure on food price rises, it could positively affect the population as a whole.
- Between policy goals. For example, a commitment to expand the production of dairy products for export, which can lead to an increase in absolute GHG emissions, and a national commitment to reducing emission under the Paris agreement.

Governments will need to be cognisant of the multiple dimensions of synergies and trade-offs in order to identify and implement appropriate policy responses. The choices made by policy-makers, therefore, should balance different environmental issues (e.g. climate mitigation and biodiversity), different types of stakeholders (e.g. farmers vs consumers), different locations (e.g. within a country, or at a transboundary level), and over time.

Secondary (i.e. indirect) impacts of policies can also be important. For example, production of palm oil in Indonesia has increased GHG emissions via land-use change from the expansion of oil palm plantations. However, the introduction of a levy on exports of palm oil or its derivatives has also helped to strengthen the Indonesian biodiesel market, and thus displace some use of fossil fuels (Wright, Rahmanulloh and Abdi, 2017[53]) (see Chapter 5).[14] Whether this displacement of fossil fuel use in Indonesia through increased biodiesel usage, has led to reduced GHG emissions, or increased GHG emission from increased land-use change is unclear.

Thus, the interaction (or lack thereof) of policies in this land use nexus can impact their effectiveness. Identifying potential interactions is important, as action will be needed by a wide variety of stakeholders in order to successfully achieve multiple goals. For example, farm-level mitigation measures will need to be implemented in order for the EU to achieve its GHG mitigation commitment, but these measures will impact food production (European Parliament, 2014[54]). It is also important to ensure that policy messages to specific stakeholders are clear. However, this is not always the case. For example, in Mato Grosso, (a key Brazilian state in terms of agricultural output that produced 31.3% of Brazil's soybean production in 2009 (Arvor et al., 2012[55]) and where 89% of forest area has been deforested since 2004 (OBT, 2017[56])), there were at least eight separate dialogues on deforestation relevant to farmers (Nepstad et al., 2013[57]).

There are both supply-side and demand-side policy options to reduce GHG emissions from land use (see e.g. Smith et al., (2014[17]); Bryngelsson et al., (2016[58]); Kiff Wilkes and Tennigkeit, (2016[59])), with various challenges associated with each. There are also some technical supply-side measures that could help to reduce emissions from the agricultural sector. For example, some rice production practices such as alternate wetting and drying can help intensify production while reducing methane emissions (CTA, 2013[60]).

Demand-side measures are also likely to have significant mitigation potential in the agricultural sector (Smith et al., 2014[17]). This is partly because the current agricultural system is not efficient, with high levels of food waste (Teuber and Jensen, 2016[61]). Further, some sources of protein (e.g. beef and dairy products) are considerably more GHG-intensive than others (e.g. poultry) (Smith et al., 2014[17]; Popp, Lotze-Campen and Bodirsky, 2010[62]).

A number of policy-related barriers have been identified to improve the ability of land use to address both climate and biodiversity concerns. These include barriers related to (Wreford, Ignaciuk and Gruère, 2017[63]) :

- Institutional structure and co-ordination: a lack of integration between land use, forestry and agricultural policies, as well as climate and biodiversity policies (e.g. some of the long-term mitigation strategies submitted to the UNFCCC do not refer to biodiversity and/or ecosystems), a lack of (or poorly-enforced) land tenure rights may incentivise environmentally-harmful practices, no requirement to manage small plots of land, lack of an investment framework for the AFOLU sector, lack of focus on a "landscape approach" to managing land[15];
- Ecosystem valuation: understanding the true value of ecosystem benefits and strengthening policies to account for positive and negative externalities;
- Policy misalignments: e.g. agricultural subsidies that link support to inputs or to specific production levels (Henderson and Lankoski, 2019[64]);
- Consumer behaviour: e.g. current behaviour can lead to large volumes of consumer waste, and consumer preferences for GHG-intensive food sources.
- Information/awareness: the role of stakeholders, including sub-national governments, financiers, farmers, is important in implementing environmentally friendly responses in the agriculture and forestry sectors. However, these stakeholders may not always be aware of possible responses, or the environmental consequences of their actions.

Overcoming these barriers could play a significant role in the transition to more sustainable land use and agricultural practices. Better aligned policies and informed decisions could help to minimise trade-offs between forestry and agriculture, climate and biodiversity. Moreover, although there are some examples of private sector corporate social responsibility initiatives in the context of sustainable land use, efforts are needed to further encourage the private sector to engage in sustainable land-use policies. The recent OECD-FAO Guidance for Responsible Agricultural Supply Chains (2016[65]) outlines the standards required to build responsible agricultural supply chains.

The need for a coherent policy framework for sustainable development to address interactions across sectors and reconciling divergent policy objectives has already been recognised. The SDG Target 17.14 calls on all governments and stakeholders to enhance policy coherence for sustainable development. However, this can be complex in practice in the land-use nexus, given the multiple interactions (Figure 1.4.

). For example, according to the ICSU scoring system, actions aimed at achieving target 2.4 on sustainable and resilient agricultural practices aligned to ecosystem protection would reinforce the conservation, restoration and sustainable use of terrestrial and inland freshwater ecosystems. In contrast, achieving SDG target 2.1 to ensure access by all people to sufficient food could potentially conflict with achieving SDG target 7.2 to increase the share of renewable energy if food crops and biofuel production compete for the same land or water (OECD, 2017[66]).

Figure 1.4. Interactions between selected SDGs

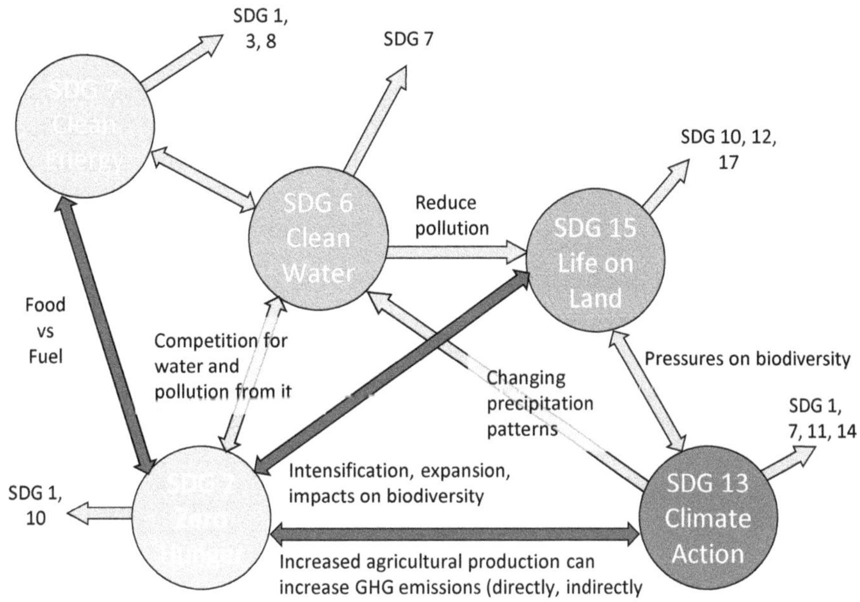

Source: Authors

As part of these efforts to encourage policy coherence, the OECD has developed a toolkit in the context of food security (OECD, 2016[25]). This is composed of a six-section checklist to help policy makers to overcome inconsistencies and promote cross-sectoral synergies for achieving SDG 2. The six overarching sections are generalised below, to apply them to the SDGs of most relevance to the land use nexus (i.e. SDG 2, 6, 7, 13, and 15):

- Consider how domestic policies influence the key dimensions of climate, biodiversity, agriculture and food security in the context of land use;
- Identify policy inter-linkages of relevance across these areas (horizontal coherence);
- Reform or remove policies that create negative spill-over effects;
- Ensure coherence of actions at and between different levels of government (vertical coherence);
- Consider diverse sources of finance to improve food security, climate mitigation and enhance biodiversity and ensure complementarities; and
- Consider contextual factors such as socio-economic circumstances and create enabling conditions.

Applying this framework would entail identifying whether national (political) interests and priorities with specific goals and targets are aligned; and whether the government has a good understanding of the many synergies and trade-offs between policy targets relating to food security, enhanced climate action, and the conservation and sustainable use of ecosystems. This would involve considering issues such as subsidies for agricultural inputs or energy use, land availability and carbon sink function of forests, water availability, trade tariffs, technology transfer, biofuel mandates, and biological pest-control. For example, Article 16 of the 2014 Indonesian law number 39 about plantations (Government of Indonesia, 2014[67]) indicates that the company to whom land rights have been given shall cultivate the whole area within six years, or face penalties. While such a policy will encourage rapid development of land, it will also impede plantation owners from setting aside a proportion of their land for conservation purposes. Food security and other policies may also need to be complemented by strengthened social protection services in many countries in particular for vulnerable groups (the poor, women and children) (OECD, 2016[25]).

Landscape approaches aim to balance the social, environmental and productivity goals in regions where there are several competing land uses. Under landscape approaches, the social, economic and ecological functions of an area are considered holistically to develop spatial and development plans that try to ensure development does not come at the expense of broader socio-economic and environmental benefits. Landscape approaches are generally defined as a set of organising principles rather than prescriptive rules and as such are flexible enough to be applicable across a broad range of socio-economic and environmental contexts (Sayer et al., 2019[68]). Consequently, landscape approaches are increasingly being used - for example the landscape approach is a key underlying principle of the World Bank Forest Action Plan (FY16-20) (World Bank, 2016[69]) and the Bonn Challenge.[16]

However, despite the emergence of landscape approaches, the high-level integration of climate and biodiversity objectives is, generally, not systematic. For example, only a third of country climate-related "nationally determined contributions" under the Paris Agreement include mention of biodiversity and food – although 78% specifically identify the importance of the agriculture sector (FAO, 2016[70]). Moreover, OCED (2012[27]) highlights that even if there is mainstreaming of biodiversity concerns into other national strategies and programmes (e.g. national development plans), this is not always implemented in practice via policies, nor monitored accordingly.

Key findings of the report

Effective land-use management is essential for achieving many national and international goals and commitments, such as the Sustainable Development Goals, the Paris Agreement and the Aichi Biodiversity Targets. Improved co-ordination and coherence between policy areas is needed to achieve effective land-use management given the inherent interconnections, synergies and trade-offs. This report explores which tools and institutions are best suited to achieving effective land-use management consistent with national and international environmental commitments. The report examines six case study countries to draw out common challenges and opportunities to align policy frameworks relevant to the land-use nexus. The report explores alignments and misalignments between different strategies, institutions and policies that can impede effective action on the ground. The areas covered are: coherence across national strategies and action plans, institutional co-ordination and coherence, and policy instruments relevant to the land-use nexus.

The case study countries in this report are Brazil, France, Indonesia, Ireland, Mexico and New Zealand. These countries were selected because they have large greenhouse emissions from the agriculture and/or forestry sectors (in absolute or relative terms), and nearly all host globally important biodiversity. The case study countries moreover represent a selection of OECD member countries and key partner countries which includes two out of the top three land-use change and forestry emitters globally, and two out of the top four agricultural emitters from OECD (CAIT Climate Data Explorer, 2017[5]).

Insights on coherence within and across **national strategies and plans** were identified by looking at the Nationally Determined Contributions, Long-Term Low Emissions Development Strategies, National Biodiversity Strategies and Action Plans (NBSAP), Agricultural Development Plans, Trade or Export Plans and National Development Plans in the six countries, suggesting that:

- The prominence of land-use issues covered in different national strategies relevant to the land-use nexus, and the degree of coherence between the strategies, varies substantially. Overall, few of the national strategies and plans examined are specific enough to facilitate the multiple Ministries (and other stakeholders) involved to take policy action in a coherent manner. Moreover, only a minority of the national strategies and plans (including the Irish NBSAP) examined identify who is responsible for what action or target to be achieved.
- Ideally, national strategies and plans should be prepared in a consultative manner, with engagement all of the Ministries whose actions are likely to impact on the national strategy in question, as well as by other key stakeholders. While stakeholder engagement is improving (i.e. compared to past policy processes), further efforts are needed to ensure that this is done consistently across the various different national strategies.
- Governments can encourage greater policy coherence by ensuring that medium-term (i.e. 5-10 year) national strategies and plans have clear objectives, actions and targets. This would allow for any misalignments to be more easily identified. Developing indicators against which progress towards the targets can be assessed also provides greater transparency and accountability. Where possible, the targets should be specific, measurable, actionable, realistic, and time-bound (SMART). In most strategies and plans reviewed, however, this is not the case.
- Existing national strategies rarely explicitly acknowledge misalignments between different national policies in an individual country. This is despite specific requests to do so at the international level, e.g. the UNFCCC requests Parties to report on policies that increase GHG emissions, and the Aichi Biodiversity Targets under the CBD include specific targets to identify and address harmful incentives (Target 3).
- National plans and strategies relevant to trade could explicitly recognise and where possible quantify the linkages between trade policy and the land-use nexus. This includes overarching national development plans and strategies. Good practice examples include France, which is developing a national Strategy to Combat Imported Deforestation (i.e. from abroad), and Ireland which includes a specific target in their NBSAP to identify and address the adverse impacts on biodiversity from trade. Mainstreaming the consideration of land-use implications into general trade policy formulation would contribute to improved policy coherence.

The land-use nexus involves multiple issues and affects multiple actors from both the public and private sectors, and at supra-national, national and sub-national levels. Examining the **institutional structures** in place in the case study countries highlights the following lessons for institutional co-ordination and coherence:

- Stronger institutional co-ordination both at the horizontal level (between different ministries) and vertical level (e.g. between national and sub-national governments) is needed to ensure the necessary degree of linkage across silos, and to facilitate the coherent design and implementation of policies. The establishment of inter-ministerial committees as well as leadership from the top (i.e. the office of the President, Prime Minister or cabinet) are needed to encourage different stakeholders to develop consistent and co-ordinated policies in the land-use nexus.
- The roles and mandates of institutions should be clearly defined, to increase horizontal alignment of land-use policy. Both lack of institutional co-ordination and overly complex institutional arrangements still occur, and can contribute to policy misalignments. For example, in Indonesia at least eight national ministries are involved in land-use decisions, the mandate of different institutions overlap, and the institution responsible for regulating peatland use has no direct authority over peatland areas. However, while good institutional co-ordination is crucial in promoting policy alignment in this nexus, it is not sufficient by itself to ensure that policies are aligned in practice.

- Countries are intensifying co-ordination of relevant policies, in part by intensifying relevant policy co-ordination mechanisms. This includes setting up an over-arching body - often in the context of national work towards the Sustainable Development Goals. Institutionalising such processes can help improve coherence and co-ordination (e.g. as between the French ministries of agriculture and food, and ministry for an ecological and solidarity transition).
- Vertical alignment of policy creation can be challenging as decision-making power in the nexus is often split between national governments, sub-national governments, and private actors. This decentralisation can undermine the implementation of nexus-relevant policies if the vertical co-ordination of goals is poor. Differing institutional priorities and capacities, and opportunity for local corruption due to lack of oversight can also be a problem. However, decentralisation provides an opportunity to develop innovative context specific solutions (especially in large heterogeneous countries), such as state-specific international conservation funds (in Brazil).
- Multi-stakeholder partnerships involving both public and private actors at national and sub-national scale have been an effective mechanism for influencing the land-use nexus implications of global supply chains. A challenge for government institutions is how to engage and coordinate with these initiatives to ensure maximum effectiveness and alignment with national policy.

Assessing **policy frameworks and instruments** has highlighted the following insights:

- Clearly defined and enforced land tenure is a prerequisite for effective implementation of policies relevant to the land-use nexus. Without clarity on who owns or has the rights to manage which areas of land, incentives for sustainable use are undermined and policy enforcement becomes challenging. Lack of clarity on land rights can also lead to illegal logging, mining and agricultural activities, issues that are still particularly prevalent in Brazil, Mexico and Indonesia. Supporting and intensifying ongoing land reform efforts, such as social forestry and the One Map initiative in Indonesia, is essential for effective land-use policies.
- The negative environmental externalities associated with land-use remain largely un- or under-priced across the case study countries. For example, environmentally related taxes are under-utilised in the land-use nexus when compared other economic instruments (such as subsidies). Greater application of taxes to price environmentally-damaging practices, such as pollution from agrochemical inputs (e.g. fertilisers and pesticides), could enhance the effectiveness of existing regulatory approaches, by providing a price signal to reduce environmentally damaging activity.
- Payments for ecosystem service programmes and agri-environment schemes do compensate land owners for ensuring the provision of certain services (generally water, carbon and biodiversity) in certain regions.[17] But the support is less than that available to support food production and the programmes are often too limited in geographic scope (with the notable exception of Mexico) to improve the sustainability of national land-use systems as a whole, as participation is limited. The balance of support for the delivery of different ecosystem services from land (e.g. food, carbon, water, habitat provision) should ensure that the growth in food production – necessary to meet growing global demand – does not compromise the delivery of other services. Paying land-managers for each ecosystem service from the same area of land (also called 'payment stacking') is a promising approach for improving the incentives available for sustainable management.
- In contrast, government support for agricultural production is larger than support for other land uses (with the exception of New Zealand). Despite recent progress, potentially market-distorting support which can lead to unsustainable practices and encourage the expansion of agriculture, although highly variable, is still prevalent across the case study countries. In all the case study countries (bar New Zealand), more effort is needed to reform potentially market-distorting and environmentally-harmful agricultural support. In addition, biofuel production subsidies and biofuel blending mandates can lead to increased emissions from land-use change, ecosystem degradation

and put pressure on food production (particularly for 1st generation biofuels), however these impacts are context- and crop-specific.

- Although the SDGs include targets relating to reducing food loss and waste, quantitative, national-level targets for reducing food loss and waste are lacking (with the exception of France). There is a clear economic and environmental rationale for action to address food loss and waste, with many potential synergies across other key national policy agendas, such as climate change and biodiversity. Better and more consistent food loss and waste monitoring at national and sub-national levels is recommended, as without these systems the setting of appropriate targets and monitoring progress is not possible.
- International trade in agricultural and forestry products facilitates the import and export of products generating negative externalities not addressed by domestic policies (e.g. climate mitigation and biodiversity protection). Better assessment of the land-use impacts of trade and supply chains and the disclosure of relevant information are key for effective and coherent polices. Improved assessment of ecosystem services and their integration into cost-benefit analysis and more broad application of life cycle assessment (LCA) approaches are important tools for achieving this.
- A number of policy instruments are available to manage interactions between trade and land use. Product-specific mechanisms, including product-specific trade agreements and memoranda of understanding, can be effective instruments, especially if they cover traded products with major land-use implications and include environmental provisions that are strictly enforced. For example, the EU has concluded voluntary partnership agreements (VPAs) for trade in forest products with a number of countries, one of which is currently in place between EU and Indonesia. Policy measures promoting and facilitating responsible business conduct (RBC) can be an effective tool for improved land-use outcomes, too.
- The range of policy approaches utilised in the nexus is broad and their interactions with each other and wider governance systems are complex. Managing the land-use nexus requires a broad policy toolkit as the dynamic, complex and contextual nature of land-use systems mean the effective policy mix in each country or landscape is likely to vary. Successfully balancing outcomes within this policy nexus requires consistent application and maintenance of many different elements, such as monitoring systems, enforcement agencies, stakeholder engagement processes, otherwise policies will cease to function effectively and previous environmental gains can be reversed. For example, increases in deforestation in the Brazilian Amazon in 2018 highlight how changing domestic political circumstances can undermine previously effective policies.

References

Adams, V., R. Pressey and J. Álvarez-Romero (2016), "Using Optimal Land-Use Scenarios to Assess Trade-Offs between Conservation, Development, and Social Values", *PLOS ONE*, Vol. 11/6, http://dx.doi.org/10.1371/journal.pone.0158350. [16]

Alkama, R. and A. Cescatti (2016), "Biophysical climate impacts of recent changes in global forest cover.", *Science (New York, N.Y.)*, Vol. 351/6273, pp. 600-4, http://dx.doi.org/10.1126/science.aac8083. [74]

Archer, D. et al. (2009), "Atmospheric Lifetime of Fossil Fuel Carbon Dioxide", *Annual Review of Earth and Planetary Sciences*, Vol. 37/1, pp. 117-134. [18]

Arvor, D. et al. (2012), "Analyzing the agricultural transition in Mato Grosso, Brazil, using satellite-derived indices", *Applied Geography*, Vol. 32/2, pp. 702-713, http://dx.doi.org/10.1016/j.apgeog.2011.08.007. [55]

Blanco G., R. et al. (2014), "Drivers, Trends and Mitigation", in *Climate Change 2014: Mitigation of Climate Change. Contribution of Working Group III to the Fifth Assessment Report of the Intergovernmental Panel on Climate Change*, Intergovernmental Panel on Climate Change, Cambridge, UK. [49]

Bonan, G. (2008), "Forests and Climate Change: Forcings, Feedbacks, and the Climate Benefits of Forests", *Science*, Vol. 320/5882, pp. 1444-1449, http://dx.doi.org/10.1126/science.1155121. [72]

Bryngelsson, D. et al. (2016), "How can the EU climate targets be met? A combined analysis of technological and demand-side changes in food and agriculture", *Food Policy*, Vol. 59, pp. 152-164, http://dx.doi.org/10.1016/j.foodpol.2015.12.012. [58]

Bustamante, M. et al. (2014), "Co-benefits, trade-offs, barriers and policies for greenhouse gas mitigation in the agriculture, forestry and other land use (AFOLU) sector", *Global Change Biology*, Vol. 20/10, pp. 3270-3290, http://dx.doi.org/10.1111/gcb.12591. [30]

CAIT Climate Data Explorer (2017), *Country Greenhouse Gas Emissions*, Washington, DC: World Resources Institute, http://cait.wri.org (accessed on 31 January 2019). [5]

Costanza, R. et al. (2014), "Changes in the global value of ecosystem services", *Global Environmental Change*, Vol. 26, pp. 152-158, http://dx.doi.org/10.1016/j.gloenvcha.2014.04.002. [41]

Cowie, A. et al. (2018), "Land in balance: The scientific conceptual framework for Land Degradation Neutrality", *Environmental Science & Policy*, Vol. 79, pp. 25-35, http://dx.doi.org/10.1016/j.envsci.2017.10.011. [43]

Cramer, W. et al. (2017), "Biodiversity and food security: from trade-offs to synergies", *Regional Environmental Change*, Vol. 17/5, pp. 1257-1259, http://dx.doi.org/10.1007/s10113-017-1147-z. [34]

Creutzig, F. et al. (2014), "Bioenergy and climate change mitigation: an assessment", *GCB Bioenergy*, Vol. 7/5, pp. 916-944, http://dx.doi.org/10.1111/gcbb.12205. [13]

CTA (2013), *Climate-smart agriculture success stories from farming communities around the world*, ELD Initiative, http://www.eld-initiative.org. [60]

de Wit, H. et al. (2014), "Climate warming feedback from mountain birch forest expansion: reduced albedo dominates carbon uptake", *Global Change Biology*, Vol. 20/7, pp. 2344-2355, http://dx.doi.org/10.1111/gcb.12483. [73]

Delzeit, R. et al. (2016), "Addressing future trade-offs between biodiversity and cropland expansion to improve food security", *Regional Environmental Change*, Vol. 17/5, pp. 1429-1441, http://dx.doi.org/10.1007/s10113-016-0927-1. [35]

Díaz, S. et al. (2019), *Summary for policymakers of the global assessment report on biodiversity and ecosystem services of the Intergovernmental Science-Policy Platform on Biodiversity and Ecosystem Services - advance unedited version*, https://www.ipbes.net/system/tdf/spm_global_unedited_advance.pdf?file=1&type=node&id=35245 (accessed on 20 May 2019). [1]

Dwyer, J. et al. (2009), "Carbon for conservation: Assessing the potential for win–win investment in an extensive Australian regrowth ecosystem", *Agriculture, Ecosystems & Environment*, Vol. 134/1-2, pp. 1-7, http://dx.doi.org/10.1016/j.agee.2009.06.003. [46]

ELD Initiative (2013), *The value of land: Prosperous lands and positive rewards through sustainable land management*. [42]

European Parliament (2014), *Measures at farm level to reduce greenhouse gas emissions from EU agriculture*, European Union, Brussels, http://www.europarl.europa.eu/RegData/etudes/note/join/2014/513997/IPOL-AGRI_NT(2014)513997_EN.pdf. [54]

FAO (2018), *FAOSTAT*, Food and Agriculture Organization of the United Nations, http://www.fao.org/faostat/en/#home (accessed on 7 February 2019). [15]

FAO (2018), *The State of the Worlds Forests 2018 - Forest pathways to sustainable development*, http://www.fao.org/3/I9535EN/i9535en.pdf (accessed on 13 September 2019). [22]

FAO (2016), *State of the World's Forests*, Food and Agriculture Organization, Rome, http://www.fao.org/3/a-i5588e.pdf. [19]

FAO (2016), *The agriculture sector in the intended nationally determined contirbutions*, Food and Agriculture Organization, http://www.fao.org/climate-changeclimate-change@fao.org. [70]

FAO (2011), *Save and grow: Part I*, Food and Agriculture Organization, http://www.fao.org/docrep/014/i2215e/i2215e.pdf. [20]

FAO et al. (2017), *The State of Food Security and Nutrition in the World 2017*, Food and Agriculture Organization. [75]

Fischer, T., D. Byerlee and G. Esmeades (2014), *Crop yields and global food security: will yield increase continue to feed the world?*, Australian Centre for International Agricultural Research, Canberra, https://www.aciar.gov.au/node/12101. [37]

Fuss, S. et al. (2014), "Betting on negative emissions", *Nature Climate Change*, Vol. 4/10, pp. 850-853, http://dx.doi.org/10.1038/nclimate2392. [71]

Government of Indonesia (2014), *Law of the Republic of Indonesia Number 39 2014 about Plantations*, Government of Indonesia, http://www.indolaw.org. [67]

Grassi, G. et al. (2017), "The key role of forests in meeting climate targets requires science for credible mitigation", *Nature Climate Change*, Vol. 7/3, pp. 220-226, http://dx.doi.org/10.1038/nclimate3227. [10]

Griscom, B. et al. (2017), "Natural climate solutions.", *Proceedings of the National Academy of Sciences of the United States of America*, Vol. 114/44, pp. 11645-11650, http://dx.doi.org/10.1073/pnas.1710465114. [9]

Haddad, N. et al. (2015), "Habitat fragmentation and its lasting impact on Earth's ecosystems", *Science Advances*, Vol. 1/2, p. e1500052, http://dx.doi.org/10.1126/sciadv.1500052. [39]

Haščič, I. and A. Mackie (2018), "Land Cover Change and Conversions: Methodology and Results for OECD and G20 Countries", *OECD Green Growth Papers*, No. 2018/04, OECD Publishing, Paris, https://dx.doi.org/10.1787/72a9e331-en. [24]

Havlik, P. et al. (2014), "Climate change mitigation through livestock system transitions", *Proceedings of the National Academy of Sciences*, Vol. 111/10, pp. 3709-3714, http://dx.doi.org/10.1073/pnas.1308044111. [48]

Henderson, B. and J. Lankoski (2019), "Evaluating the environmental impact of agricultural policies", *OECD Food, Agriculture and Fisheries Papers*, No. 130, OECD Publishing, Paris, https://dx.doi.org/10.1787/add0f27c-en. [64]

ICSU (2017), *Introduction: A Framework for Understanding Sustainable Development Goal Interactions*, ICSU, https://sustainabledevelopment.un.org/?menu=1300. [36]

IEA (2017), *Energy Technology Perspectives 2017*, International Energy Agency, Paris. [11]

IPCC (2018), "Summary for Policymakers", in Masson-Delmotte V., Z. et al. (eds.), *Global Warming of 1.5°C. An IPCC Special Report on the impacts of global warming of 1.5°C above pre-industrial levels*, World Meteorological Organisation, Geneva, Switzerland, https://www.ipcc.ch/sr15/chapter/spm/ (accessed on 12 August 2019). [12]

Kaim, A., A. Cord and M. Volk (2018), "A review of multi-criteria optimization techniques for agricultural land use allocation", *Environmental Modelling & Software*, Vol. 105, pp. 79-93, http://dx.doi.org/10.1016/j.envsoft.2018.03.031. [45]

Kennedy, C. et al. (2016), "Optimizing land use decision-making to sustain Brazilian agricultural profits, biodiversity and ecosystem services", *Biological Conservation*, Vol. 204, pp. 221-230, http://dx.doi.org/10.1016/j.biocon.2016.10.039. [47]

Kiff, L., A. Wilkes and T. Tennigkeit (2016), *The technical mitigation potential of demand-side measures in the agri-food sector: A preliminary assessment of available measures - CCAFS Report N. 15*, CGIAR Research Program on Climate Change, Agriculture and Food Security, http://www.ccafs.cgiar.org (accessed on 26 September 2018). [59]

Krausmann, F. and E. Langthaler (2019), "Food regimes and their trade links: A socio-ecological perspective", *Ecological Economics*, Vol. 160, pp. 87-95, http://dx.doi.org/10.1016/J.ECOLECON.2019.02.011. [51]

Montanarella, L., R. Scholes and A. Brainich (eds.) (2018), *The IPBES assessment report on land degradation and restoration.*, Secretariat of the Intergovernmental Science-Policy Platform on Biodiversity and Ecosystem Services, Bonn. [2]

Munaretto, S. and M. Witmer (2017), *Water-land-energy-food-climate nexus: policies and policy coherence at European and international scales*, Netherlands Environmental Assessment Agency (PBL), Den Haag. [32]

Nelson, E. et al. (2008), "Efficiency of incentives to jointly increase carbon sequestration and species conservation on a landscape", *Proceedings of the National Academy of Sciences*, Vol. 105/28, pp. 9471-9476, http://dx.doi.org/10.1073/pnas.0706178105. [40]

Nepstad, D. et al. (2013), "More food, more forests, fewer emissions, better livelihoods: linking REDD+, sustainable supply chains and domestic policy in Brazil, Indonesia and Colombia", *Carbon Management*, Vol. 4/6, pp. 639-658, http://dx.doi.org/10.4155/cmt.13.65. [57]

Nkonya, E. et al. (2015), "Global Cost of Land Degradation", in *Economics of Land Degradation and Improvement – A Global Assessment for Sustainable Development*, Springer International Publishing, Cham, http://dx.doi.org/10.1007/978-3-319-19168-3_6. [77]

OBT (2017), *Monitoramento da Floresta Amazônica Brasileira por Satélite*, Observacao da Terra, http://www.obt.inpe.br/OBT/assuntos/programas/amazonia/prodes. [56]

OECD (2018), *Cost-Benefit Analysis and the Environment: Further Developments and Policy Use*, OECD Publishing, Paris, https://dx.doi.org/10.1787/9789264085169-en. [44]

OECD (2018), *Water and Agriculture*, OECD, Paris. [8]

OECD (2017), "Tracking progress on policy coherence for sustainable development at the national level: What and how to measure?", *Coherence for Sustainable Development* 9, http://file:///C:/Users/Falduto_C/Downloads/Coherence%20for%20Development_Issue_9.pdf. [66]

OECD (2016), *Alternative Futures for Global Food and Agriculture*, OECD Publishing, Paris, http://dx.doi.org/10.1787/9789264247826-en. [21]

OECD (2016), *Better Policies for Sustainable Development 2016: A New Framework for Policy Coherence*, OECD Publishing, Paris, https://sustainabledevelopment.un.org/content/documents/commitments/493_12066_commitment_Better%20Policies%20for%20Sustainable%20Development%202016.pdf. [25]

OECD (2014), *Green Growth Indicators for Agriculture: A Preliminary Assessment*, OECD Green Growth Studies, OECD Publishing, Paris, http://dx.doi.org/10.1787/9789264223202-en. [28]

OECD (2012), *OECD Environmental Outlook to 2050: The Consequences of Inaction*, OECD Publishing, Paris, https://dx.doi.org/10.1787/9789264122246-en. [27]

OECD and FAO (2016), *OECD-FAO Guidance for Responsible Agricultural Supply Chains*, OECD Publishing, http://www.oecd.org/daf/inv/investment-policy/rbc-agriculture-supply-chains.htm. [65]

Phalan, B. et al. (2011), "Reconciling Food Production and Biodiversity Conservation: Land Sharing and Land Sparing Compared", *Science*, Vol. 333/6047, pp. 1289-1291, http://dx.doi.org/10.1126/science.1208742. [38]

Popp, A., H. Lotze-Campen and B. Bodirsky (2010), "Food consumption, diet shifts and associated non-CO2 greenhouse gases from agricultural production", *Global Environmental Change*, Vol. 20/3, pp. 451-462, http://dx.doi.org/10.1016/j.gloenvcha.2010.02.001. [62]

Power, A. (2010), "Ecosystem services and agriculture: tradeoffs and synergies", *Philosophical Transactions of the Royal Society B: Biological Sciences*, Vol. 365/1554, pp. 2959-2971, http://dx.doi.org/10.1098/rstb.2010.0143. [31]

Ravishankara, A., J. Daniel and R. Portmann (2009), "Nitrous oxide (N2O): the dominant ozone-depleting substance emitted in the 21st century.", *Science (New York, N.Y.)*, Vol. 326/5949, pp. 123-5, http://dx.doi.org/10.1126/science.1176985. [7]

Sayer, J. et al. (2019), "Ten principles for a landscape approach to reconciling agriculture, conservation, and other competing land uses", *PNAS*, Vol. 110/21, pp. 8349-8356, http://dx.doi.org/10.1073/pnas.1210595110. [68]

Smith, P. et al. (2014), "Agriculture, Forestry and Other Land Use (AFOLU)", in [Edenhofer, O., R., J. Pichs-Madruga, Y. Sokona, E. Farahani, S. Kadner, K. Seyboth, A. Adler, I. Baum, S. Brunner, P. Eickemeier, B. Kriemann and T. Savolainen, S. Schlömer, C. von Stechow (eds.), *Climate Change 2014: Mitigation of Climate Change. Contribution of Working Group III to the Fifth Assessment Report of the Intergovernmental Panel on Climate Change*, Cambridge University Press, Cambridge and New York, https://www.ipcc.ch/pdf/assessment-report/ar5/wg3/ipcc_wg3_ar5_chapter11.pdf (accessed on 26 September 2018). [17]

Tallard, G., P. Liapis and G. Pilgrim (2016), "The Implications of Agricultural Trade and Market Developments for Food Security"*, OECD Food, Agriculture and Fisheries Papers*, No. 95, OECD Publishing, Paris, https://dx.doi.org/10.1787/5jlr579rkqwk-en. [50]

Teuber, R. and D. Jensen (2016), *Food losses and food waste – Extent, underlying drivers and impact assessment*, University of Copenhagen, http://www.ifro.ku.dk/english. [61]

The Economics of Ecosystems and Biodiversity (TEEB) (2018), *Measuring what matters in agriculture and food systems: a synthesis of the results and recommendations of TEEB for Agriculture and Food's Scientific and Economic Foundations report*, UN Environment, Geneva, http://www.teebweb.org/agrifood/home/scientific-and-economic-foundations-report. (accessed on 20 May 2019). [4]

The Royal Society (2007), *Biodiversity - climate interactions: adaptation, mitigation and human livelihoods*, The Royal Society. [33]

Tilman, D. et al. (2017), "Future threats to biodiversity and pathways to their prevention", *Nature*, Vol. 546/7656, pp. 73-81, http://dx.doi.org/10.1038/nature22900. [6]

Tonosaki, M. (2009), "Harvested wood products accounting in the post Kyoto commitment period", *Journal of Wood Science*, Vol. 55/6, pp. 390-394, http://dx.doi.org/10.1007/s10086-009-1052-2. [78]

UCS (2014), *Deforestation Success Stories Tropical Nations Where Forest Protection and Reforestation Policies Have Worked*, Union of Concerned Scientists, http://www.ucsusa.org/forestsuccess. [23]

UNCCD (2013), *A Stronger UNCCD for a Land-Degradation Neutral World.* [76]

UNDESA (2017), *Synthesis of Voluntary National Reviews 2017 Prepared by DSD/DESA Prepared with inputs from: Division for Sustainable Development Department of Economic and Social Affairs United Nations*, United Nations Department of Economic and Social Affairs, https://sustainabledevelopment.un.org/. [52]

United Nations, Department of Economic and Social Affairs, Population Division (2019), *World Population Prospects 2019: Highlights*, United Nations. [26]

V. Masson-Delmotte, P. Zhai, H. O. Pörtner, D. Roberts, J. Skea, P.R. Shukla, A. Pirani, W. Moufouma-Okia, C. Péan, R. Pidcock, S. Connors, J. B. R. Matthews, Y. Chen, X. Zhou, M. I. Gomis, E. Lonnoy, T. Maycock, M. Tignor, T. (ed.) (2018), *Strengthening and implementing the global response*, In press. [14]

Van der Esch, S. et al. (2017), *Exploring future changes in land use and land condition and the impacts on food, water, climate change and biodiversity: Scenarios for the Global Land Outlook*, PBL Netherlands Environment Agency, The Hague, https://www.pbl.nl/sites/default/files/cms/publicaties/pbl-2017-exploring-future-changes-in-land-use-and-land-condition-2076b.pdf (accessed on 11 January 2019). [29]

Willett, W. et al. (2019), "Food in the Anthropocene: the EAT-Lancet Commission on healthy diets from sustainable food systems.", *Lancet (London, England)*, Vol. 0/0, http://dx.doi.org/10.1016/S0140-6736(18)31788-4. [3]

World Bank (2016), *World Bank Group Forest Action Plan FY16-20*, World Bank, Washington DC. [69]

Wreford, A., A. Ignaciuk and G. Gruère (2017), "Overcoming barriers to the adoption of climate-friendly practices in agriculture", *OECD Food, Agriculture and Fisheries Papers*, No. 101, OECD Publishing, Paris, https://dx.doi.org/10.1787/97767de8-en. [63]

Wright, T., A. Rahmanulloh and A. Abdi (2017), *Indonesia Biofuels Annual Report 2017*, USDA Foreign Agricultural Service, https://gain.fas.usda.gov/Recent%20GAIN%20Publications/Biofuels%20Annual_Jakarta_Indonesia_6-20-2017.pdf. [53]

Notes

[1] There is a strong link between agriculture and climate adaptation, e.g. via agricultural demand for water. However, the scope of this report focuses on the climate mitigation aspects of land-use.

[2] Various modelling of stringent mitigation goals requires the ability to deliver significant "negative emissions" - biomass with carbon capture and storage (CCS) is one of the most feasible ways to do this – alongside but different to afforestation/reforestation (Fuss et al., 2014[71]).

[3] The climate effects of changes in forest area can vary significantly depending on where this occurs. For example, while all forests have a low albedo (i.e. reflectivity of solar radiation), increased areas of tropical forests can reduce the impacts of global warming via the cooling effect of increased evapotranspiration. In contrast, increased boreal forests can exacerbate global warming, under some limited conditions, especially at high elevation and latitude. See e.g. Bonan (2008[72]), de Wit *et al.* (2014[73])and Alkama and Cescatti (2016[74])

[4] MSA is an indicator of naturalness or biodiversity intactness. It is defined as the mean abundance of original species relative to their abundance in undisturbed ecosystems. An MSA of 0% means a completely destroyed ecosystem, with no original species remaining.

[5] Food security refers to the supply of food and individuals' physical, social and economic access to it (FAO et al., 2017[75]).

[6] See footnote 3.

[7] Given the inter-connectedness of land-use, biodiversity, climate and food with other areas, there are also synergies and trade-offs outside this nexus. For example, increased use of biomass for cooking can lead to negative health impacts associated with increased indoor biomass burning.

[8] Manure management systems can include the collection and storage of manure, in order to capture and use or flare the methane produced from manure decomposition. This reduces total levels of GHG emissions, as methane is a more potent, albeit short-lived, GHG than carbon dioxide.

[9] The causes of land degradation include both direct anthropogenic impacts such as deforestation, and unsuitable land management practices (e.g. the cultivation of steep slopes, overgrazing, and overcutting of vegetation) and indirect anthropogenic impacts (e.g. climate change induced drought) and natural disasters (e.g. flooding and forest fires).

[10] UNCCD (UNCCD, 2013[76]) for example, estimated that the global costs of land degradation amount to USD 490 billion. According to the Economics of Land Degradation Initiative (ELD Initiative, 2013[42]), land degradation is costing the world as much as USD 10.6 trillion every year, equivalent to 17% of global gross domestic product.

[11] Nkonya et al. (2015[77]) estimate that the annual global costs of land degradation due to land use and land cover change (LUCC) are about USD 231 billion per year.

[12] In terrestrial and freshwater ecosystems, InVEST models habitat quality (terrestrial only) and the benefits of: carbon sequestration; annual water yield for hydropower, water purification (for nutrients); erosion

control (for reservoir maintenance), crop pollination; timber production, and non-timber forest product harvest.

[13] Another example are harvested wood products (HWP), which influence the carbon cycle by storing and releasing carbon from forests. The current reporting practice for Annex I parties under the Kyoto Protocol is to report HWP emissions and removals for domestically harvested wood only (UNFCCC/ 2/CMP.7). While this production approach allows for comparability and aggregation, other accounting approaches have been suggested to more accurately capture carbon fluxes associated with internationally traded HWP (Tonosaki, 2009[78]).

[14] The lifecycle GHG benefits of biofuels will depend on the level of fossil fuel and other non-renewable inputs needed for their production, as well as any associated land-use clearing.

[15] Among multiple initiatives and ways to overcome these policy-related barriers, REDD+ is aiming to address this first category of barriers, *inter alia* through the development of a national plan or strategy addressing them (see chapters 4 and 5 for more detail).

[16] http://www.bonnchallenge.org/content/forest-landscape-restoration

[17] These schemes are different to mandatory environmental conditions on agricultural support payments, such as the greening of basic payments under the EU Common Agricultural Policy, because the level of payment is contingent on increasing the level of delivery of a certain ecosystem service (e.g. carbon sequestration or habitat provision).

2 Data and trends relevant to sustainable land use

This chapter highlights some of the important data and trends in areas relevant to the land-use, biodiversity, climate and food nexus across the case study countries (Brazil, France, Indonesia, Ireland, Mexico and New Zealand), regionally and globally. This includes information on trends in land-cover change and ecosystems, greenhouse gas emissions from agriculture and LULUCF (land use, land use change and forestry), the emissions intensity of agricultural production and trends in protected area coverage. The chapter also highlights the economic importance of international trade in agricultural and forestry products, and its impact on land use in the case study countries.

This chapter presents data and trends relevant to land use, land cover change (partially as a proxy for biodiversity), GHG emissions from LULUCF, food loss and waste and international trade for the six case study countries, Brazil, France, Indonesia, Ireland, Mexico and New Zealand, as well as at OECD and global levels, for comparative purposes. Global and regional trends in food security are also highlighted.

Land cover and ecosystems

The contribution of land cover types to total land in 2015, based on recently available data from the Climate Change Initiative-Land Cover (CCI-LC),[1] is depicted in Figure 2.1. Land cover types analogous with unmanaged areas are tree-covered area, grassland, wetland and shrubland. Overall, most of the conversion of natural land since 1992 has been to cropland.

Figure 2.2 shows land-cover conversion patterns in Indonesia, Brazil and the OECD between 1992-2015. The extent of land conversion is highly variable between the different countries and the OECD. For example, 2.3% of total land area in Ireland and 8.4% of total land area in Indonesia was converted from one land cover to another. There are also differences in the patterns of land-cover change between countries. The majority of Indonesian land-cover change was from tree-covered areas to cropland, whereas in OECD as a whole, slightly more land was converted to tree-covered areas than from tree-covered areas. In Brazil, more tree-covered areas were converted to cropland between 1992 and 2015 than in all OECD countries combined. However, the data for conversion between some individual IPCC categories in Figure 2.2 must be treated with caution, as some are difficult to distinguish reliably via remote sensing.[2]

Figure 2.1. Contribution of primary land cover types to total, 2015

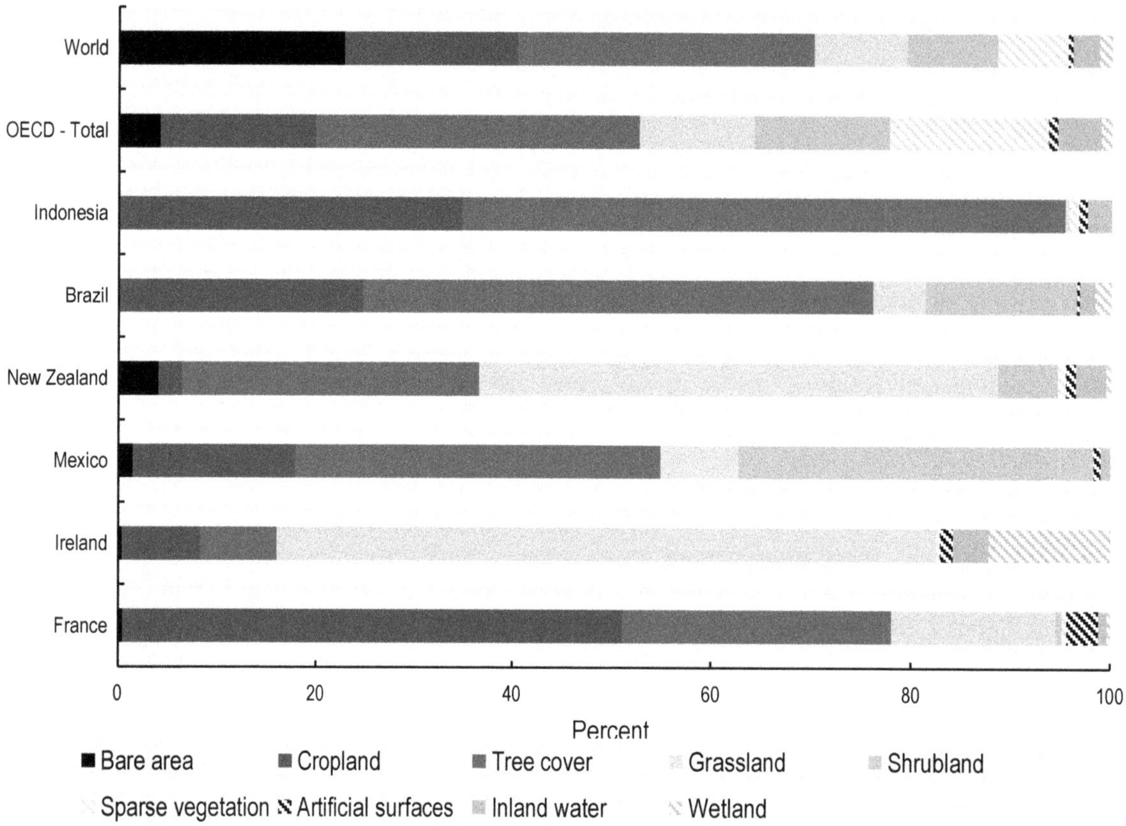

Note: The definitions used to categorise these data differ from those used by the FAO to characterise land use classes. For example, the changes in 'Tree Covered Areas' reported in this figure are not analogous to changes in forest area as a share of land area reported in Figure 2.3.
Source: (Haščič and Mackie, 2018[1]), *Land cover change and conversions: Methodology and results for OECD and G20 countries*, https://doi.org/10.1787/22260935.

Figure 2.2. Land conversion in Brazil, Indonesia and OECD countries

1992-2015, thousand km2

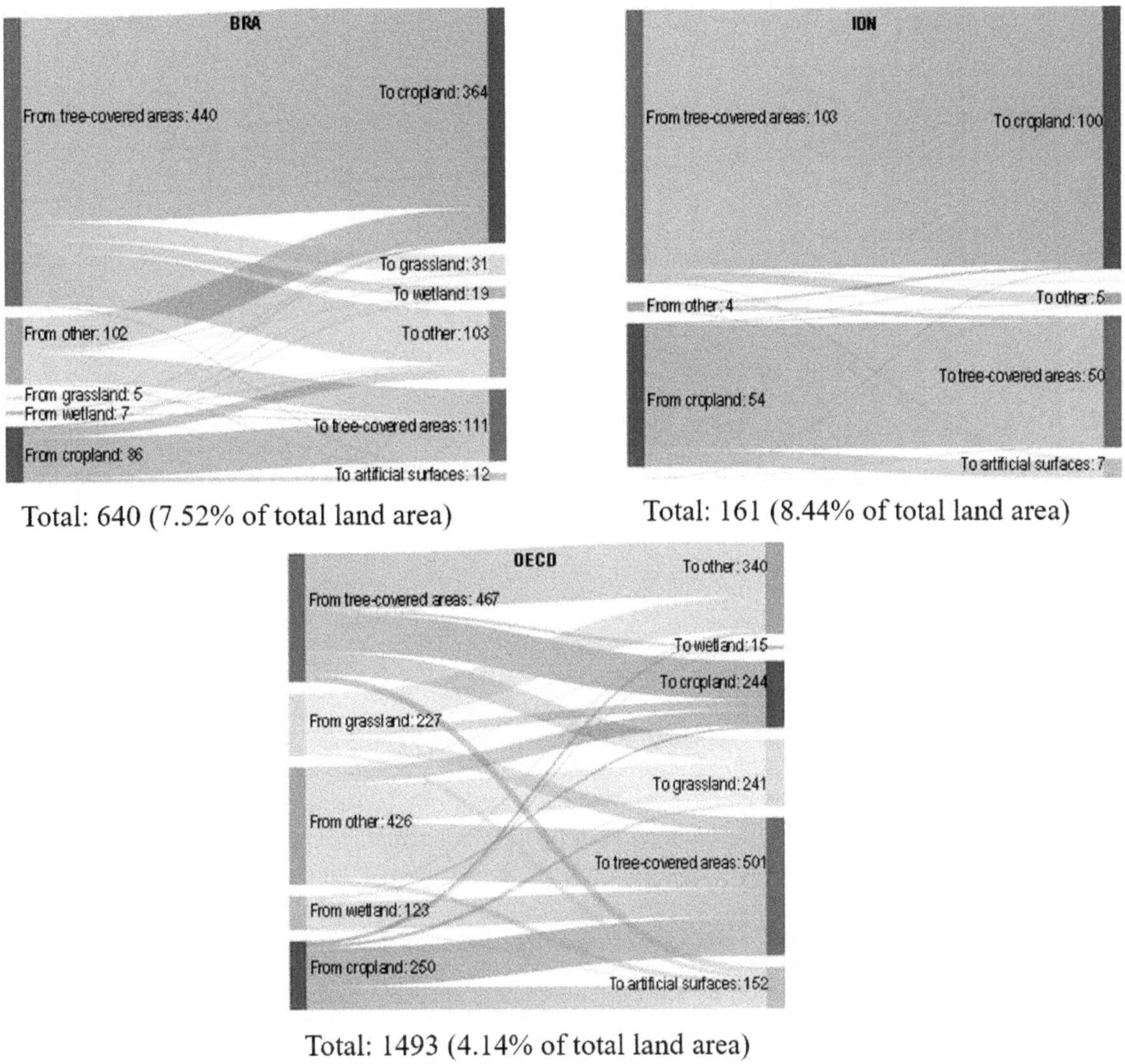

Note: Six IPCC-like top-level categories. "Other" consists of water, bare land, shrubland, and sparse vegetation. Flow sizes are indicated numerically for flows of more than one thousand km2. Due to the different order of magnitude of land area converted in France, Ireland, Mexico and New Zealand, land conversion diagrams for these countries are reported in the Annex.
Source: (Haščič and Mackie, 2018[1]), Land cover change and conversions: Methodology and results for OECD and G20 countries, https://doi.org/10.1787/22260935.

Trends in forest area – to be distinguished from 'tree-covered areas' referred to above due to the different definitions used by the various data sources – since 1990 for the six countries, the OECD and the world are depicted in Figure 2.3. While at the global scale, the total forest area has remained stable (from 31.7% of total land area in 1990, to 30.6% of total land area in 2014), this can obscure large variations between different countries. In particular, there was significant forest loss in tropical areas (FAO, 2016[2]), including large declines in forest area in Brazil and Indonesia (FAOSTAT, 2017[3]). In contrast, afforestation, most notably in China, but also in several OECD countries, has increased forest area in temperate regions. The area of primary forest stayed relatively constant in OECD countries (from 10% in 1990 to 9.9% in 2014). There were, however, reductions in primary forest area in Indonesia (from 27.3% of land area in 1990 to 25.5% in 2014) and Brazil (from 26.1% of land area in 1990 to 24.3% of land area in 2014).

Figure 2.3. Trends in forest area (as a share of total land area)

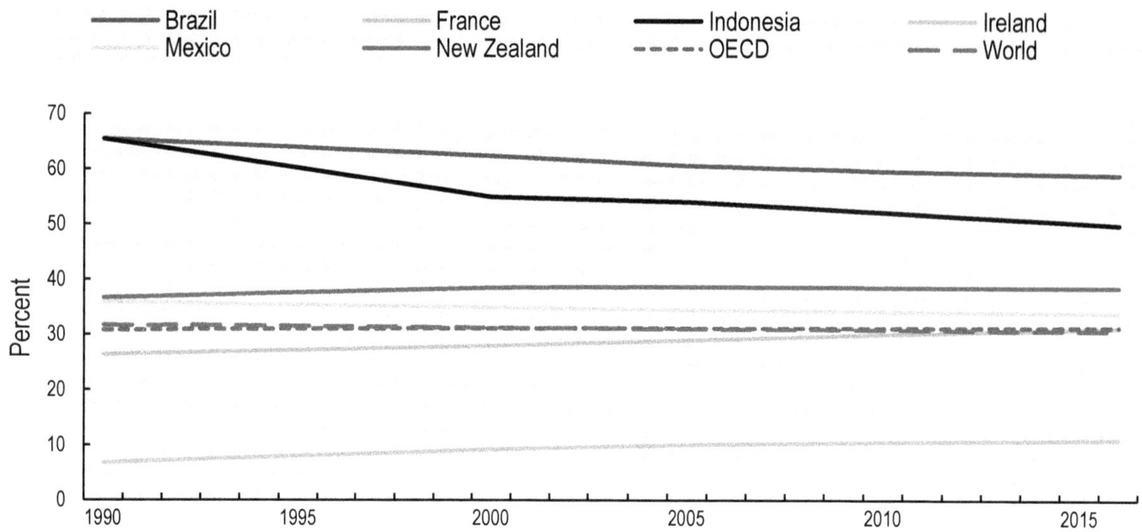

Source: FAOSTAT (2017[3]), *Food and Agriculture data*, http://www.fao.org/faostat/en/#data

Greenhouse gas emissions

Turning to GHG emissions from the agricultural and forestry sectors, Figure 2.4 illustrates that there is significant variation between the countries. In Indonesia, where deforestation levels have been high and the carbon content of forest areas is high (particularly in peatlands), forestry-related emissions accounted for approximately half of national GHG emissions in 2014. Contrastingly, in many OECD countries (with the notable exception of New Zealand, where agriculture accounted for almost half of national GHG emissions, albeit with significant emissions removals from the forestry sector), GHG emissions from land use, land-use change and forestry contributed a relatively low proportion of total GHG emissions in 2014.

Figure 2.4 also shows the contribution of the agriculture and forestry sectors to GDP in the case study countries. While this is not true for OECD in general, the contribution of agriculture to GDP is higher than forestry sector in all case study countries. The latter remains below 2% for all the countries bar New Zealand where it represents 2.4%, whereas the agricultural share of GDP diverges more substantially across countries. The contribution of agriculture to GDP ranges between 1.9% and 3.2% for France, Ireland and Mexico and between 6 and 13.3% for Brazil, New Zealand and Indonesia, suggesting this sector is significantly more economically important to this latter group of countries.

Figure 2.4. Emissions from land use, land-use change and forestry (LULUCF) and agriculture, and proportion of GDP from forests and agriculture (2014)

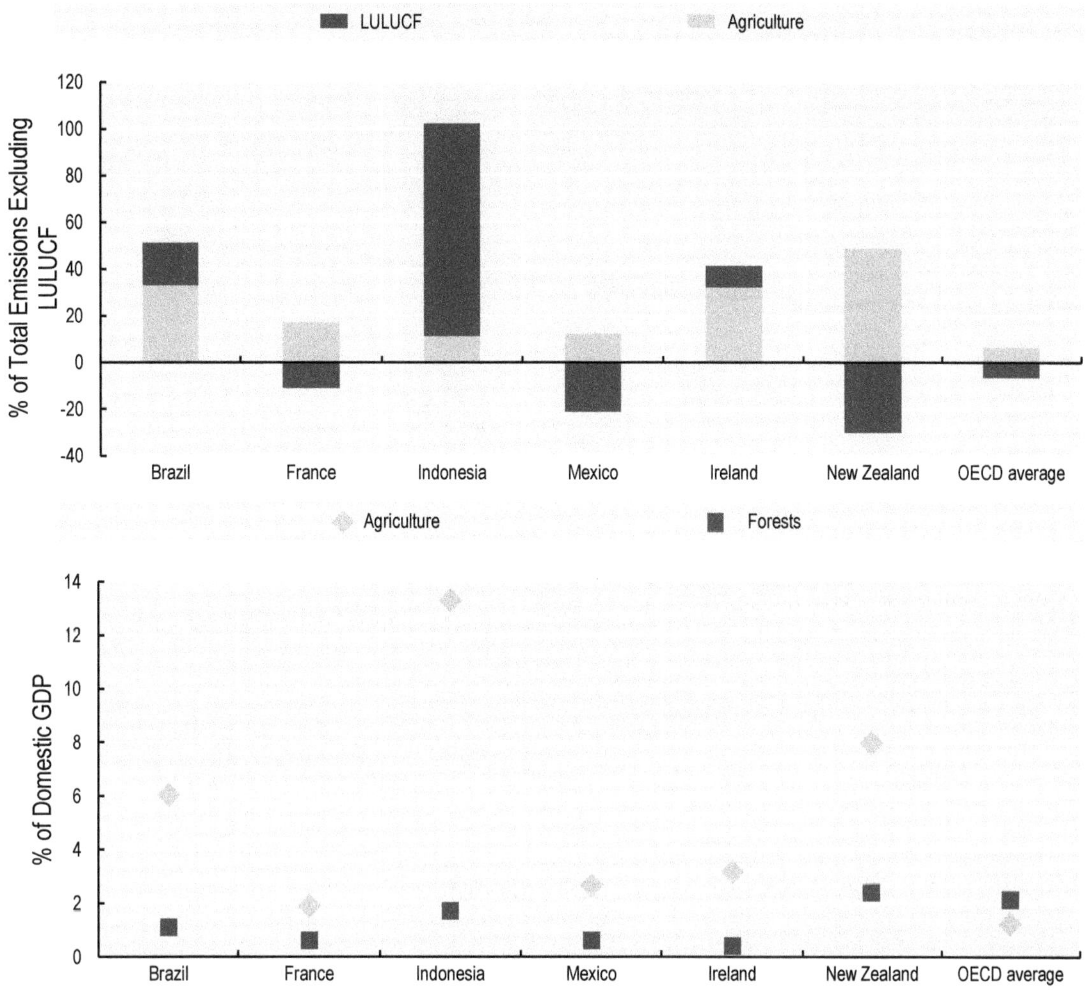

Note: To separate out the different trends for GHG emissions from the agriculture and forestry sectors, the y axis is expressed as a percentage of national emissions excluding LULUCF. Data on LULUCF emissions, in accordance with the 1996 IPCC Gudelines for National Greenhouse Gas Inventories and the IPCC's Good Practice Guidance on Land Use, Land-Use Change and Forestry comes from OECD.stat and is used for comparability between data reported by Annex I- and non-Annex I-Parties to the UNFCCC. LULUCF emissions largely correspond to emissions from forestry and other land use (FOLU) reported by Annex I-Parties following the 2006 IPCC Guidelines.

Sources: Authors based on OECD.stat (2017[4]) *National Inventory Submissions 2017 to the United Nations Framework Convention on Climate Change (UNFCCC, CRF tables), and replies to the OECD State of the Environment Questionnaire*, http://dotstat.oecd.org/?lang=en, FAOSTAT (2017[3]), *Food and Agriculture data*, http://www.fao.org/faostat/en/#data, and FAO (2014[5]) *Contribution of the Forestry Sector to National Economies, 1990-2011*, http://www.fao.org/3/a-i4248e.pdf.

Global GHG emissions from agriculture increased by 11.0% between 1990 and 2010, while those from OECD countries decreased by 9.5% over the same period (Figure 2.5). The gross production value derived from global agriculture increased by a greater proportion than global emissions, demonstrating a relative decoupling. Among OECD countries the data suggest an absolute decoupling of emissions and value from agriculture over the period, as value increases were realised while absolute levels of GHG emissions declined. However, rising food prices between 2000 and 2012 probably explain at least some of the growth in value both inside and outside OECD countries. Figure 2.6 shows GHG emissions intensities from agriculture by country measured in gigagrams of CO_2 equivalent per million US dollars of agricultural revenue. This suggests substantial convergence in direct GHG emissions intensities from the agricultural sector across countries over time. However, it should be noted that indirect emissions due to land-use change are not included, which are substantial in some countries.

Figure 2.5. Direct agricultural GHG emissions and gross production value from agriculture

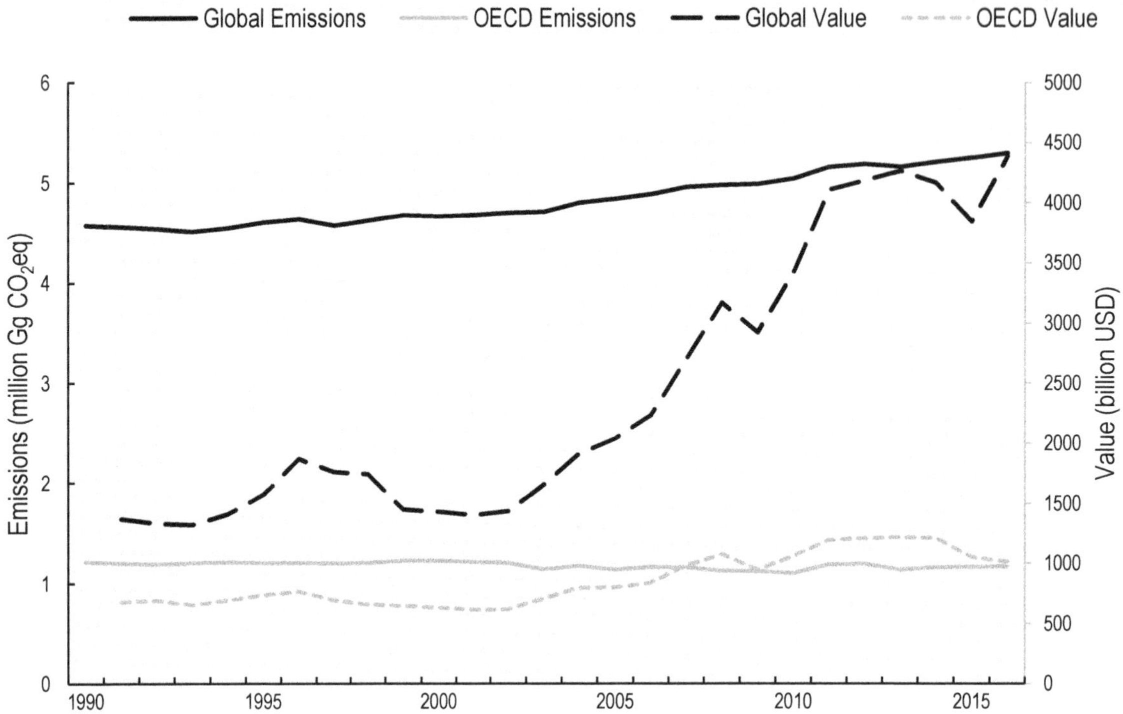

Note: Data for agricultural value in the OECD are incomplete prior to 2000.
Source: FAOSTAT (2017[3]), *Food and Agriculture data*, http://www.fao.org/faostat/en/#data

The sources of agricultural GHG emissions differed markedly between countries over time (Figure 2.7). As for OECD as a whole, agricultural emissions declined in France over time. This occurred largely through reductions in emissions from enteric fermentation and synthetic fertilisers. By contrast, GHG emissions from enteric fermentation and synthetic fertilisers have driven substantial increases in agricultural emissions in Brazil. Emissions from synthetic fertilisers have similarly increased in Indonesia, and have added to substantial increases in methane emission from rice cultivation in the country. New Zealand showed little change in agricultural emissions over the time period, as increases in the contribution from synthetic fertilisers were similar in size to decreases in emissions from enteric fermentation. GHG emissions intensities by product, namely for beef and dairy production are depicted in Figure 2.8 and Figure 2.9 respectively, in most cases indicating a decline in emissions intensities, albeit at differing rates.

Figure 2.6. Direct GHG emissions intensities from agriculture

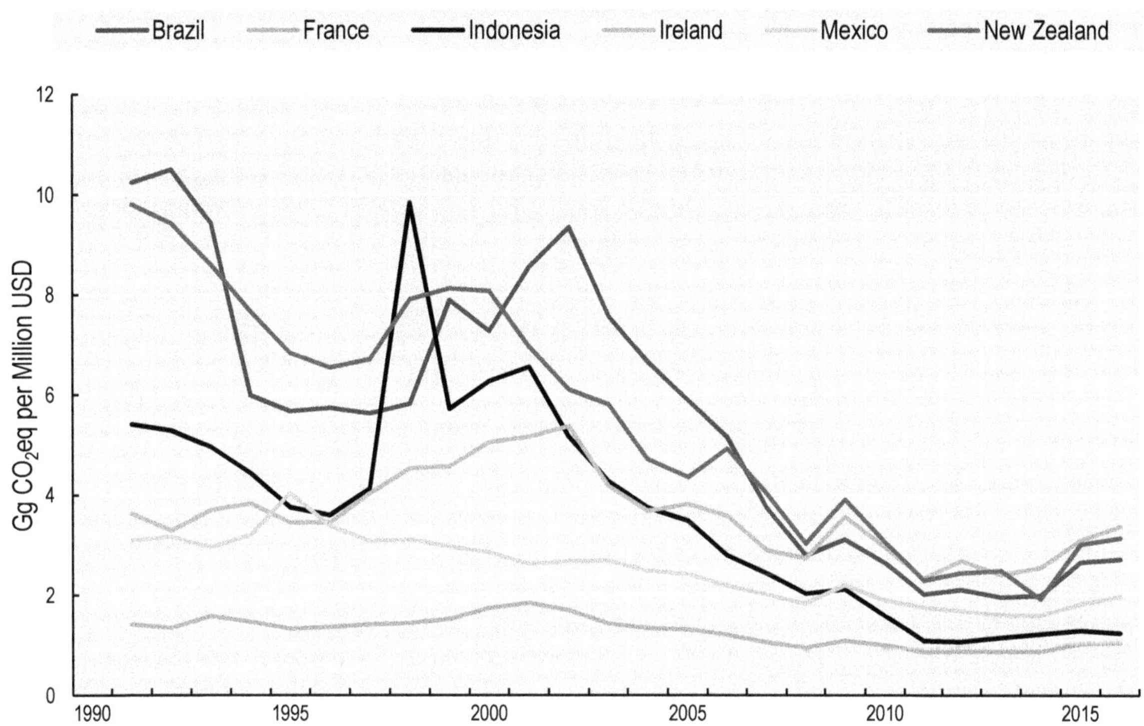

Note: Increases in emissions intensities between 1998 and 2002, most notably in Indonesia, Brazil and New Zealand, reflect reductions in gross agricultural revenue over the period. These reductions may reflect the impacts of the 1997/98 El Niño which have been linked to severe drought and wildfires in Indonesia, drought and severe flooding in Brazil, and substantial reductions in crop and livestock revenue in New Zealand (National Drought Mitigation Center, n.d.[6]). They may also reflect decreases in the value of traded agricultural products resulting from dips in the Indonesian Rupiah in 1998 and the Brazilian Real in 2002 (Trading Economics, 2018[7]). This graph does not include indirect emissions from agriculture, e.g. those associated with land-clearing.
Source: Authors based on FAOSTAT (2017[3]),*Food and Agriculture data,* http://www.fao.org/faostat/en/#data and OECD.stat (2017[4]) , *National Inventory Submissions 2017 to the United Nations Framework Convention on Climate Change (UNFCCC, CRF tables), and replies to the OECD State of the Environment Questionnaire*, http://dotstat.oecd.org/?lang=en.

Box 2.1. Livestock production systems and trade

Livestock production systems, in particular cattle-rearing dairy and beef production systems, are economically important to almost all case study countries. At the same time, cattle rearing accounts for a significant share of nexus impacts, through land-use change for pastureland or feed production, direct GHG emissions from manure, and pollution. Dairy and beef production systems range from extensive, pasture-based production systems, to intensive feedlot-based systems. These systems differ in both their economic performance and environmental impacts.

For example, Gerber *et al.* (2013[8]) argue that milk and beef from intensive, high-yielding production systems are less emissions-intensive due to scale effects and productivity gains from emissions-reducing practices, such as high-quality feed and herd management. Figure 2.8 and Figure 2.9 confirm that per-unit emissions are indeed lower in countries such as New Zealand, Ireland and France when compared to the more extensive production systems in Indonesia and Brazil.

However, important differences exist between intensive cattle-rearing systems, which are not discernible from the figures showing only emissions from within the *farm gate*. Life-cycle analysis which accounts for upstream (and downstream) emissions (see chapter 5)[3], shows the predominantly grass-based dairy systems in New Zealand and Ireland to be less emissions-intensive than France, for example, due to their lower reliance on imported feed (Weiss and Leip, 2012[9]). Consequently, indirect land-use change from cattle feed production – which accounts for up to one third of EU GHG emissions in the study by Weiss and Leip (2012[9]) – can severely constrain the scope for intensification to lower the livestock sector's GHG footprint (Bowles, Alexander and Hadjikakou, 2019[10]; Styles et al., 2018[11]).

Livestock product trade

If a higher proportion of global beef and dairy production originates from the most efficient production systems, international trade can in theory contribute to global production efficiency, reducing GHG emissions and other environmental impacts. Rising (domestic and) international demand is boosting the beef and dairy export industry in the case study countries particularly in New Zealand, Ireland, Brazil, and Mexico. Ireland, for instance, exported 85% of its beef production and 90% of its dairy production in 2016 (Agriculture and Food Development Authority, 2017[12]; Fitzgerald, 2019[13]). While Ireland and New Zealand are relatively efficient producers from a GHG emissions perspective, the increases in production are undermining their ability to meet domestic emissions pledges. Further, whether the wider environmental impacts associated with export-oriented production can be sustained in the long term, is questionable. In New Zealand, for instance, where dairy products accounted for a quarter of total goods exports in 2018 (Stats NZ, 2019[14]), dairy farming has now replaced lower impact sheep farming leading to significant increases in water pollution (Ministry for the Environment, 2019[15]). Despite being an economic boon, the societal costs from environmental impacts of the dairy industry have, however, been found to outweigh the export revenues (Foote, Joy and Death, 2015[16])

Figure 2.7. Agricultural emissions by source

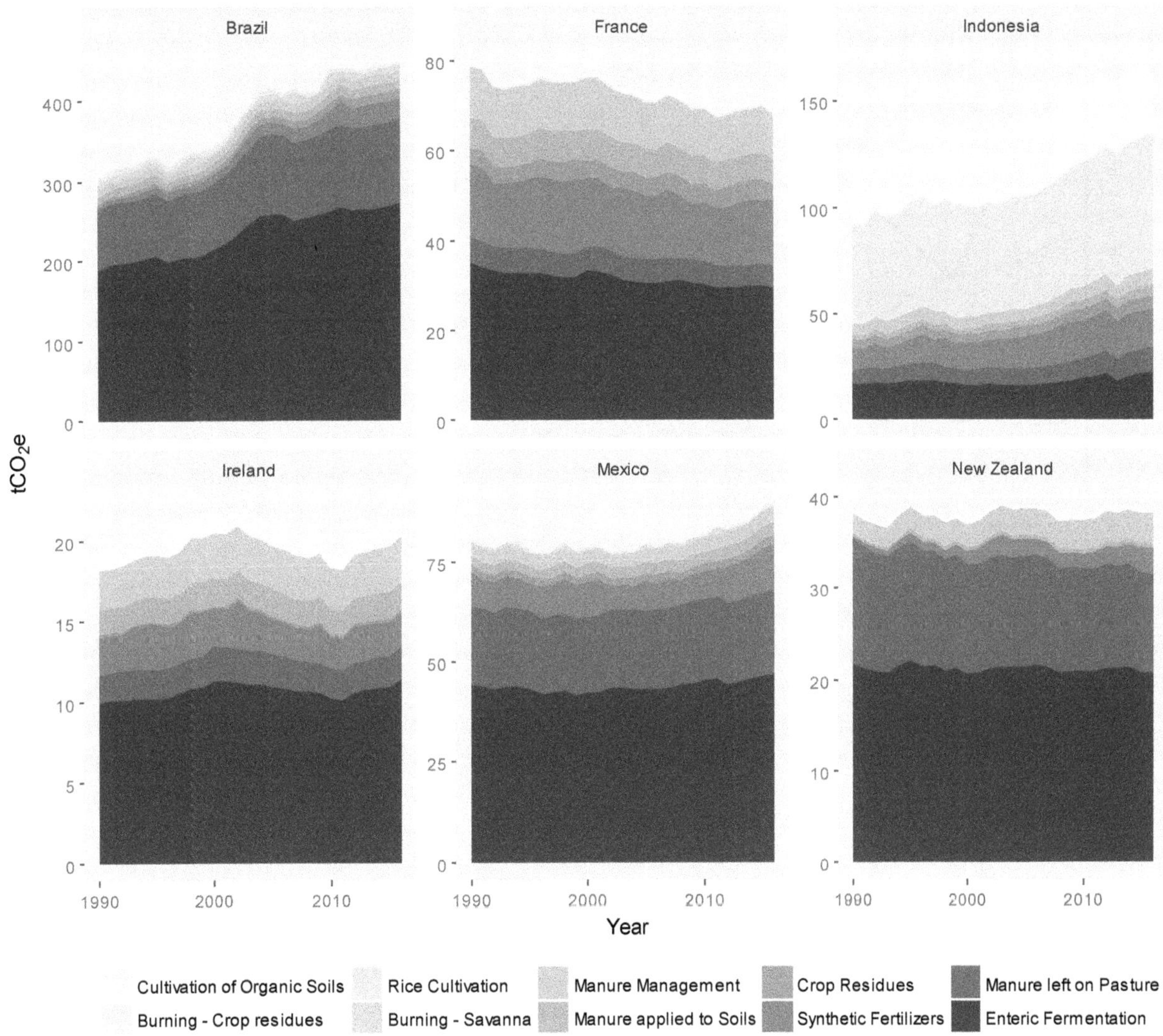

Note: Y-axes on different scales

Source: FAOSTAT (2017[3]), Food and Agriculture data, http://www.fao.org/faostat/en/#data

Figure 2.8. GHG emissions generated within farm gate per kilogram of beef production

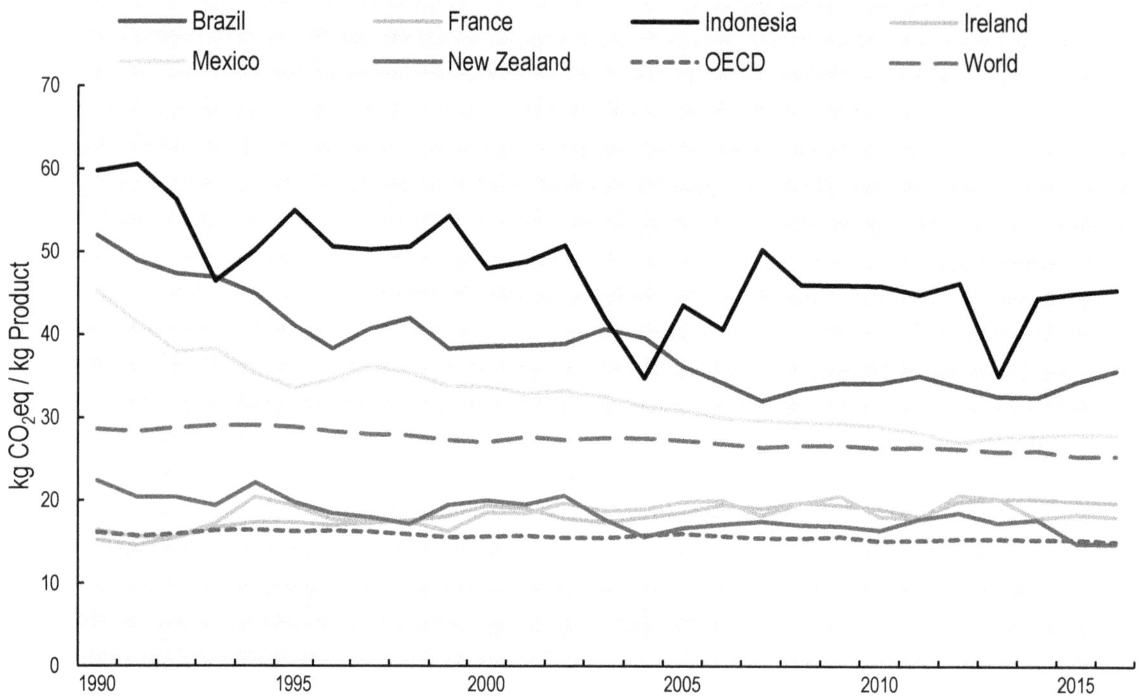

Source: FAOSTAT (2017[3]), *Food and Agriculture data*, http://www.fao.org/faostat/en/#data

Figure 2.9. GHG emissions generated within farm gate per kilogram of milk production

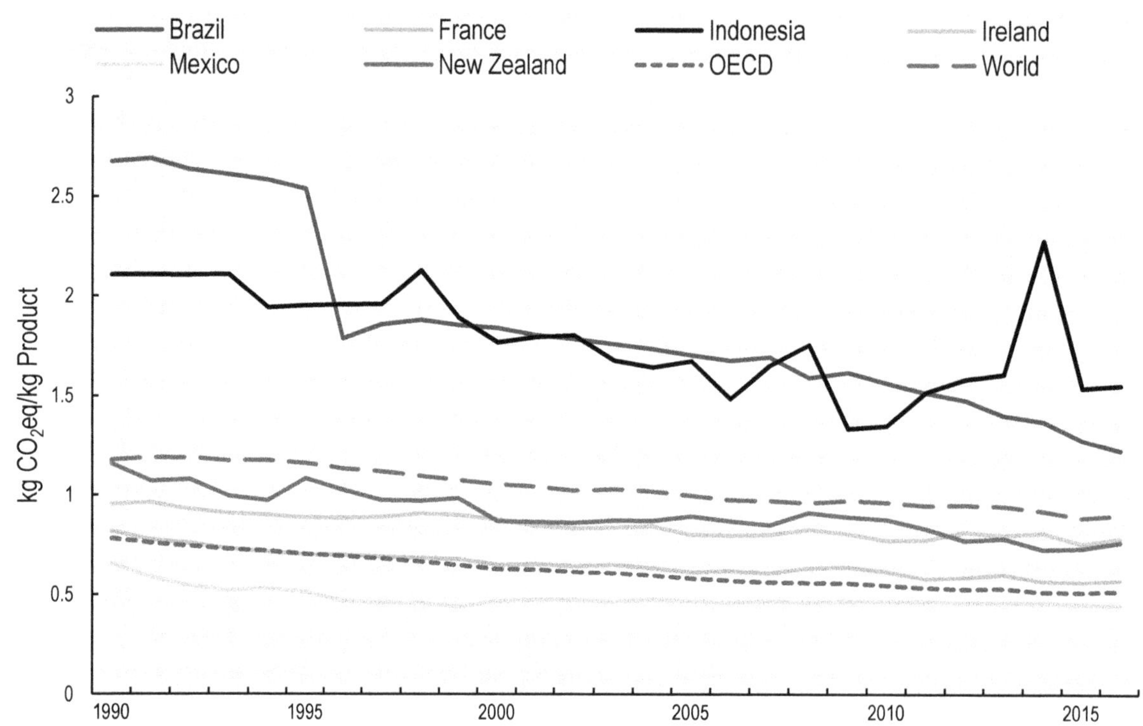

Source: FAOSTAT (2017[3]), *Food and Agriculture data*, http://www.fao.org/faostat/en/#data

Food systems

Other agri-environment indicators also exist, such as the farmland bird index, pesticide sales and nutrient balance. These indicators provide additional information on the sustainability of agriculture.[4] The OECD tracks this information for OECD and some other countries, though complete data is not always available for all countries. For example, time-series data on the farmland bird index is available for France (showing a decline over time). Data on pesticide sales is available for France, Mexico, and New Zealand.

Food security is a growing concern globally, according to FAO et al. (2017[17]), the estimated number of undernourished people – having been on the decline for the past decade – increased from 777 million in 2015 to 815 million in 2016 (i.e. to 11% of global population). Food security issues are in part caused by inefficiencies in global food systems and the recent increases can be traced to the greater number of conflicts. These issues are often exacerbated by climate-related shocks, which are expected to increase in frequency and severity as a result of human GHG emissions, and the reduced resilience of ecosystems from degradation and biodiversity loss. Contrastingly, the same inefficiencies combined with unhealthy consumption patterns also produce the opposite issues in different regions. The global prevalence of obesity is rapidly on the rise, with 13% of the world adult population classified as obese in 2014. The problem is most severe in Northern America, Europe and Oceania, where 28% of adults are classified as obese, compared with 7 % in Asia and 11 % in Africa. In Latin America and the Caribbean, roughly one-quarter of the adult population is currently considered obese (FAO et al., 2017[17]). Addressing the inefficiencies in global food systems, reducing anthropogenic GHG emissions and tackling ecosystem degradation is a key addressing food security issues, especially under environmental change in the future.

The *OECD-FAO Agricultural Outlook 2018-2027* (2018[18]) projects that across most commodities, the growth in total demand (including non-food uses) will slow considerably compared to the previous decade (Figure 2.10). Future growth in crop production is expected to come mostly from increasing yields. Yield growth is projected to decrease slightly, but output could be raised by closing large yield gaps, especially in Sub-Saharan Africa. Nevertheless, the *Outlook* indicates that food insecurity will remain a critical global concern. Further, because the areas of projected food demand growth differ from the areas where supply can be increased sustainably, international trade will become increasingly import for adapting to and mitigating climate change and achieving the SDGs.

Food waste and food loss (FLW) also has major implications for land use, biodiversity, climate change and water. An estimated one third of all food produced for human consumption is either lost or wasted (FAO, 2013[19]). This equates to approximately 1.3 billion tonnes a year, worth an estimated USD 936 billion and generating around 4.4 $GtCO_2$. Compared to countries FLW is the third biggest emitter globally (behind only the USA and China) (FAO, 2013[19]; FAO, 2015[20]; FAO, 2013[21]). Importantly for the land-use nexus, the production from approximately 30% of global agricultural land is wasted every year, which equates to 1.4 billion hectares (FAO, 2013[21]), an area larger than the total land area of all the case study countries combined.

Figure 2.10. Annual growth in consumption for key commodity groups, 2008-17 and 2018-27

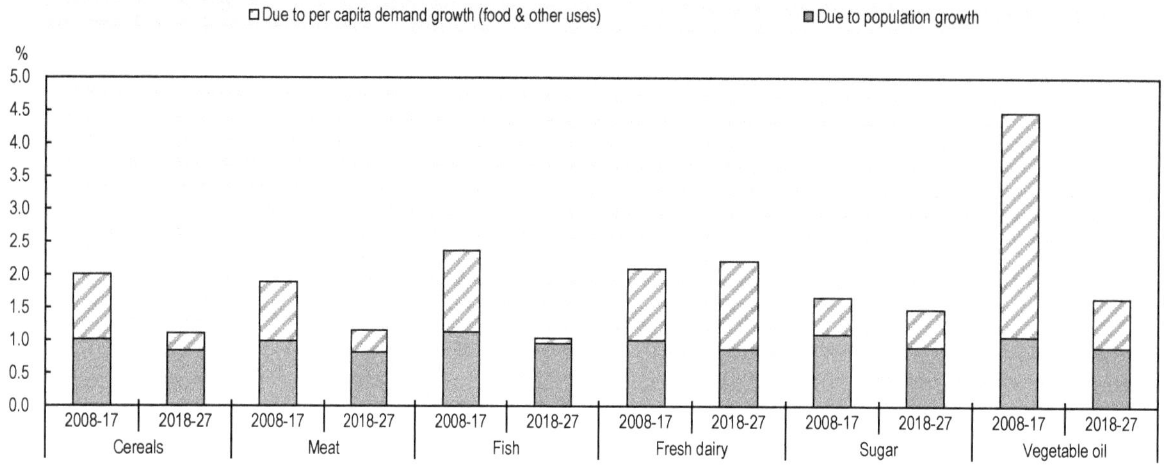

Note: The population growth component is calculated assuming per capita demand remains constant at the level of the year preceding the decade. Growth rates refer to total demand (for food, feed and other uses).
Source: OECD/FAO (2018[18]), *OECD-FAO Agricultural Outlook*, http://dx.doi.org/10.1787/agr-outl-data-en.

Figure 2.11. Kilograms of food waste per capita per year

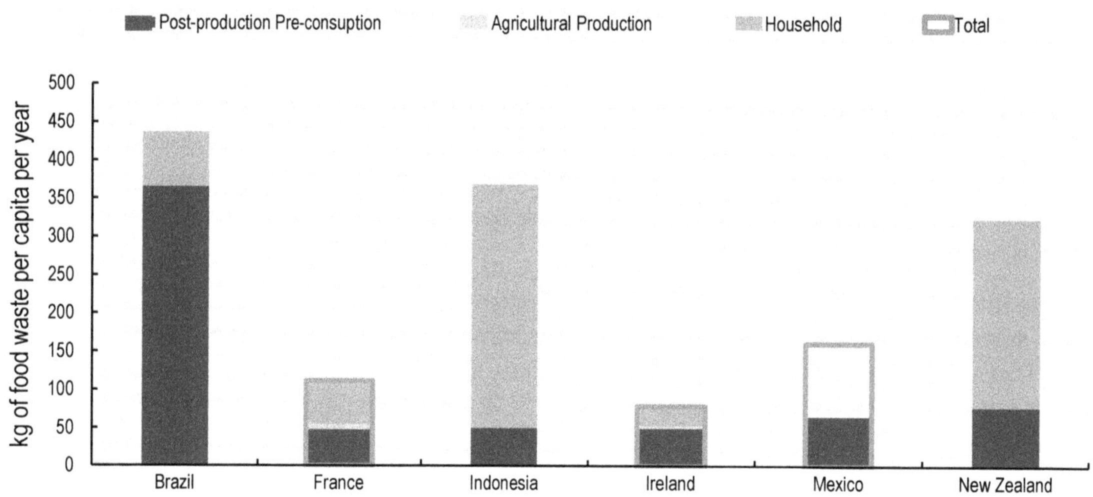

Note: The estimates of food waste in this graph should not be directly compared between countries as different methodologies were used in the estimation.
Source: Brazil and Indonesia: EIU (2018[22]) *Food Sustainability Index, Country Index and Data,* http://foodsustainability.eiu.com/
France and Ireland: OECD (2018[23]) *Food Waste database,* https://stats.oecd.org/viewhtml.aspx?datasetcode=FOOD_WASTE&lang=en;
Mexico: Aguilar Gutiérrez (2016[24]) *Food Losses and food Waste in Mexico,* http://www.cec.org/sites/default/files/pdf/fww/wb-presentations/6-genaro-aguilar.pdf; New Zealand: Yates (2013[25]), *Summary of existing information on domestic food waste in New Zealand Document quality control*, http://www.wasteminz.org.nz/wp-content/uploads/Report-on-Food-Waste-in-NZ-2013-Final-1.1.pdf and Reynolds *et al.* (2016[26]), *New Zealand's Food Waste: Estimating the Tonnes, Value, Calories and Resources Wasted*, http://dx.doi.org/10.3390/agriculture6010009.
All countries: FAOSTAT (2018[27]), *Food Balance Sheets*, http://www.fao.org/faostat/en/#data/FBS

Estimates for per capita food waste in the six case study countries vary substantially. The volumes presented in Figure 2.11 are not all directly comparable (due to the differing methodologies used to derive them), and should be treated with caution. Generally, household level FLW is comprised of edible food and is potentially avoidable, whereas feasibility and desirability of avoiding post-production, pre-consumption FLW varies with both the type of food and the position the loss occurs in the food supply chain. There is also considerable uncertainty within the data. Indonesia for example has, according to some sources, both the second highest per capita level of household food waste globally (315kg/capita/year) (behind Saudi Arabia) (EIU, 2018[22]) and over 30% of children under 5 are malnourished (WFP, 2018[28]). However, other estimates of household food waste in Indonesia show large variation from 6kg/capita/year (EIU, 2019[29])[5] to 253kg/capita/year (Meidiana and Gamse, 2010[30]) highlighting the considerable uncertainty associated with these data. The high level of post-production pre-consumption waste seen in Brazil (much higher than other countries) is probably a result of viewing the data on a per capita basis which tends to lead to inflated figures in countries which export large volumes of agricultural produce. When viewed as a proportion of production, post-production pre-consumption food waste in Brazil is similar to Indonesia and only marginally more than Mexico and New Zealand. In general, household level food waste is higher in developed than developing countries.

International Trade

The consumption of goods traded internationally accounts for an estimated 25% of agricultural and forestry impacts on bird extinctions, and for 21% of impacts on terrestrial carbon sequestration (Marques et al., 2019[31]). Globally, 20% of wheat, 12% of maize and more than 60% of global soy production is exported (Fischer, Byerlee and Esmeades, 2014[32]). Indeed, Brazil exports two-thirds (41 Mt of 62Mt) of its soybean production (ibid). Indonesia is the world's largest producer of palm oil, with 76.5% of palm oil production exported in 2013 (FAOSTAT, 2017[3]). Production of palm oil in Indonesia has grown at 4.9% per year between 1991-2010 (Fischer, Byerlee and Esmeades, 2014[32]). Beyond these examples, international trade in goods whose production significantly impacts the nexus is important for all case study countries. When comparing trade in forest products to trade in agricultural products, the latter emerges as the more important category both (i) economically and, in most cases, (ii) in terms of land-use nexus impacts. [6] However, when forest products originate from primary forests, nexus impacts per traded unit, in particular biodiversity impacts, are high and often irreversible.

In economic terms, export revenues from agriculture exceeded those from forest products by a factor of between four (Indonesia) and 52 (Mexico) in 2016 (FAO, 2018[33]). Figure 2.12 illustrates the economic importance of international trade in agricultural products in terms of the case study countries' exports share of agricultural GDP for 10 years from 2005. The importance of agricultural exports varies significantly between the countries, and has grown in all case study countries except Indonesia (where it slightly declined) in this time period.

Figure 2.12. Share of exports in agricultural GDP

Domestic Value-Added Content of Exports from the Agriculture, Forestry and Fisheries in percent of total Value-Added by these sectors

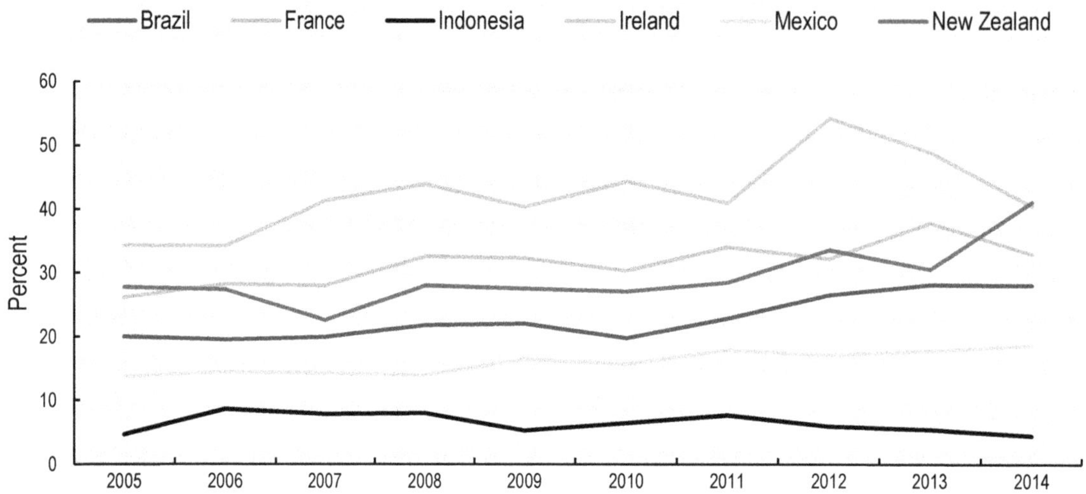

Note: The low Indonesian ratio is partly related to the fact that a large share of the value addition of main Indonesian export products such as palm oil and rubber occurs during their processing and manufacturing, which in accordance with the ISIC4 Classification of Economic Activities is not captured here. Because values for fisheries are reported in conjunction with forestry and agriculture under this classification, fisheries are included here although they are not the focus of this report. Since the economic contribution of fisheries to the variables considered here is marginal for all case study countries, the reported trends are however valid for land-based components of agricultural GDP, too.
Source: OECD (2018[34]), *Trade in Value Added* (database), oe.cd/tiva

Figure 2.13 shows the economic importance of international trade in agricultural products by another measure, their share in total goods trade. While the share of agricultural products in goods imports lies between 7% (Brazil) and 12.3% (Indonesia) for all case study countries, the share of agricultural exports in total goods exports varies more substantially, ranging from 7.5% (Mexico) to 57.1% (New Zealand). Figure 2.13 also facilitates the interpretation of trends in Figure 2.12 above. Those countries with the highest share of exports in agricultural GDP (Ireland, New Zealand, France) tend to export more higher-value products (such as animal products, processed foods and beverages), the other case study countries tend to export primary commodities such as soy and rubber.

Figure 2.13. Share of different agricultural products in total goods trade (by value), 2016

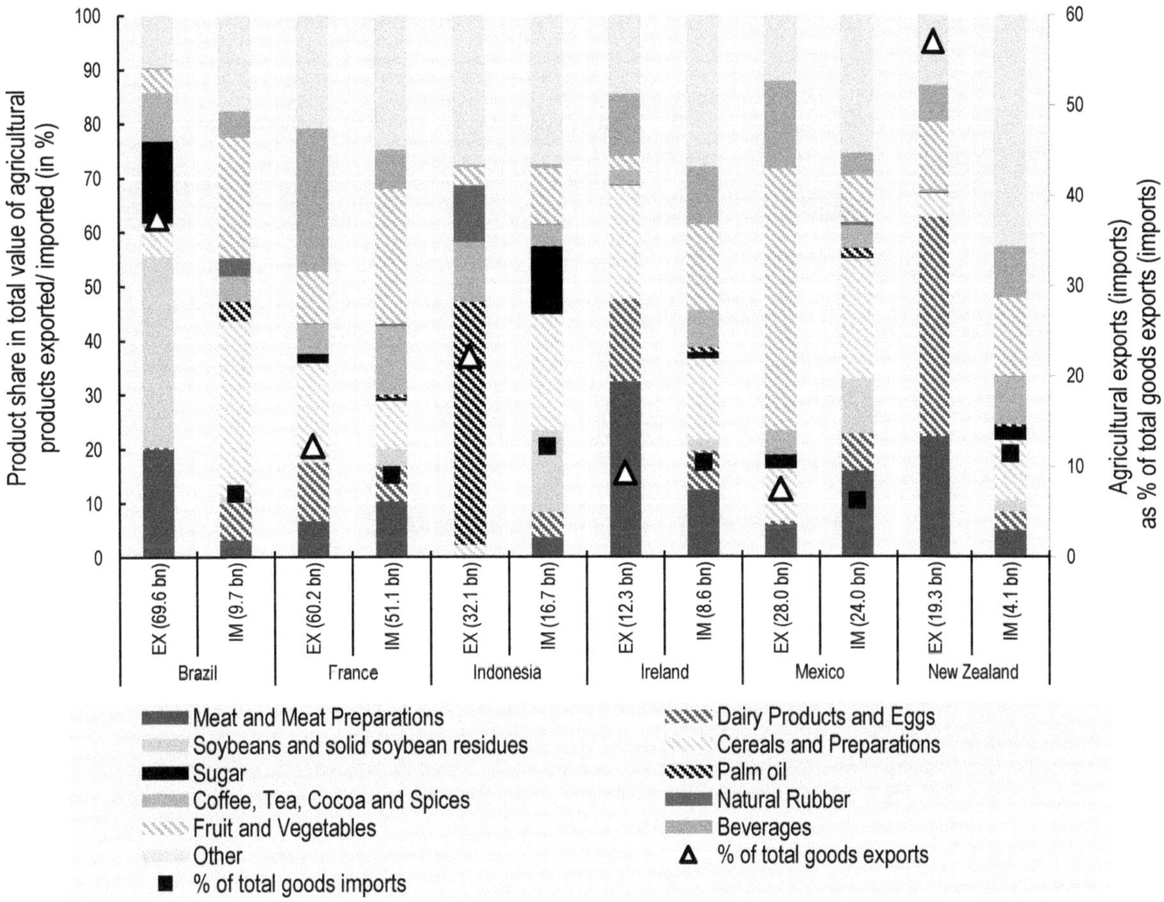

Note: The total value of all agricultural exports (EX) and imports (IM), indicated in the bar labels, is given in billion (bn) USD.
Source: Authors based on FAOSTAT (2018[33]), *Food and Agriculture data* (database), http://www.fao.org/faostat/en/#data and (UN Comtrade, n.d.[35]), *International Trade Statistics* (database), http://comtrade.un.org.

One way to compare the land-use nexus impacts embodied in international trade across countries is the land footprint of national production and consumption. Figure 2.14 illustrates results of the estimation approach adopted by the Global Footprint Network (2018[36]) disaggregated by land type, and shows that land requirements embodied in international flows of goods are substantial for some countries.[7] In fact, countries whose ecological footprint of consumption exceeds their export production footprint (Ireland, Mexico) are in effect net importers of land. The other case study countries are net "exporters" of biocapacity, meaning more biologically productive land is embodied in their exports than in their imports. While for Brazil, cropland contributes more than twice as much as forest or grazing land to net biocapacity exports, for both New Zealand and Indonesia forest land constitutes the largest source of net biocapacity exports.[8] Lastly, given the important export share of its livestock sector, Ireland is a net "importer" of cropland but a net "exporter" of grazing land. While Figure 2.14 displays the net trade balance of land flows embodied in production and consumption ("virtual land flows"), it must be noted that gross virtual land flows exceed net flows substantially due to circular loops in increasingly integrated markets for agricultural products (Harchaoui and Chatzimpiros, 2017[37]).

Figure 2.14. Net biocapacity exports, 2014

Percentage values: Share of net biocapacity exports in a country's total biocapacity from cropland, grazing land and forest land

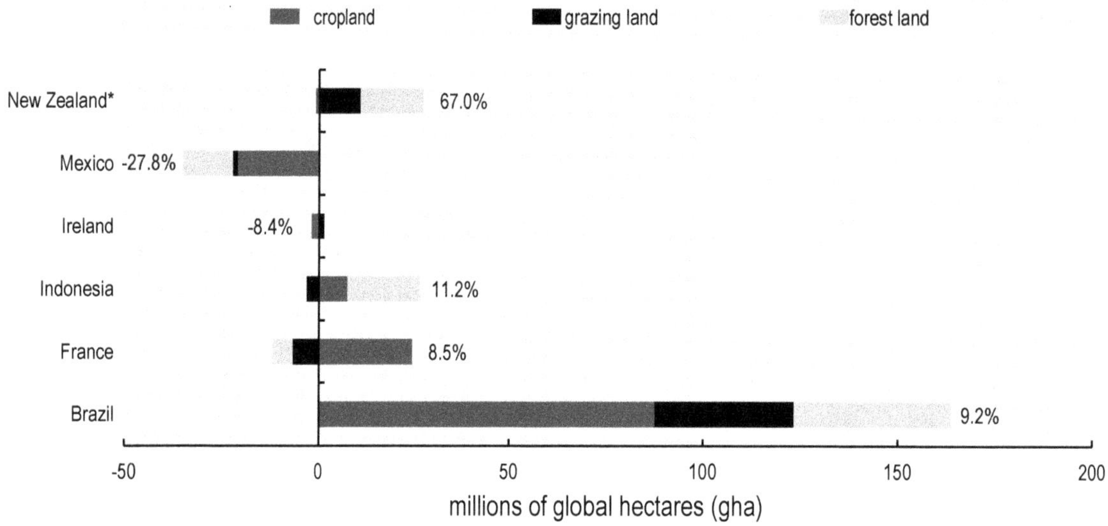

Note: *Note that data displayed for New Zealand refers to 2013. Percentage values indicate the share of net biocapacity exports in a country's total biocapacity from cropland, grazing land and forest land. Biocapacity is the capacity of a country's ecosystems to regenerate what people demand from those surfaces including space for growing food, fibre production, and timber regeneration. Cropland is defined as the area needed to grow 177 agricultural products contained in the FAOstat database. Grazing land is defined as the area required to grow grass feed required for feeding a country's livestock under national average grazing land productivity and after accounting for other feed sources. Forest land represents the area of forest land needed to supply wood for fuel, construction, and paper. The Ecological Footprint of Production indicates the consumption of biocapacity resulting from production processes within a country, and the Ecological Footprint of Consumption indicates biocapacity actually consumed by a country's inhabitants. Differences between production and consumption footprints result in biocapacity imports or exports attributable to international trade. Biocapacity is measured in global hectares, a productivity-weighted measurement unit making biologically productive areas of different land types comparable.
Source: Authors based on Global Footprint Network (2018[36]), *National Footprint Accounts*, **http://data.footprintnetwork.org/#/**

Patterns of trade illustrated by Figure 2.12, Figure 2.13., and Figure 2.14 have important land-use nexus impacts in the case study countries and beyond. In Brazil, for instance, more than 50% of tree cover loss between 2005 and 2015 have been attributed to commodity-driven deforestation (Global Forest Watch, 2019[38]), primarily associated with beef and soy production, two of Brazil's main export commodities (Henders, Persson and Kastner, 2015[39]). While more recent trends in land use mean that this proportion might have changed, a number of earlier studies estimate that an approximate share of 30% of Brazil's LUC emissions were historically embodied in exports (Saikku, Soimakallio and Pingoud, 2012[40]; Karstensen, Peters and Andrew, 2013[41]). In Indonesia, quantitative data on the drivers of deforestation are rare, but an estimated 23% to 50% of deforestation after 2000 has been attributed to the expansion of oil palm plantations (Austin et al., 2019[42]; Henders, Persson and Kastner, 2015[39]), used to produce palm oil, a key export commodity. Adverse biodiversity impacts attributable to the production of export commodities have also been estimated. Chaudhary and Kastner (2016[43]), for instance, report that among all countries Indonesia has the highest biodiversity impacts in terms of species loss attributable to food exports, more than twice that of second-ranked Thailand.[9]

In Mexico, research suggests that while the global environmental impacts of agricultural production have been reduced due to trade liberalisation under the North American Free Trade Agreement (NAFTA), more severe environmental impacts have shifted from the US to Mexico (Martinez-Melendez and Bennett, 2016[44]). In fact, agricultural intensification in the wake of NAFTA is likely to have led to significant biodiversity impacts through the wide-scale replacement of traditional cropping systems by input-intensive modern production systems (Orozco-Ramírez et al., 2017[45]; UNCTAD, 2013[46]). In the case of France, studies have focused on the extent to which imported goods embody deforestation and biodiversity threats abroad. Envol Vert (2018[47]), for instance, reports that the deforestation footprint of the average French consumer is 352 m^2 per year, 59% of which is attributable to soy (mainly from Brazil) embodied in animal products.

Domestic impacts on the land-use nexus attributable to international trade also occur in developed countries. New Zealand and Ireland both export large quantities of, dairy and beef, which are emission-intensive to produce. While exports of these products continue to grow, this growth model is starting "to show its environmental limits" in New Zealand (OECD, 2017, p. 15[48]). Beyond domestic land-use and emissions impacts, animal feed imports imply impacts on land-use outcomes abroad, too. In Ireland, for instance, among agricultural products, animal feed imports constitute the most important import category (in volumetric terms)[10] reported by (Department of Agriculture; Food and the Marine, 2018[49]).

References

Agriculture and Food Development Authority (2017), *Agriculture in Ireland - Teagasc | Agriculture and Food Development Authority*, https://www.teagasc.ie/rural-economy/rural-economy/agri-food-business/agriculture-in-ireland/ (accessed on 22 May 2019). [12]

Aguilar Gutiérrez, G. (2016), *Food Losses and Food Waste in Mexico: Quantification and Some Proposals for Public Policy*, International Workshop on Food Loss and Food Waste, November 7–9. [24]

Austin, K. et al. (2019), "What causes deforestation in Indonesia?", *Environmental Research Letters*, Vol. 14/2, p. 024007, http://dx.doi.org/10.1088/1748-9326/aaf6db. [42]

Bowles, N., S. Alexander and M. Hadjikakou (2019), "The livestock sector and planetary boundaries: A 'limits to growth' perspective with dietary implications", *Ecological Economics*, Vol. 160, pp. 128-136, http://dx.doi.org/10.1016/J.ECOLECON.2019.01.033. [10]

Chaudhary, A. and T. Kastner (2016), "Land use biodiversity impacts embodied in international food trade", *Global Environmental Change*, Vol. 38, pp. 195-204, http://dx.doi.org/10.1016/J.GLOENVCHA.2016.03.013. [43]

Department of Agriculture; Food and the Marine (2018), *Annual Review and Outlook for Agriculture, Food and the Marine 2018*, Government of Ireland, Dublin, https://www.agriculture.gov.ie/media/migration/publications/2018/AnnualReviewandOutlook2018310818.pdf (accessed on 4 February 2019). [49]

EIU (2019), *Food Sustainability Index 2018: Data*, http://foodsustainability.eiu.com/wp-content/uploads/sites/34/2018/11/Food-Sustainability-Index-2018_EIU_BCFN_23-November.xlsm. [29]

EIU (2018), *Food Sustainability Index, Country Index and Data*, http://foodsustainability.eiu.com/ (accessed on 18 October 2018). [22]

Envol Vert (2018), *L'Empreinte Foret des Francais*, Author, Paris, http://envol-vert.org/wp-content/uploads/2018/11/Envol_Vert_Rapport_Empreinte_Foret_Final.pdf (accessed on 6 February 2019). [47]

FAO (2018), *FAOSTAT*, Food and Agriculture Organization of the United Nations, http://www.fao.org/faostat/en/#home (accessed on 7 February 2019). [33]

FAO (2016), *State of the World's Forests*, Food and Agriculture Organization, Rome, http://www.fao.org/3/a-i5588e.pdf. [2]

FAO (2015), *Food wastage footprint and Climate Change*. [20]

FAO (2014), *Contribution of the Forestry Sector to National Economies 1990-2011*, Food and Agriculture Organization. [5]

FAO (2013), *Food Wastage Footprint: Full-cost Accounting*, Food and Agriculture Organisation of the United Nations, Rome. [19]

FAO (2013), *Food wastage footprint: Impacts on natural resources - Summary report*, Food and Agriculture Organisation, http://www.fao.org/docrep/018/i3347e/i3347e.pdf (accessed on 29 November 2018). [21]

FAO et al. (2017), *The State of Food Security and Nutrition in the World 2017. Building resilience for peace and food security.*, FAO, Rome, http://www.fao.org/3/a-I7695e.pdf (accessed on 17 September 2019). [17]

FAOSTAT (2018), *Food Balance Sheets*, http://www.fao.org/faostat/en/#data/FBS (accessed on 18 October 2018). [27]

FAOSTAT (2017), *Food and Agriculture data*, Food and Agriculture Organization, http://www.fao.org/ag/save-and-Grow/en/1/index.html. [3]

Fischer, T., D. Byerlee and G. Esmeades (2014), *Crop yields and global food security: will yield increase continue to feed the world?*, Australian Centre for International Agricultural Research, Canberra, https://www.aciar.gov.au/node/12101. [32]

Fitzgerald, C. (2019), *Dairy in the Irish Economy!*, Teagasc, https://www.teagasc.ie/media/website/publications/2019/Dairy-in-the-Irish-economy!.pdf. [13]

Foote, K., M. Joy and R. Death (2015), "New Zealand Dairy Farming: Milking Our Environment for All Its Worth", *Environmental Management*, Vol. 56/3, pp. 709-720, http://dx.doi.org/10.1007/s00267-015-0517-x. [16]

Galli, A. et al. (2016), "Questioning the Ecological Footprint", *Ecological Indicators*, Vol. 69, pp. 224-232, http://dx.doi.org/10.1016/J.ECOLIND.2016.04.014. [51]

Gerber, P. et al. (2013), *Tackling Climate Change through Livestock: A Global Assessment of Emissions and Mitigation Opportunities*, Food and Agriculture Organization of the United Nations, Rome, Italy, http://www.fao.org/publications (accessed on 13 May 2019). [8]

Global Footprint Network (2018), *National Footprint Accounts*, http://data.footprintnetwork.org/#/ (accessed on 5 June 2019). [36]

Global Forest Watch (2019), *Brazil Country Profile*, https://www.globalforestwatch.org/dashboards/country/BRA?treeLossTsc=eyJoaWdobGlnaHRlZCI6ZmFsc2V9 (accessed on 18 March 2019). [38]

Harchaoui, S. and P. Chatzimpiros (2017), "Reconstructing production efficiency, land use and trade for livestock systems in historical perspective. The case of France, 1961–2010", *Land Use Policy*, Vol. 67, pp. 378-386, http://dx.doi.org/10.1016/J.LANDUSEPOL.2017.05.028. [37]

Haščič, I. and A. Mackie (2018), "Land Cover Change and Conversions: Methodology and Results for OECD and G20 Countries", *OECD Green Growth Papers*, No. 2018/04, OECD Publishing, Paris, https://dx.doi.org/10.1787/72a9e331-en. [1]

Henders, S., U. Persson and T. Kastner (2015), "Trading forests: land-use change and carbon emissions embodied in production and exports of forest-risk commodities", *Environmental Research Letters*, Vol. 10/12, p. 125012, http://dx.doi.org/10.1088/1748-9326/10/12/125012. [39]

Karstensen, J., G. Peters and R. Andrew (2013), "Attribution of CO2 emissions from Brazilian deforestation to consumers between 1990 and 2010", *Environmental Research Letters*, Vol. 8/2, p. 024005, http://dx.doi.org/10.1088/1748-9326/8/2/024005. [41]

Marques, A. et al. (2019), "Increasing impacts of land use on biodiversity and carbon sequestration driven by population and economic growth", *Nature Ecology & Evolution*, Vol. 3/4, pp. 628-637, http://dx.doi.org/10.1038/s41559-019-0824-3. [31]

Martinez-Melendez, L. and E. Bennett (2016), "Trade in the US and Mexico helps reduce environmental costs of agriculture", *Environmental Research Letters*, http://dx.doi.org/10.1088/1748-9326/11/5/055004. [44]

Meidiana, C. and T. Gamse (2010), *Development of Waste Management Practices in Indonesia*, http://www.eurojournals.com/ejsr.htm (accessed on 10 January 2019). [30]

Ministry for the Environment (2019), *Environment Aotearoa 2019*, Government of New Zealand, Wellington, https://www.mfe.govt.nz/sites/default/files/media/Environmental%20reporting/environment-aotearoa-2019.pdf. [15]

National Drought Mitigation Center (n.d.), *Reported Effects of the 1997-98 El Niño*, http://jrscience.wcp.muohio.edu/studentresearch/climatechange03/elnino/elninoanalysis.pdf. [6]

OECD (2018), *Food Waste Database*, https://stats.oecd.org/viewhtml.aspx?datasetcode=FOOD_WASTE&lang=en (accessed on 28 November 2018). [23]

OECD (2018), *Trade in Value Added*, http://www.oecd.org/sti/ind/measuring-trade-in-value-added.htm (accessed on 5 June 2019). [34]

OECD (2017), *OECD Environmental Performance Reviews: New Zealand 2017*, https://www.oecd-ilibrary.org/docserver/9789264268203-en.pdf?expires=1548772643&id=id&accname=ocid84004878&checksum=34BA8F8BD5F9B3671D35BB832DFAA3C1 (accessed on 29 January 2019). [48]

OECD (2013), "Biodiversity: Farmland bird populations and agricultural land cover", in *OECD Compendium of Agri-environmental Indicators*, OECD Publishing, Paris, https://dx.doi.org/10.1787/9789264186217-15-en. [50]

OECD/FAO (2018), *OECD-FAO Agricultural Outlook 2018-2027*, OECD Publishing, Paris/Food and Agriculture Organization of the United Nations, Rome, https://dx.doi.org/10.1787/agr_outlook-2018-en. [18]

OECDSTAT (2017), *National Inventory Submissions 2017 to the United Nations Framework Convention on Climate Change (UNFCCC, CRF tables), and replies to the OECD State of the Environment Questionnaire*, OECD Publishing, http://dotstat.oecd.org/?lang=en. [4]

Orozco-Ramírez, Q. et al. (2017), "Agricultural Land Use Change after NAFTA in Central West Mexico", *Land*, Vol. 6/4, p. 66, http://dx.doi.org/10.3390/land6040066. [45]

Reynolds, C., M. Mirosa and B. Clothier (2016), "New Zealand's Food Waste: Estimating the Tonnes, Value, Calories and Resources Wasted", *Agriculture*, http://dx.doi.org/10.3390/agriculture6010009. [26]

Saikku, L., S. Soimakallio and K. Pingoud (2012), "Attributing land-use change carbon emissions to exported biomass", *Environmental Impact Assessment Review*, Vol. 37, pp. 47-54, http://dx.doi.org/10.1016/J.EIAR.2012.03.006. [40]

Stats NZ (2019), *Overseas merchandise trade: December 2018 | Stats NZ*, https://www.stats.govt.nz/information-releases/overseas-merchandise-trade-december-2018 (accessed on 15 May 2019). [14]

Styles, D. et al. (2018), "Climate mitigation by dairy intensification depends on intensive use of spared grassland", *Global Change Biology*, Vol. 24, pp. 681-693, http://dx.doi.org/10.1111/gcb.13868. [11]

Trading Economics (2018), *Trading Economics Currency Data*, https://tradingeconomics.com/indonesia/currency. [7]

UN Comtrade (n.d.), *International Trade Statistics*, 2019, https://comtrade.un.org/data/ (accessed on 5 June 2019). [35]

UNCTAD (2013), *Mexico's Agriculture Development: Perspectives and outlook*, Author, Geneva, Switzerland, https://unctad.org/en/PublicationsLibrary/ditctncd2012d2_en.pdf (accessed on 7 February 2019). [46]

Weiss, F. and A. Leip (2012), "Greenhouse gas emissions from the EU livestock sector: A life cycle assessment carried out with the CAPRI model", *Agriculture, Ecosystems & Environment*, Vol. 149, pp. 124-134, http://dx.doi.org/10.1016/J.AGEE.2011.12.015. [9]

WFP (2018), *Indonesia Country Brief*, World Food Programme, http://www.wfp.org/countries/Indonesia (accessed on 29 November 2018). [28]

Yates, S. (2013), *Summary of existing information on domestic food waste in New Zealand Document quality control*, Waste Not Consulting. [25]

Annex 2.A. Land-cover change in France, Ireland, Mexico and New Zealand

Annex Figure 2.A.1. Land Conversion in France, Ireland, Mexico and New Zealand

1992-2015, thousand km^2

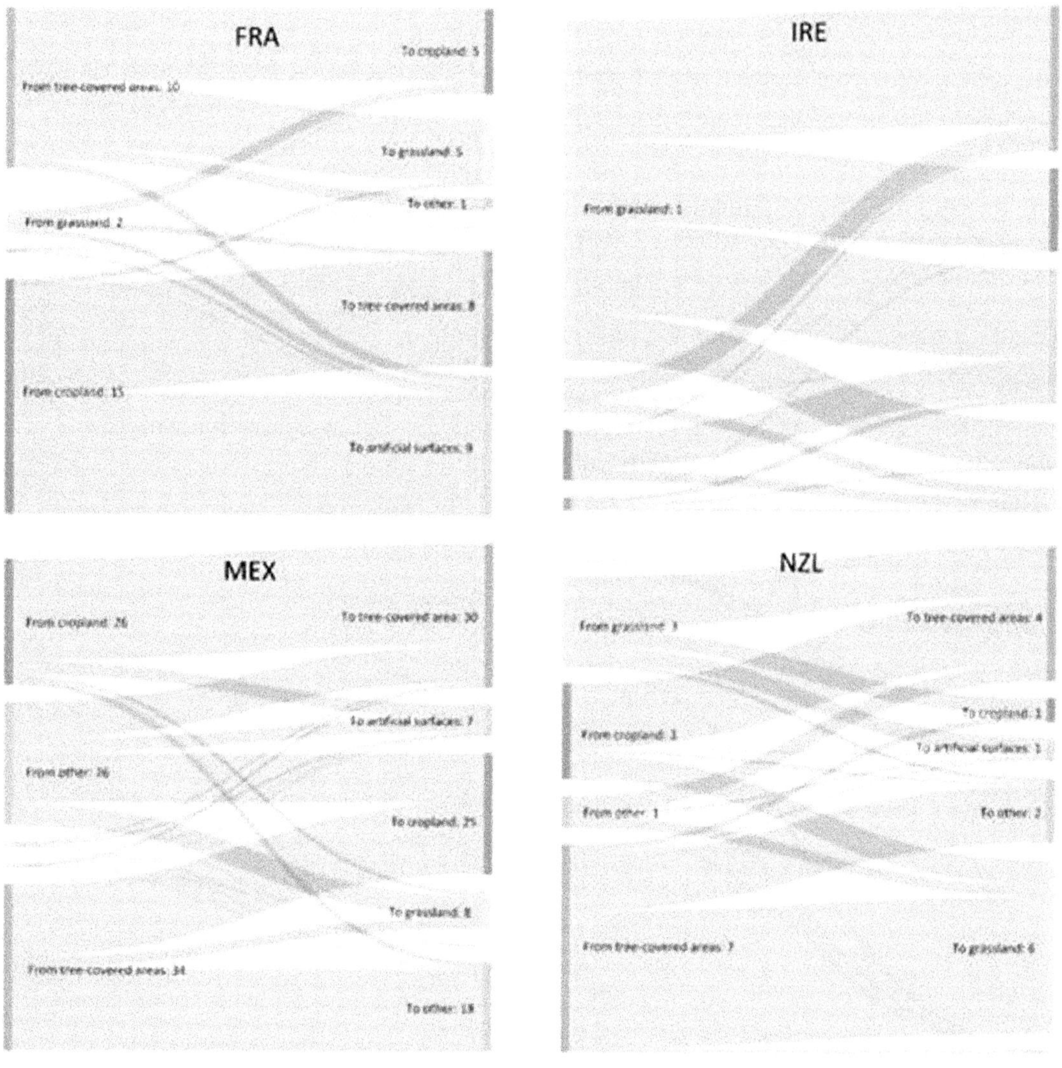

Note: Six IPCC-like top-level categories. "Other" consists of water, bare land, shrubland, and sparse vegetation. Flow sizes are indicated numerically for flows of more than one thousand km2.
Source: OECD calculations based on CCI-LC database in "Land cover change and conversions: Methodology and results for OECD and G20 countries" (Haščič and Mackie, 2018[1]).

Notes

[1] The CCI-LC datasets are currently the only available global datasets that can provide some acceptably harmonised indication of the type and intensity of change *between* different land cover types. See (Haščič and Mackie, 2018[1]) for a description of the dataset.

[2] Misclassification is more likely between different vegetated land types as these classes are often similar and are more difficult to reliably distinguish. For example, the observed conversions from wetlands to tree-cover seen in Figure 2.1 is partly an ambiguous classification issue: the observable biophysical difference between the wetland definition (*Shrub or herbaceous cover, flooded, fresh-saline or brackish water*) and the flooded forest classes (*Tree cover, flooded, fresh or brackish water, Tree cover, flooded, saline water*) is small and difficult to distinguish reliably via remote sensing (Haščič and Mackie, 2018[1]).

[3] The methodology used to assess the impacts of particular land uses has important implications for decision making as it directly influences the perceived size of any trade-offs and synergies between areas in the land use nexus.

[4] For example, the farmland bird index is an average trend in a group of species suited to track trends in the condition of farmland habitats. In general, a decrease in the index means that the balance of bird species population trends are negative, representing biodiversity loss (OECD, 2013[50]).

[5] Methodological changes between the 2017 and the 2018 food sustainability index caused the household food waste estimates for Indonesia to change from 315kg/capita/year to 6kg/capita/year, for full details see http://foodsustainability.eiu.com/wp-content/uploads/sites/34/2018/11/FSI-2018-Methodology-Paper_full_December-2018.pdf

[6] Clearly, subsistence agriculture and other forms of agricultural production for domestic consumption are important in some contexts, accounting for an important share of both economic value-creation and land-use impacts of total agricultural production. This, however, is not captured in the trade statistics presented in this chapter.

[7] The debate about the robustness of this approach is ongoing for reasons including the accurateness of the proxy adopted (land use) for the variable of interest (environmental impact), and the difficulty of comparing heterogeneous environmental impacts across locations (see e.g. (Galli et al., 2016[51]) for a discussion). In Figure 2.14, for instance, land-use nexus impacts associated with virtual exports of forest land are likely to substantially differ between the tropical forests of Indonesia and Brazil and the temperate forests of other case study countries.

[8] From an environmental perspective, net biocapacity exports of forest land will not have negative nexus impacts as long as they are produced from sustainably managed forests.

[9] Species loss attributable to food exports is estimated using the countryside species area relationship (SAR) model. For full details, see (Chaudhary and Kastner, 2016[43]).

[10] Since land-use nexus impacts often represent externalised costs imperfectly reflected in prices, volumetric measures of trade can usefully complement monetary accounts and enhance a quantitative understanding of land-use impacts associated with imports and exports.

3 Coherence across national strategies and plans for sustainable land use

National strategies and plans establish a country's medium- to long-term priorities across a range of sectors. This chapter analyses the extent to which land use, biodiversity, climate and food considerations are included in the strategies and action plans developed in the case study countries (Brazil, France, Indonesia, Ireland, Mexico and New Zealand). The chapter analyses the coherence between land-use relevant targets in Nationally Determined Contributions (NDCs) (developed in response to the Paris Agreement), long-term Low Emissions Development Strategies (LEDS), National Biodiversity Strategies and Action Plans (NBSAP) (developed in response to the UN Convention on Biological Diversity), Agricultural Development Plans, National Development Plans (or similar), National Forestry Plans and National Trade or Export Plans.

National strategies establish a country's medium- to long-term priorities in various areas. They are intended to guide and steer national actions in particular sectors or policy areas. In some cases (notably for biodiversity), strategies also include associated action plans. National strategies, therefore, should develop, in a consultative manner, common objectives that various Ministries will need to work towards. National strategies should provide clear and actionable objectives that the national government – and all relevant Ministries – should be striving to achieve. To this end, strategies and action plans that set specific, measurable, time-bound targets, and that also identify indicators against which progress can be assessed, can strongly facilitate this process. Given the various potential synergies and trade-offs across sectors and policy areas, the various multiple strategies should be coherent with one another.

In some cases, the development of national strategies are encouraged or required by overarching international multilateral agreements or initiatives. This is true, for example, for National Biodiversity Strategies and Action Plans (NBSAPs) required under the Convention on Biological Diversity, or for National Strategy or Action Plans required for implementation of REDD+ under the UNFCCC. Nevertheless, even without international agreements in other areas of the land-use nexus, nearly all governments have established national agricultural strategies or plans, forestry plans, and overarching economic growth or development plans.

Key strategies and plans that are relevant to the land-use nexus include Nationally Determined Contributions (NDCs), long-term Low Emissions Development Strategies (LEDS), NBSAPs, Agricultural Development Plans, National Development Plans (or similar), and National Trade or Export Plans. This Chapter begins with a brief overview of the relevant multilateral agreements in the land-use nexus, and the requirements or guidelines to transpose these at the national level, thereunder. It then proceeds to compare relevant national strategies and plans across the six case study countries, to examine their degree of coherence.

The role of multilateral agreements in guiding national strategies

At the international level, the 2030 Agenda and the Sustainable Development Goals have spurred efforts to examine, more holistically, how actions to achieve one goal may interact, both positively and negatively, to achieve others (outlined in chapter 1). The specific targets, as well as the indicators, set a framework for action across the multiple sustainable development areas, including the need for policy coherence (SDG 17). Similarly, though focussing on specific environmental areas, the UNFCCC and the CBD set the international framework for action on climate change and on biodiversity, respectively.[1] These differ in various ways in terms of the information that countries are invited or required to submit, including with respect to national strategies and plans (Table 3.1), as well as the timelines covered.

Under the Paris agreement, Parties are required to submit NDCs stating their GHG emission targets. These NDCs are relatively short-term, with the first running until 2025 or 2030 (to be followed by subsequent NDCs). It is for countries to determine the level and sectoral coverage of such targets. Some of the NDCs include explicit references to forests[2] and agriculture and may have associated targets, others do not.

The Paris Agreement, agreed in 2015, also invited Parties to submit, by 2020, long-term low GHG emissions development strategies to 2050 (Paris Agreement, Article 4.19).[3] Ten countries had done so by February 2019, including France and Mexico.[4] Given the longer-term nature of these strategies, it is more difficult for governments to establish specific action plans. Parties to the UNFCCC are also required to submit National Communications, which highlight, *inter alia*, climate policies and measures planned or undertaken. In addition, Annex I[5] countries are required to outline progress towards their climate targets in biennial reports; a requirement extended in the Katowice Climate Package to all countries in the "biennial transparency reports" to be produced at latest by the end of 2024.

Under the CBD, the twenty 2011-2020 Aichi Biodiversity Targets include targets related to forests (Targets 5 and 7), agriculture (e.g. Targets 7 and 8), climate change (Targets 10 and 15)[6], ecosystem services (Target 15) and many relate to land use more generally. Parties to the CBD are encouraged to use the Aichi Biodiversity Targets as a guiding framework to develop their NBSAPs.

As a result, the overarching CBD framework encourages a more coherent approach with respect to the development of NBSAPs and the land-use nexus at the national level, than does the UNFCCC. This is because as there are limited guidelines on what information to include in an NDC, and no requirements on the form or coverage it should take, there are wide variations in form, content and coverage. On the other hand, the timeframes for documents under this CBD framework are significantly more near-term (i.e. to 2020) than under the UNFCCC framework.

Table 3.1. Comparison of national strategy requirements and timelines under the UNFCCC and the CBD

	UNFCCC (and Paris Agreement)	CBD (and 2011-2020 Aichi Biodiversity Targets)
Long-term vision or plan (to 2050)	Long-Term LEDS: Not mandatory in either developed or developing countries. Several countries have established GHG targets to 2050.	"Living in Harmony with Nature" where "By 2050, biodiversity is valued, conserved, restored and wisely used, maintaining ecosystem services, sustaining a healthy planet and delivering benefits essential for all people."
Short to medium-term strategy/contributions and action plans	NDCs: Mandatory for all Parties (often targets up to 2030)	NBSAP (targets and action plans on how these will be achieved, usually until 2020. Some also include indicators)
Reporting on progress	National Communication (NC) (subject to provision of support for developing countries) includes information on mitigation and adaptation Mandatory for all Parties	National Reports (on progress made towards targets and challenges encountered)
	Biennial Reports (BRs for developed countries) and Biennial Update Reports (BURs) for developing countries – focus on mitigation	

Note: While Parties to the UNFCCC are, in theory, all required to submit NCs, and "biennial (update) reports" (BUR), only 41 (of 154) developing countries have ever reported a BUR. In addition, 66 developing countries have not reported anything since January 2015 (Ellis et al., 2018[1]). Of the 196 Parties to the CBD, 160 have submitted NBSAPs since COP-10, and in terms of overall NBSAP submission to date, 190 of 196 (97%) Parties have developed NBSAPs in line with Article 6 of the CBD.
Source: Authors.

Other relevant agreements and fora

Other relevant international multilateral agreements include the UN Strategic Plan for Forests, developed by the United Nations Forum on Forests (UNFF) and subsequently adopted by the UN General Assembly in 2017. The Strategy contains six voluntary global forest goals and 26 associated targets to be achieved by 2030. Member States are invited to announce their "voluntary national contributions" towards achieving these goals and targets at upcoming sessions of the UNFF. As of 31 July 2018, five countries had submitted such announcements. At the supranational level, through the European Union, the 28 Member States are also governed by various EC Directives that are relevant to the nexus area. These include EU legislation on the Climate and Energy Package, EC Nature Directive, the Habitats Directive, the Sustainable Use Directive (for pesticides), the Water Framework Directive, and the Common Agricultural Policy (CAP). This supranational framework therefore strongly influences agricultural policy in France and Ireland.

SDG goal 12.3 directly addresses food loss and waste (FLW); "by 2030, halve per capita global food waste at the retail and consumer levels and reduce food losses along the production and supply chains, including post-harvest losses", but beyond the SDGs international agreements tackling FLW are lacking. At the EU level the Waste Framework Directive defines a timeline for adopting common measurement methodologies and will produce a report by 2023 that considers the introduction of legally binding targets for food waste prevention (Champions 12.3, 2018[2]). There is also the EU Platform on Food Losses and Waste, which brings together key stakeholders from government, industry and NGOs to understand the issues of FLW, and highlight good practices from member countries. Despite several other international initiatives, such as the FAOs global initiative on Food Losses and Waste Reduction (SAVE FOOD), the integration measures to reduce FLW in other nexus relevant agreements, such as NDC or NBSAPs is lacking. Greater consideration of FLW in such agreements would likely raise the profile of this issue leading to emission savings and reduced pressure on managed and unmanaged lands and other impacts from agriculture.

Coherence across key national strategies and action plans relevant to the nexus

As noted, coherence across relevant national strategies in the land-use nexus is a key entry point to help ensure that domestic actions and policies across multiple sectors and areas are aligned. Clear and quantified objectives can provide strong signals for the level of ambition that is necessary across different sectors and policy areas.

In what follows, the key national strategy documents across the six case study countries are compared and discussed. Overall, the analysis suggests that there is still large scope to strengthen coherence and clarity across the national strategies relevant to the land-use nexus. Few of the NDCs and LEDS refer to land-use nexus issues (e.g. forests, agriculture). Those that do specifically refer to the land-use nexus tend to provide quantitative targets, however, at least in selected areas (e.g. as in France, Indonesia and Mexico – see Table 3.2)

The monitoring of GHG emissions and removals from all sectors has already been underway for a number of years, and the indicator for GHG emissions, tCO_2e, is well established, facilitating the creation of quantitative targets. In contrast, nearly all of the NBSAPs make reference and include some kind of target relevant to forestry, agriculture and climate change (as noted above, this is due, at least in part, to the overarching Aichi Biodiversity Targets that also refer specifically to these issues). While being more coherent in this general sense, many of the targets relevant to the land-use nexus in the NBSAPs are not quantified.

For example, New Zealand's Target 7 to implement a national environmental standard for plantation forestry by 2018, and France's target 3.2 to integrate biodiversity in forest management plans, do not provide clear direction on the level of ambition that is needed. In contrast, Brazil's target to restore at least 15% of degraded land, and France's target on zero net artificialisation provide much clearer signals to relevant Ministries on the objectives they are intended to achieve.

Agricultural development plans tend to be vaguer than NBSAPs with respect to land-use nexus issues. While pressures on climate change, biodiversity/ecosystems and forests are generally acknowledged across the plans of all six countries, the language therein is limited to phrases such as "improve efficiency", "support efforts", "minimise risk". Given the large proportion of GHG emissions stemming from this sector, and the pressures that agricultural land use and management practices exert on biodiversity, the lack of specificity in these plans creates large potential for various Ministries to interpret the language in different ways, and for eventual policy misalignments. Ideally, relevant agriculture-relevant targets in, for example, the NBSAPs should also be reflected in the countries' agricultural development plan. Such an approach would send consistent signals to the various Ministries in the land-use nexus.

References to land-use nexus issues in the National Development Plans (or similar strategies) are similarly ambiguous. New Zealand and Ireland are, to some degree, exceptions: New Zealand's Economic Plan specifically calls for the planting of 1 billion trees, and Ireland's plan refers to afforestation targets to rise incrementally by a quantified amount each year. A closer examination of the strategies is provided below.

Box 3.1. Coherence across national strategies in Ireland, and a look at its NBSAP

Looking across the various national strategies and plans relevant to the nexus in Ireland indicates that there is significant coordination and integration between land-use, climate mitigation, ecosystems/biodiversity and food objectives. In all cases, the main documents in each policy area were created with input from one or more of the other areas. However, references to biodiversity/ecosystems in the agricultural development plans and the national development plan are fairly general. Despite this, its importance is recognised in all the key policy documents such as the National Mitigation Plan, Food Wise 2025, as well as the Rural Development Plan.

Ireland's NBSAP is particularly clearly defined (i.e., in comparison to its other national strategies) in that it includes clear targets, actions and has also defined indicators in order to monitor progress towards achieving these (though some are SMARTer than others). The targets are cross-cutting, with specific references and measures relating to agriculture and forestry (e.g. NBSAP Target 4.1 and the actions thereunder, which refer to Agri-Environment Schemes, High Nature Value farmland, etc, and associated indicators). The role of Protected Areas in enabling adaptation to climate change is also recognised, with specific targets to increase peatland area. In contrast, Ireland's National Development Plan (2018-2027) does not include specific (quantitative) targets and indicators. Mention to e.g. biodiversity is made, but it basically refers back to the NBSAP.

GHG mitigation targets in the NDCs and LEDS and the inclusion of land-use nexus issues

References to land-use, ecosystems and food security issues in the NDCs and LEDS across the six case study countries are compared in Table 3.2 providing an indication of the extent to which these issues are mainstreamed in national climate change strategies. Land-use issues, agriculture, and forestry are explicitly referred to in three of the six Parties' NDCs (Brazil, Indonesia, and Mexico)[7] with specific targets included for several of these. Looking across these three NDC's, it is difficult to compare the relative ambition of these targets given the lack of consistency in the way they are expressed.[8] Overall, explicit reference to interlinkages with biodiversity or ecosystems is made rarely in these documents.[9]

In addition to NDCs, certain countries have developed national strategies or plans that are more detailed. In France, for example, the National Low-Carbon Strategy (SNBC)[10] was published in November, 2015, with a revised version published in 2018. It outlines strategic guidelines for implementing the transition to a sustainable, low-carbon economy across all sectors of activity including agriculture (see Table 3.2). It also highlights the importance of individual behaviour, including dietary changes, for reaching national GHG mitigation targets.

In addition, the Climate Plan (July 2017)[11] specifies both long-term objectives and shorter term milestones and explicitly strengthens the French GHG 2050 target from 'Factor 4'[12] up to carbon neutrality. The Climate Plan, drawn up at the request of the President and Prime Minister, calls on all government departments across the board to step up the pace of the energy and climate transition and of the Paris Agreement's implementation. The Plan aims to foster coherence between climate change mitigation and land use, ecosystems and food. It focusses on these elements in its fifth part ('Mobilising the potential of ecosystems and agriculture in order to tackle climate change'), from axis 15 to 19: axis 15 and 17 emphasise the importance of the sustainable management of forests to achieve climate ambitions, directly on the French territory (axis 17) but also through improved consumption to reduce deforestation (axis 15) (the latter is discussed below).

Inclusion of land-use nexus issues in the NBSAPs

Overall, fewer countries have specific targets relating to forest and agriculture in their (climate) NDCs and LT-LEDS, than specific targets relating to climate, forest and agriculture in their national biodiversity strategies. Table 3.3 summarises the information on forestry, agriculture and climate change in the National Biodiversity Strategies and Action Plans. While all NBSAPs refer to various areas of the land-use nexus however, a review of the six NBSAPs indicates that often these references are not specific, not ambitious or both (e.g. Indonesia: "improvement of forestry areas"; Ireland: "continue forest research programmes"). Most of the targets are not quantified and hence do not provide sufficiently specific guidance for relevant Ministries to act. Exceptions include France for some of their targets such as on zero net artificialisation of land[13]; Brazil, with respect to the target to restore at least 15% of degraded land, and Ireland, with a target to achieve 30% broadleaf afforestation.

The lack of quantification of many of the targets also implies that they are not measurable. Several of the NBSAPs do include the use of indicators with the targets, namely those of Brazil, Indonesia, Ireland and France; some are more specific than others however. Brazil brought together nearly 280 institutions to develop its NBSAP, and established a multi-stakeholder Panel for Biodiversity (PainelBio) to develop the indicators. Mexico and New Zealand do not include indicators. Overall, it is very difficult to guide national action in a coherent, transparent way if targets are not specific, measurable, actionable, realistic and time-bound (SMART).

Some of the case study countries' NBSAPs moreover refer to the protection of certain core forested areas (Brazil) or "stewardship lands with high conservation value" (New Zealand), and to targets to reduce and curb forest (Mexico, Brazil) or habitat (Ireland, France) fragmentation. Action 7 under Target 5 of the Brazilian NBSAP, for instance, is to "reduce fragmentation of remaining forest patches, as well as promote the connection of forest fragments". Related targets, however, mostly remain qualitative.[14]

Table 3.2. GHG targets stated in first NDCs and LEDS and references to land-use nexus issues

	GHG emissions reduction targets in NDCs NDCs	Targets relevant to land use, ecosystems and food in NDCs	Targets relevant to land use, ecosystems and food in LEDS
Brazil (Government of Brazil, 2016)	Country-wide target to reduce GHG emissions by 37% below 2005 levels in 2025; and by 43% in 2030 as an indicative value	By 2030, the Government of Brazil (2015) will restore an additional 15 Mha of degraded pasturelands (besides the 15 million targeted by 2020); enhance 5 Mha of integrated cropland-livestock-forestry systems; achieve zero illegal deforestation and restore 12 Mha of forest in Amazonia.	None submitted to date
European Union (France/Ireland) (European Commission, 2016)	Binding target of at least 40% domestic reduction in GHG emissions by 2030 compared to 1990	Policy on how to include Land Use, Land Use Change and Forestry into the 2030 greenhouse gas mitigation framework will be established as soon as technical conditions allow and in any case before 2020.	NA
France (National Low-Carbon Strategy, 2015)	Country-wide target	See EU above for the NDC	Reduce agricultural emissions by more than 12% by the 3rd carbon budget period (i.e. 2024-28) compared to 2013 and by half by 2050 through the agro-ecology project. Store and conserve carbon in soils and biomass.
Ireland (Climate Action Plan 2019)	Country-wide target	See EU above for the NDC	Reduce emissions from agriculture, forestry and land use to be between 17.5–19.0 $MtCO_2eq$ by achieving between 16.5 -18.5 $MtCO_2eq$ cumulative abatement over the period 2021 – 2030. 34 Actions and 120 sub-actions assigned to specific institutions.
Indonesia	29% reduction by 2030 from baseline (41% conditional i.e. with international support)	By 2030: Agriculture emissions reduction of 0.32% (0.13% conditional) Forestry (including peat fires) emissions reduction of 17.2% (23% conditional)	None submitted to date
Mexico (Climate change Mid-Century Strategy 2016)	25% below BAU in 2030 and further conditional reduction target up to 40%	Includes LULUCF and agriculture. Target of 0% deforestation by 2030.	Reduce emissions by 50% by 2050 relative to 2000. Objective 2: Conserve, restore and sustainably manage ecosystems to guarantee their environmental services to promote climate change mitigation and adaptation (with 6 strategies and 45 actions; none are quantified) Various actions specified for agriculture and forestry under M series. None are quantified. (e.g. "encourage local communities to plan"...)
New Zealand (New Zealand Government, 2016)	Country-wide target to reduce GHG emissions to 30% below 2005 levels by 2030.	No specific targets but included as part of economy-wide commitment in New Zealand's first NDC.	Reduce emissions by 50% by 2050 relative to 1990 (Formal steps have recently been taken for carbon neutrality)

Note: Long-term LEDS have not yet been submitted by Brazil, Indonesia and New Zealand.
Source: Authors based on relevant country NDC submissions, available at http://www4.unfccc.int/ndcregistry/Pages/All.aspx; and others referenced above: (Ministère de l'Écologie, du Developpement Durable et de l'Energie, 2015[3]), Stratégie Nationale Bas-Carbone, https://www.ecologique-solidaire.gouv.fr/sites/default/files/SNBC_France_low_carbon_strategy_2015.pdf, ; (Government of Ireland, 2018[4]) Climate action plan 2019: To tackle climate breakdown; (SEMARNAT-INECC, 2016[5]), Mexico's Climate Change Mid-Century Strategy. https://unfccc.int/files/focus/long-term_strategies/application/pdf/mexico_mcs_final_cop22nov16_red.pdf

France has also developed a National Forests and Woodlands Programme (MAA, 2016[6]), proposed by the MAA and adopted in 2016, which defines the main objectives of the French forest policy for the 2016-26 timeframe. It notes the role of forests in reducing GHG emissions, and the interrelations between biodiversity and climate change policies. Similarly, Ireland's Department of Agriculture, Food and the Marine developed in 2014 a forest policy strategy in its document "Forests, products and people, Ireland's forestry policy – a renewed vision". This includes a cost-benefit analysis of future afforestation programmes, where the benefits considered include timber, carbon sequestration, biodiversity, water quality, among others.

The Aichi Biodiversity Targets also explicitly recognise the need to eliminate, phase out or reform incentives, including subsidies, harmful to biodiversity under its Target 3. Nevertheless, very few of the NBSAPs refer to incentives, including subsidies, harmful to biodiversity, despite market-distorting and potentially-harmful subsidies being in place in all the case study countries (see chapter 5). Similar language on reforming harmful incentives is also in the reporting guidelines for national communications on climate change, yet few countries have done this. Identifying and assessing existing incentives that are not coherent with international environmental goals is a key first step. Commitments to undertake these assessments, such as through national assessments (e.g. France and biodiversity) or international peer-review processes (e.g. Indonesia fossil fuel subsidy G20 peer-review) are an important first step.

Such commitments include Ireland wherein the NBSAP states they will undertake a study in the 2017-2019 timeframe, and Brazil, which takes on Aichi Target 3 at national level nearly verbatim, stating that by 2020, at the latest, incentives harmful to biodiversity, including the so-called perverse subsidies, are eliminated, phased out or reformed.[15] More specifically for Ireland under Target 1, Action 1.1.15. is to: Identify and take measures to minimise the impact of incentives and subsidies on biodiversity loss, and develop positive incentive measures, where necessary, to assist the conservation of biodiversity. The performance indicator defined is: 1. Policies and practices that generate perverse incentives identified; 2. Number of appropriate reform policies designed and implemented. This language presents a clear, time-bound commitment to tackle this issue. In contrast, in France, while a report on domestic public subsidies harmful to biodiversity has already been undertaken (CAS, 2011[7]), it is not referred to in the NBS nor the NBP.

In Brazil, some states, including São Paulo, Paraná and Rio Grande do Sul, have also developed biodiversity strategies and action plans or programmes. However, ensuring consistency and synergy with the federal biodiversity policies, programmes and targets has been challenging (OECD, 2015[8]).

Table 3.3. Forestry, agriculture and climate change in the NBSAPs

	Forestry	Agriculture	Climate change
Brazil (NBSAP 2016-2020)	Yes, target 7 incorporate sustainable management practices in forest and fauna management	Yes, target 7; target 8 on excess nutrients. Includes associated indicators	Yes, target 15 to enhance carbon stocks and restore at least 15% degraded land
France (NBS 2011 and NBP 2018)	No in the National Strategy (refers to logging but vaguely so) (NBS, 2011); Yes in the National Plan, target 1.3 zero net artificialisation; target 3.2 integrate biodiversity in forest management plans (NBP, 2018)	No in the National Strategy (NBS, 2011); Yes in the National Plan: target 1.3 zero net artificialisation; target 2.2 transition to agroecology (NBP, 2018)	No (NBS, 2011); Yes, interspersed, no specific targets (NBP, 2018)
Indonesia (IBSAP 2015-2020)	A few e.g. Development of forestry plan and improvement of forestry areas; sustainable management of protected forests	Yes, several e.g. expansion and sustainable management of lands for agriculture, plantations and animal husbandry (p. 236)	Yes, improvement of activities dealing with climate change adaptation and mitigation at national and local levels
Ireland (BAP, 2017-2021)	Yes, target 4.1: optimised opportunities under forestry to benefit biodiversity, with various specific actions and associated indicators	Yes, target 4.1: optimised opportunities under agriculture to benefit biodiversity, with various specific actions and associated indicators	Yes, 1.1.14. Implement actions from Ireland's Biodiversity Climate Change Sectoral Adaptation Plan; 2.1.10. continue forest research programmes, including on carbon stocks
Mexico (NBSAP, 2016-2030)	Yes, Multiple targets relevant to forestry. None are quantified.	Yes, multiple targets relevant to agriculture. None are quantified.	Yes, multiple references to climate change; no specific targets
New Zealand (2016-2020)	Yes, Target 7, implement National Environmental Standard for Plantation Forestry by 2018	Yes, target 7, improve efficiency of agriculture production systems (e.g. by increasing flexibility in land management and farming practices)	Yes, Target 16.1 monitoring of carbon stocks in forests and habitats

Note: Brazil's national target 7, for example, states: By 2020 the incorporation of sustainable management practices is disseminated and promoted in agriculture, livestock production, aquaculture, silviculture, extractive activities, and forest and fauna management, ensuring conservation of biodiversity (Government of Brazil, 2018[9]).
Source: Authors based on relevant country NBSAP submissions, available at: https://www.cbd.int/nbsap

Inclusion of land-use nexus issues in agricultural development plans

In contrast to climate change and biodiversity, there is no overarching multilateral agreement that requires or invites governments to develop national agricultural development plans. Nevertheless, most (if not all) countries have developed such strategies. For France and Ireland, agricultural policies are determined, to a large extent at the European level, by the CAP. Table 3.4 summarises the references to climate mitigation, forestry, and biodiversity/ecosystems in the national agricultural development plans (or other similar national documents).

Table 3.4. Climate mitigation, biodiversity/ecosystems and forests in agriculture development plans or similar

	Climate mitigation	Biodiversity/ecosystems	Forests
Brazil (National Plan for Low Carbon Emissions in Agriculture, (2016[10]); and Agriculture and Livestock Plan 2018/19 (2018[11]))	Specific actions identified together with quantified targets and estimated mitigation potential	Improve efficiency of natural resource use	Support efforts to reduce the role livestock farming expansion plays in deforestation
France (Agroecological project (2013[12]))	Mentioned but in vague terms. Not quantified	Mentioned but in vague terms. Not quantified	-
Indonesia[1] (Strategic Plan of Agriculture 2015-2019)	Refers to climate mitigation, indicating agriculture should be more sustainable	Mentioned	Targets conversion of 4.5 million ha of forest estate to agricultural land
Ireland (Food Wise 2025) (2015[13])	Well integrated but no specific targets	Biodiversity is mentioned in the context of monitoring and developing impacts, but no specific targets	Detailed plan for forestry for production and afforestation, integrated with climate but not biodiversity
Mexico (Agriculture Development Plan 2013-2018 (2013[14]))	Section on diagnosis refers to impact of climate change on sector	Section on diagnosis refers to impact of natural resource degradation on sector	-
New Zealand (Good Farming Practice Action Plan for Water Quality) (2018[15])[2]	Very vague	Aim is to improve ecological health of waterways. References made to e.g. minimise risk of fertiliser spillage, leaching and loss into waterways	-

Notes: [1] The Indonesian Plan does not seem to be available in English. Content for this table is taken from here: http://ap.fftc.agnet.org/ap_db.php?id=416

[2] For New Zealand, see also Table 3.2 on their national development strategy.

Source: Authors based on documents referenced in-table.

Looking across the six countries and the nexus areas, only Brazil has clearly defined actions, together with quantified targets in the context of climate mitigation. While references to the nexus areas are made in nearly all of the six countries' agriculture development plans, these are all fairly general.

France has however developed a Plan for Agroforestry Development for 2015-2020, released in 2015 by the MAA (Government of France, 2015[16]). This presents actions to encourage farmers to adopt practices coupling trees, crops and farming. It underlines the role hedges and trees play for timber and fodder production, limiting erosion, waterborne and microclimate regulation, carbon storage or climate change adaptation. The Plan argues for research and development and a better understanding of agroforestry systems, a better regulatory framework and stronger financial incentives, and the development of a national sector enhancing the economic value of agroforestry by-products. It also includes the promotion of agroforestry at an international level as an objective. None of the actions outlined, however, have clear specific targets associated with them.

Inclusion of land-use nexus issues in national development plans (or similar strategies)

Perhaps the politically weightiest and overarching national strategies are the national development plans (or similar documents). References to the land-use nexus issues across these documents are compared in Table 3.5. France does not have a national development plan *per se*, but rather has established a National Strategy for Sustainable Development which covers all aspects of the land-use nexus and makes the case for action. It does not, however, lay out specific targets to be achieved.

Indonesia's Master Plan for Economic Development 2011-2021 (the long-term plan) does not refer to the environmental impacts of the development (other than as a side-effect of the growth in palm oil production). However, the medium-term development plan (RPJMN 2015-2019) does refer to forest conservation and the NBSAP. The importance of environmental issues, including ecosystems and climate change, are recognised in Indonesia's development planning process. The long-term development strategy set for 2005-2025 recognises environmental sustainability as one of the nine development missions for Indonesia to pursue. It also has the aim of exploiting Indonesia's comparative advantage in agriculture and mining to achieve food self-sufficiency and middle-income status by 2025. The RPJMN is based on the concept of the green economy, specifying concrete targets for achieving the overall missions set out in the long-term strategy.

The next phase of the medium-term national development plan (RPJMN 2020-24) provides an opportunity to ensure greater effort to reconcile the specific goals of developmental policy with the climate change, land use and ecosystems targets. As part of the preparations for the future RPJMN 2020-2024, BAPPENAS undertook modelling to strengthen coherence between relevant sectoral targets and to facilitate discussion between stakeholders. The elaboration of sectoral targets, however, does not appear to have fully considered interactions between objectives. Given that there is only a finite stock of land, the implicit demands for land from each objective need to be consistent. Increases in production will require a combination of increased productivity and increased land area. The consequences for ecosystems and climate depends on where expansion occurs. However, the production objectives for food and energy crops make claims on degraded land and convertible production forest.

Ireland's NDP refers to multiple aspects of the land-use nexus and defines investment priorities that include references to these areas. It also provides indicative (monetary) resource allocations for delivery of the various National Strategic Objectives thereunder. While resource allocation is quantitative by definition, since this is an input indicator, rather than an outcome or impact indicator, it will be difficult to determine whether progress is being made towards the ultimate objectives of the NDP in relation to the land-use nexus.

Brazil's Multi-Year Plan (Plano Plurianual (PPA) 2016-2019), on the other hand, defines both monetary inputs dedicated to specific government programmes and overarching objectives along with detailed, quantitative programme targets and indicators. Among the 54 strategic government programmes set out in the PPA, topics of relevance to the land-use nexus figure prominently. Various programmes pertain to agriculture and food security (i.e. programmes 2012, 2066, 2069) and set quantitative targets relating to, *inter alia*, the provision of rural credit, technical assistance and extension services, the registration and regularization of forest and agricultural land, the expansion of support to agroecological practices in family agriculture, and food assistance and school feeding programmes. Specific programmes are devoted to climate change mitigation and adaptation action (Programme 2050: Climate Change) and the protection of biodiversity (Programme 2078: Conservation and Sustainable Use of Biodiversity). Notable targets specified for these programmes include: (i) absolute emissions reductions from reduced deforestation in the Amazon region of 737,465,122 tCO_2e (target 047B) and of 70,000,000 tCO_2e from the agricultural sector against baseline projections (target 047E); and (ii) the reduction of the risk of extinction of 20% of the species listed in the Official National List of Species threatened by extinction (target 4084). The PPA moreover designates the government ministry responsible for the delivery of the specified objectives and targets.

Table 3.5. Land-use nexus issues in national development plans or similar strategies

	Climate mitigation	Ecosystems/biodiversity	Agriculture/Food	Other
Brazil (Multi-Year Plan 2016-2019) (2016[17])	Reference to the policy goal of economy-wide emission reductions of 36.1-38.9% by 2020 compared to BAU. Includes emission reduction targets for the AFOLU sector. Indicative resource allocations are provided.	Reference to Brazil's domestic and international engagement in this area. Details the scope of and monetary resources for achieving detailed related quantitative targets.	Includes quantitative targets on the strengthening of family agriculture, agrarian reform, land governance, and food and nutrition security. Provides indicative resource allocations.	Refers to a government programme (Programme 2083: Environmental Quality) aiming at broader environmental quality, waste management and atmospheric air pollutants management is presented. Indicative resource allocations are provided.
France (National Strategy of Ecological Transition Towards Sustainable Development 2015-2020) (2014[18])	Yes, though no targets are specified	Yes, though no targets are specified	Yes, though no targets are specified	-
Indonesia (Master Plan for Economic Development 2011-2025) (2011[19]) (Medium term development plan 2015-2019) (2014[20])	No	No Refers to the NBSAP	No	Refers to forest conservation
Ireland (National Development Plan 2018-2027) (2018[21])	National Strategic Outcome (NSO) 8: Transition to a Low-Carbon and Climate-Resilient Society. Provides indicative resource allocations for delivery of NSOs and specific actions thereunder.	NSO 9. Sustainable Management of Water and other Environmental Resources. Provides indicative resource allocations for delivery of NSOs. Refers to NBSAP.	States: Public capital investments in the agri-food sector will seek to enable the sustainable development of the sector in accordance with the ambition in Food Wise 2025 and any successor strategy (Huge growth target for agriculture in Food Wise)	Forestry: States: The current Programme for a Partnership Government has targets for afforestation which rise incrementally to 8,100 hectares per annum in 2020. More than EUR100 million will be invested in 2018 alone.
Mexico (National Development Plan 2013-2018) (2013[22])	-	Goal 4 is to enhance sustainable use of natural resources. Strategy 4.2 is to promote sustainable agriculture and livestock practices	Quantitative targets to expand agriculture production. Objectives included to address food security	-
New Zealand (Growing and Protecting New Zealand) (2018[23])	Yes, but vague	Accelerating Predator Free 2050 programme and other initiatives relevant to the biodiversity strategy Government goal to plant one billion trees between 2018 and 2027	-	

Note: For example, relevant references in the Irish NDP include: Achieving a transition to a competitive, low-carbon, climate-resilient and environmentally sustainable economy by 2050; and Safeguarding Ireland's abundant natural and environmental resources through the sustainable management of water, waste and other environmental resources.
Source: Authors

In New Zealand, the Ministry for Primary Industries (MPI) has set out a strategy for achieving its purpose of "Growing and Protecting New Zealand" (MPI, 2017[24]). This strategy comprises four key outcomes, the first of which is growth in production and the second is sustainability. Ecosystems and climate change are not explicitly mentioned in this strategy (though they could be seen as implied by the sustainability objective). The MPI also reports on its performance. The MPI "Strategic Intentions 2015-2020" includes indicators for measuring progress, including on sustainability. These indicators refer most predominantly to water, nutrient management and fisheries. There is no specific reference to biodiversity in the document.

Looking beyond national jurisdictional boundaries: Consideration of land-use nexus issues in trade policy

Given the close interlinkages between land-use outcomes and international trade it is important that trade policy is coherent with sustainable land use. Commonly conceived of as a driver of economic growth, international trade receives significant policy attention across the case study countries. While the promotion of international trade is part of most of the overarching national development plans or strategies, few of these explicitly acknowledge interactions of trade and land-use nexus issues (table 3.6).

Similarly, most of the case study countries' trade or export strategies and plans do not explicitly account for the land-use nexus implications of trade policy. For most countries, these documents provide further detail of the plans for trade in nexus-relevant products (Table 3.7). However, while the plans and strategies that do so primarily lay out sub-targets and strategies to grow agri-food exports, only some make limited reference to the attainment of environmental objectives, or domestic (Indonesia) or international (Brazil) food security objectives. The relative lack of consideration of land-use nexus issues in general trade policy represents a potential challenge to policy coherence.

Table 3.6. Trade targets in national development plans or similar strategies

	Quantitative trade targets	Qualitative goals and specific references to trade in nexus-relevant goods	Examples of possible land-use nexus implications
Brazil (Multi-Year Plan 2016-2019) (2016[17])	Several quantitative input indicators and targets for trade support programmes are specified.	Improvement of Brazil's trade performance through increased value-added and technological content in exports and through the diversification of export composition and destination, but no reference to nexus relevant implications of trade.	The diversification of the export base could reduce pressures on land, if land products are replaced by other goods and services.
France (National Strategy of Ecological Transition Towards Sustainable Development 2015-2020) (2014[18])	-	Commitment to reorient production, trade and consumption patterns as part of the transition towards a circular and low carbon economy. Pledge to strive for tighter environmental trade rules under the WTO.	More environmentally-friendly production, trade and consumption patterns could reduce land-use pressures domestically and abroad. Reduced trade volumes could equally increase pressures on domestic land.
Indonesia (Master Plan for Economic Development 2011-2025) (2011[19]) (Medium term development plan 2015-2019) (2014[20])	Detailed annual export growth targets, including growth of non-oil and –gas exports of 8 – 14.3% (2015-2019), an increase in the services exports-to-GDP ratio from 2.7% (2015) to 3.5% (2019), and an increase in the share of manufactured products in total exports from 44% (2015) to 65% (2019).	Aim to become one of the world's main food suppliers, and a processing centre for agricultural, fishery, and natural resources by 2025. Announcement of export restrictions for energy commodities. Reference to safeguards ensuring the environmental integrity and social inclusiveness of the trade sector.	Increases in export-oriented agricultural production may or may not increase deforestation by increasing demand for land. Depending on domestic bioenergy policy, energy commodity export restrictions could benefit standing forests or not, and they can potentially counteract trade efficiency and mitigation efforts abroad. Strictly enforced adherence to environmental safeguards could reduce adverse land-use impacts of trade.
Ireland (National Development Plan 2018-2027) (2018[21])		Aim to broaden Ireland's global exporting footprint, and to build resilience to external shocks in the Irish trade sector	Depending on the export composition and effects on global trade and production patterns, ambiguous effects on domestic and international land-use outcomes are possible.
Mexico (National Development Plan 2013-2018) (2013[22])		Intention to intensify trade relations under various regional agreements, to increase the logistical capacity for trade, to diversify the Mexican export base and to increase the share of domestic value-added content of Mexican exports	Depending on export and import composition and effects on global trade and production patterns, ambiguous effects on domestic and international land-use outcomes are possible.
New Zealand (Growing and Protecting New Zealand) (2018[23])	The "food and primary sector" in particular shall grow the value of its exports. Aim to achieve FTA coverage for 90% of goods exports by 2030.	Commitment to advance WTO work on agricultural domestic production subsidies	On current trends, primary sector export growth could would likely increase adverse nexus outcomes given the emphasis on cattle and dairy.

Note: Quantitative targets of the Brazilian Multi-Year Plan (PPA) are not specified in the main PPA document referenced here, but in the accompanying monitoring plan available at http://www.planalto.gov.br/ccivil_03/_ato2015-2018/2016/Lei/L13249.htm
Source: Authors

This is true also in countries where dedicated initiatives to tackle adverse land-use nexus impacts of international trade exist already. France and Ireland have noteworthy initiatives aimed at addressing these impacts.[16] France, for instance, has a National Strategy to Combat Imported Deforestation (SNDI)[17] (Ministère de la transition écologique et solidaire, 2018[25]) in place. As announced under Axis 15 in its Climate Plan, the SNDI was developed in 2018 in a consultative manner by the French Ministry of Agriculture, in collaboration with the French Ministries of the Environment, Foreign Affairs, Economy, and Research and Innovation, and the involvement of all stakeholders gathered in the National Group on

Tropical Forests (GNFT). The GNFT, has itself been recently expanded to include representatives of the agri-food sector. The SNDI is intended to contribute to several international goals on climate and forest (i.e., the SDGs, New York Declaration on Forests, Paris Agreement, Amsterdam declarations). Its main orientations are to increase cooperation with producer countries, systematically integrate deforestation in public policies, mobilise and empower the private sector and develop research. The SNDI also aims to establish a national platform to provide reliable information on imported deforestation, value commitments, and help the private sector monitor its commodities supply chains through an early alert mechanism. As France is among the top 10 timber importers globally, this initiative is potentially important globally (for more detail on the SNDI, see also Chapter 5).

In a similar vein, Target 7.4 in Ireland's NBSAP is: Reduction in the impact of Irish trade on global biodiversity and ecosystem services. More specifically the action identified is 7.4.1. "Adopt measures to significantly reduce negative impacts of trade on biodiversity and to enhance positive impacts". The lead agencies tasked with this action are clearly defined (i.e., DCHG, DFAT, DAFM), and two indicators have been identified to assess progress towards this: 1. Knowledge of the pressures placed on biodiversity by trading activity and trade routing; and 2. Measures implemented to reduce or offset those pressures and their impacts. The progress on this initiative is unclear but, if successful, it could serve as a model for other countries considering the same approach.

While these initiatives are laudable from an nexus perspective, their impacts will be constrained if the policies recommended are not mainstreamed into general trade policy. Despite the existence of a dedicated strategy in form of the SNDI, the French Government Foreign Trade Strategy (Premier Ministre de la Rèpublique Francaise, 2018[26]) does not acknowledge land-use nexus impacts of French trade policy.

Mainstreaming of land-use nexus issues in trade policy formulation and implementation therefore represents a necessary and promising avenue for improved land-use outcomes and greater policy coherence. In order for trade policy to effectively reduce land-use impacts abroad (including by pursuing quantitative targets that would complement export growth targets), a quantitative understanding of the nature and magnitude of these impacts should be gained (Chapter 5) and considered in trade policy formulation.

Table 3.7. Land-use nexus issues in national trade or export strategies and plans

	Agricultural and forest products	Food security	Climate change, biodiversity and other
Brazil (Plano Nacional de Exportações, PNE 2015-2018) (2015[27])	Identification of key market segments for export growth in 32 target countries, many of which comprise parts of the agri-food sector. Commitment to "satisfactory results" in agriculture under the WTO.	Expansion of a programme under which agricultural machinery is exported, partly to meet food security objectives abroad.	-
France (Stratégie du gouvernement en matière de commerce extérieur, (2018[26]))	-	-	-
Indonesia (Strategic Plan 2015-2019, Ministry of Trade (2015[28]))	The export growth targets in table 1.1 also explicitly apply to products of the agro-forestry sector, although no export growth targets from this specific sub-sector are quantified. Export growth in this sector should first and foremost be achieved in processed food and forestry products. Aim to translate Indonesia's share of international production into a price-setting role on international commodity markets, including for coconut, oil palm (CPO), cocoa, coffee and rubber.	The need to provide staple foods at affordable, stable prices that are similar between regions is acknowledged and a unifying policy coordinating food production, food imports and food distribution is called for.	Among seven guiding principles mentioned, two are of particular relevance to nexus issues: 2. Improve Sustainable Management of and Value-Addition from Natural Resources 4. Improve the quality of the environment, disaster risk reduction, nature and climate change
Ireland (*Ireland Connected: Trading and Investing in a Dynamic World*, (2017[29]))	Target to increase indigenous exports, including food, to reach EUR26 billion by 2020 (up by 26% from 2015). Reference to the Foodwise 2025 target to increase exports in agri-food and drink by 85% over the period to 2025 to reach EUR19 billion. 60-70% of growth in food, drink and horticulture exports are to be achieved in Asia, North America and Africa. Target to increase value added in exported food, fisheries and wood products by 70% over the period to 2025 to reach in excess of EUR13 billion.	-	Reference to the protection of a rules-based trade order under different international trade organisations and fora with special reference to "environmental issues".
Mexico (National Innovative Development Programme 2013-2018, (2013[30]))	-	-	Reference to the objective to promote environmental performance of SMEs and sustainability certification schemes, although not directly in the context of trade.
New Zealand (2030 Trade Agenda, (2017[31]))	Reference to the removal of agricultural export subsidies under the WTO.	-	Discussion of environmental regulation, including the Paris Agreement, in the context of FTAs that "reinforce common understanding and commitments" (p.5)

Note: Mexico does not have a trade strategy as such. Instead, trade goals and strategies are specified in the sectoral programme of the Ministry of the Economy (SE), which in turn is based on the National Development Plan.
Source: Authors

References

Allen, C. et al. (2018), *Good Farming Practice Action Plan for Water Quality 2018*, Good Farming Practice Governance Group, Wellington, http://www.hortnz.co.nz/assets/Our-Work-files/Good-farming-practice-for-water-action-plan-2018.pdf (accessed on 6 June 2019). [15]

CAS (2011), *Public Subsidies Harmful to Biodiversity*, Centre d'analyse statégique, https://www.strategie.gouv.fr/sites/strategie.gouv.fr/files/atoms/files/aides-publiques-contre-biodiversit-fr-en-101020141.pdf (accessed on 18 September 2019). [7]

Champions 12.3 (2018), *2018 Progress Report: An annual update on behalf of Champions 12.3*, http://www.champions123.org. [2]

Coordinating Ministry for Economic Affairs (2011), *Master Plan for Acceleration and Expansion of Indonesia's Economic Development 2011-2025*, Government of Indonesia, Jakarta, Indonesia. [19]

DAFM (2015), *Food Wise 2025*, Department of Agriculture, Food and the Marine. [13]

Department of Foreign Affairs and Trade (2017), *Ireland Connected: Trading and Investing in a Dynamic World*, Government of Ireland, Dublin, https://www.dfa.ie/media/dfa/alldfawebsitemedia/ourrolesandpolicies/tradeandpromotion/Ireland-Connected_Main-Report.pdf (accessed on 21 March 2019). [29]

Department of Public Expenditure and Reform (2018), *National Development Plan 2018-2027*, Government of Ireland, Dublin, Ireland. [21]

EC (2011), "Roadmap to a Resource Efficient Europe", *COMMUNICATION FROM THE COMMISSION TO THE EUROPEAN PARLIAMENT, THE COUNCIL, THE EUROPEAN ECONOMIC AND SOCIAL COMMITTEE AND THE COMMITTEE OF THE REGIONS*, No. COM/2011/0571, European Commission, https://eur-lex.europa.eu/legal-content/EN/TXT/?uri=CELEX:52011DC0571 (accessed on 12 June 2019). [35]

Ellis, J. et al. (2018), "Operationalising selected reporting and flexibility provisions in the Paris Agreement", *Climate Change Expert Group Paper*, No. 3, OECD/IEA, Paris, http://www.oecd.org/environment/cc/ccxg.htmwww.iea.org (accessed on 3 June 2019). [1]

Government of Brazil (2018), *National Biodiversity Strategy and Action Plan*, Ministry of the Environment Secretariat of Biodiversity, https://www.cbd.int/doc/world/br/br-nbsap-v3-en.pdf. [9]

Government of France (2017), *France's Climate Plan*, https://www.gouvernement.fr/en/climate-plan (accessed on 28 September 2018). [33]

Government of France (2017), *Plan Climat*, Ministry for an Ecological and Solidary Transition, https://www.ecologique-solidaire.gouv.fr/sites/default/files/2017.07.06%20-%20Plan%20Climat_0.pdf. [34]

Government of France (2015), *Plan de developpement de l'agroforesterie*, Ministre de l'Agriculture, de l'Agroalimentaire et de la Forêt, http://agriculture.gouv.fr/sites/minagri/files/151215-ae-agrofesterie-v2_plan.pdf (accessed on 28 September 2018). [16]

Government of Ireland (2018), *Climate Action Plan 2019: To tackle climate breakdown*, https://www.dccae.gov.ie/en-ie/climate-action/publications/Documents/16/Climate_Action_Plan_2019.pdf (accessed on 4 October 2019). [4]

Government of Mexico (2013), *Plan Nacional De Desarollo 2013-2018 [National Development Plan 2013-2018]*, Government of Mexico, Mexico City, https://observatorioplanificacion.cepal.org/sites/default/files/plan/files/MexicoPlanNacionaldeDesarrollo20132018.pdf (accessed on 21 March 2019). [22]

MAA (2016), *Programme National de la Forêt et du Bois 2016-2026*, Ministére de l'Agriculture et de l'Alimentation , Paris. [6]

Ministère de la transition écologique et solidaire (2018), *Strategie nationale de lutte contre la deforestation importee 2018-2030*, Government of France, Paris, https://www.ecologique-solidaire.gouv.fr/sites/default/files/2018.11.14_SNDI_0.pdf (accessed on 4 February 2019). [25]

Ministère de l'Agriculture et de l'Alimentation (2013), *Projet Agro-écologique pour la France*, Government of France, Paris, https://agriculture.gouv.fr/ministere/projet-agro-ecologique-pour-la-france. [12]

Ministère de l'Écologie, du Developpement Durable et de l'Energie (2015), *Stratégie Nationale Bas-Carbone*, Government of France, Paris, https://www.ecologique-solidaire.gouv.fr/sites/default/files/SNBC_France_low_carbon_strategy_2015.pdf (accessed on 5 June 2019). [3]

Ministère de l'Ecologie; du Développement durable et de l'Energie (2014), *Stratégie nationale de transition écologique vers un développement durable 2015-2020*, Government of France, Paris, https://www.ecologique-solidaire.gouv.fr/sites/default/files/SNTEDD%20-%20La%20strat%C3%A9gie.pdf (accessed on 21 March 2019). [18]

Ministério da Agricultura, Pecuária e Abastecimento (2018), *Plano Agrícola e Pecuário 2018/19 [Agriculture and Livestock Plan 2018/19]*, Government of Brazil, Brasilia, http://www.agricultura.gov.br/assuntos/politica-agricola/plano-agricola-e-pecuario/arquivos-pap/copy_of_PlanoAgricolaePecurio20182019.pdf (accessed on 6 June 2019). [11]

Ministério da Agricultura, Pecuária e Abastecimento (2016), *Plano Setorial de Mitigação e de Adaptação às Mudanças [National Plan for Low Carbon Emissions in Agriculture]*, Government of Brazil, Brasilia, http://www.agricultura.gov.br/assuntos/sustentabilidade/plano-abc/arquivo-publicacoes-plano-abc/download.pdf/view (accessed on 6 June 2019). [10]

Ministério de Planeamiento, P. (2016), *Plano Plurianual 2016-2019 [Multi-Year Plan 2016-2019]*, Government of Bazil, Brasilia, http://www.siteal.iipe.unesco.org/sites/default/files/sit_accion_files/siteal_brasil_0577.pdf (accessed on 21 March 2019). [17]

Ministry for Primary Industries (2018), *Our strategy*, https://www.mpi.govt.nz/about-us/our-strategy/ (accessed on 21 March 2019). [23]

Ministry of Development; Industry and Foreign Trade (2015), *Plano Nacional de Exportações 2015-2018 [National Export Plan 2015-2018]*, Government of Brazil, Brasilia. [27]

Ministry of Foreign Affairs and Trade (2017), *Trade Agenda 2030*, Government of New Zealand, Wellington, https://www.mfat.govt.nz/assets/Trade2030/Trade-Agenda-2030-Strategy-document.pdf (accessed on 21 March 2019). [31]

Ministry of National Development Planning and National Development Planning Agency (2014), *National Medium Term Development Plan 2015-2019*, Government of Indonesia, Jakarta, Indonesia, http://www.lse.ac.uk/GranthamInstitute/wp-content/uploads/laws/1328.pdf (accessed on 21 March 2019). [20]

Ministry of the Economy (2013), *Programa Nacional de Desarrollo Innovador 2013-2018.* [30]

Ministry of Trade (2015), *RENCANA STRATEGIS KEMENTERIAN PERDAGANGAN TAHUN 2015 - 2019*, Government of Indonesia, Jakarta. [28]

MPI (2017), *Afforestation Grant Scheme.* [24]

OECD (2015), *OECD Environmental Performance Reviews: Brazil 2015*, OECD Environmental Performance Reviews, OECD Publishing, Paris, https://dx.doi.org/10.1787/9789264240094-en. [8]

Premier Ministre de la République Francaise (2018), *Stratégie du Gouvernement en matière de commerce extérieur*, Government of France, Roubaix, https://www.gouvernement.fr/sites/default/files/document/document/2018/02/dossier_de_presse_-_presentation_de_la_strategie_du_gouvernement_en_matiere_de_commerce_exterieur-_23.02.2018.pdf (accessed on 7 March 2019). [26]

Richards, M. et al. (2015), *Agriculture's prominence in the INDCs. CCAFS Info Note.*, CGIAR Research Program on Climate Change, Agriculture and Food Security (CCAFS), http://space.cgiar.org/handle/10568/68990. [32]

SAGARPA (2013), *Programa Sectorial de Desarrollo Agropecuario, Pesquero y Alimentario 2013-2018 [Livestock, Fisheries and Agriculture Development Plan 2013-2018]*, Government of Mexico, Mexico City, https://www.gob.mx/fnd/documentos/programa-sectorial-de-desarrollo-agropecuario-pesquero-y-alimentario-2013-2018_dof (accessed on 6 June 2019). [14]

SEMARNAT-INECC (2016), *Mexico's Climate Change Mid-Century Strategy*, Ministry of Environment and Natural Resources (SEMARNAT) and National Institute of Ecology and Climate Change (INECC),, https://unfccc.int/files/focus/long-term_strategies/application/pdf/mexico_mcs_final_cop22nov16_red.pdf (accessed on 5 June 2019). [5]

Notes

[1] Under the UNFCCC's Paris Agreement, there is an overarching goal of limiting global warming to well below 2 degrees of warming, with the agreed objective to pursue efforts to keep warming well below 1.5 degrees. Under the CBD, a guiding framework has been agreed upon, with 20 Aichi Biodiversity Targets. Parties are encouraged, but not required, to use the Aichi Biodiversity Targets as a framework for developing their own national strategies and associated targets.

[2] Article 5 of the Paris Agreement states Parties should take action to conserve and enhance, as appropriate, sinks and reservoirs of GHGs, including forests. It also encourages Parties to take action relating to REDD.

[3] Parties were also encouraged to do this at COP17 in 2011.

[4] https://unfccc.int/process/the-paris-agreement/long-term-strategies

[5] Parties include the industrialized countries that were members of the OECD (Organisation for Economic Co-operation and Development) in 1992, plus countries with economies in transition, including the Russian Federation, the Baltic States, and several Central and Eastern European States.

[6] Target 15 states: By 2020, ecosystem resilience and the contribution of biodiversity to carbon stocks has been enhanced, through conservation and restoration, including restoration of at least 15 per cent of degraded ecosystems, thereby contributing to climate change mitigation and adaptation and to combating desertification.

[7] NB: France and Ireland have country-wide targets, hence agriculture and forestry are included by definition.

[8] Guidance on NDCs is currently being negotiated. The aim of such guidance is to facilitate clarity, transparency and understanding of NDCs.

[9] According to Richards et al. (2015[32]) who examined 162 Party submissions, AFOLU is well represented in most Parties NDC's and appears to be a key strategy for climate change mitigation in a majority of countries. Forest-related mitigation measures are even more frequently mentioned in Parties' NDCs than agriculture, with 80% of the submitted NDCs including targets related to the LULUCF sector, compared to 64% that specifically included agriculture.

[10] See https://unfccc.int/files/focus/long-term_strategies/application/pdf/snbc_4pager_fr_en.pdf

[11] See (Government of France, 2017[33]) https://www.gouvernement.fr/en/climate-plan and https://www.ecologique-solidaire.gouv.fr/sites/default/files/2017.07.06%20-%20Plan%20Climat_0.pdf (Government of France, 2017[34])

[12] Factor 4 specifies a 75% reduction in total GHG emissions in 2050 compared to 1990 levels.

[13] This refers to activities that result in extensive sealing of the soil in unmanaged, agricultural or forest lands due to *inter alia* urban sprawl and transport infrastructure. The French objective is in line with the EU's "zero net land take" objective (EC, 2011[35]).

[14] In Brazil, a Landscape fragmentation and connectivity index that could potentially inform quantitative targets is currently under assessment for use in future iterations of the NBSAP.

[15] Examples of potentially harmful subsidies that could be included in these assessments include concessional loans, preferential credit, market price support for soy and subsidised insurance for farmers that could encourage agricultural land conversion in Brazil, and distortive subsidies to unsustainable farming practices under the EU CAP in Ireland. More detail on potentially harmful subsidies along with examples from other case study countries is provided in chapter 5.

[16] In a sense, France has adopted a sector-like approach, focusing on forests, whereas Ireland covers trade-related issues more generally, but for an environmental policy area, namely biodiversity.

[17] Imported deforestation refers to imported products that are directly or indirectly the result of deforestation or forest degradation (e.g., wood coming from environmentally sensitive forests that have been chopped down; and products such as beef or palm oil that were produced in areas of slash-and-burn cultivation) (source: https://frenchfoodintheus.org/3977).

4 Institutional co-ordination and coherence for sustainable land use

National and sub-national institutions play a key role in land use. Ensuring co-ordination both between national institutions (horizontal co-ordination) and national and sub-national institutions (vertical co-ordination) is important for policy alignment in the land-use, biodiversity, climate and food nexus. This chapter highlights the degree of co-ordination between relevant government institutions and the mechanisms for co-ordination in the case study countries (Brazil, France, Indonesia, Ireland, Mexico and New Zealand). The chapter provides examples of horizontal co-ordination and how relevant national level ministries work together to produce policy and manage nexus areas. It then highlights the challenges facing existing mechanisms for vertical co-ordination. The chapter also discusses the role of institutions in international trade including the role of the private sector for managing nexus impacts.

The need for strong institutional co-ordination in the land-use nexus

Strong institutional co-ordination is particularly important for the effective management of the land-use nexus. This is true for both horizontal co-ordination (between different national government ministries) and vertical co-ordination (between national and sub-national stakeholders). In general, the roles and mandates of institutions should be clearly defined to facilitate transparency and accountability.

As the importance of simultaneously addressing multiple policy goals has grown, many countries are in the process of identifying effective institutional frameworks. Allowing for potential institutional changes e.g. to address areas of emerging concern, or to encourage integration of two or more specific areas of policy is therefore also important. Top-down inter-ministerial committees have been established by some of the case study countries. The advantages of such committees include that they can help to move away from silo approaches by facilitating multi-stakeholder dialogue and engagement in decision-making processes. But, these committees can create conflict and resistance from existing institutions. For the relevant institutions to effectively undertake their responsibilities, adequate capacity, technical expertise and funding are also required.

The institutional structures in place can be particularly complex in in large, decentralised countries, such as in Brazil, Indonesia and Mexico. In Indonesia, for example, relevant policies are created by at least 8 different national-level ministries, 6 non-departmental bodies, and the Office of the President. Local authorities also have significant authority over forest management (Wardojo and Masripatin, 2002[1]). It is particularly important therefore that mandates and roles are clearly defined, and that overlap is avoided. In Brazil, two co-ordination bodies relevant to climate change have been established: an Inter-ministerial Committee on Climate Change (CIM) as well as an Inter-ministerial Commission on Global Climate Change (CIMGC). Each of these groups includes several stakeholders: 15 ministries participate in the CIM, which is co-ordinated by the Presidency (CIM, 2007[2]).It is unsurprising that a complex institutional structure is used to address multiple interlinked issues that affect a myriad of stakeholders. Indeed, a structure involving multiple ministries is positive, inasmuch as it is explicitly recognising that cross-sectoral expertise are needed to address issues related to the nexus of land-use, biodiversity, climate and food.

Level of horizontal co-ordination in domestic policy development

Countries recognise the importance of horizontal policy co-ordination, and have developed different institutional means to promote it. This includes developing cross-cutting co-ordination mechanisms. These can bring together multiple different Ministries and other relevant stakeholders, and can provide a platform for communication. An example is New Zealand's "Natural Resources Sector" (NRS), which aims to "improve the productivity of New Zealand's resource-related industries while reducing their environmental impact to build a more productive and competitive economy" (MfE, 2015, p. 1[3]).[1] Brazil and Mexico have also established inter-ministerial committees to help foster coherence, e.g. Brazil's National Environmental Council (CONAMA), which is a high level advisory and deliberative committee and also includes representatives from civil society, academia, and trade unions, and the business sector.

Inter-ministerial co-ordination mechanisms are particularly important where issues relevant to the climate, land-use, ecosystems and food nexus are split between the responsibility of several different ministries. This is the case in Indonesia, where the issues of forestry, agriculture, energy (including bioenergy) and spatial planning are under the purview of four different ministries (Ministry of Environment and Forestry - MoEF, Ministry of Agriculture, Ministry of Energy and Mineral Resources, Ministry of Agrarian and Spatial Planning, respectively). The current structure of individual ministries in Indonesia should ensure some horizontal policy co-ordination in the nexus, as for example MoEF also has responsibility for setting policy regarding biodiversity and ecosystems. However, biodiversity/ecosystem policy and climate policy are created independently, despite clear synergies (e.g. REDD+) and the MoEF having responsibility for both sectors. Indonesia acknowledges in its NBSAP that "it is necessary to synchronise the issue of climate change and biodiversity that is implemented in the scope of MoEF" (Government of Indonesia, 2016[4]).

Institutional co-ordination can be on an ad hoc basis or it can be institutionalised. In France, Ireland and Mexico, it is institutionalised – which facilitates co-ordination. For example, in France, two ministries (MTES and MAA) are jointly responsible for identifying and addressing trade-offs and promoting synergies between agricultural productivity growth, biodiversity conservation, and climate change mitigation and adaptation. In France, for matters that involve multiple ministries, the general secretariat of European affairs (SGAE) oversees policy co-ordination and ensures that a consensus is reached. In Ireland, institutions to coordinate action for climate change mitigation are being established. For example, under the new Climate Action Plan 2019, a Climate Action Delivery Board, jointly chaired by the office of the Taoiseach and the DCCAE, will be established to oversee the implementation of the plan (Government of Ireland, 2018[5]). The Climate Action Delivery Board will be responsible for reviewing key projects, identifying challenges for implementation and reporting on the progress of the plan.

Box 4.1. Governance of peatlands in Indonesia and Ireland

Peatlands have globally significant biodiversity, are an important carbon sink, and conversely a potentially significant source of GHG emissions (via direct use of carbon-rich peat, or via drying and subsequent oxidation of peat soils) (UNEP; GEF; Global Environment Centre; Wetlands International, 2008[6]). Ensuring coherent governance of peatlands is therefore important to the nexus.

Peatlands are governed by a specific body both in Indonesia and Ireland. This governance arrangement has led to some misalignments and inconsistencies in both countries. For example, the Indonesian Peatland Restoration Agency (BRG) is a non-departmental institution created by presidential decree. As such, the BRG is not eligible for state funding, and funding for its actions must come from relevant departmental budgets (MoA, MoEF) and other domestic or international sources (BRG, 2016[7]) Further, despite being responsible for peatland restoration, the BRG has no direct authority over any peatland areas. The result is an organisation that lacks the resources or authority to realistically achieve its goals, of 2 million ha restored by 2021.

In Ireland, Bord na Móna is a quasi-state organisation responsible for the development and management of Ireland's peat resources. It operates an extensive peat harvesting operation as well as two of Ireland's three peat-fired power stations. It also owns and manages 80,000ha of land, including around 7% of the total extent of peat bogs (Bord na Móna, 2018[8]). However, policies relating to peatlands are formulated by a different body (the National Parks and Wildlife Service). Subsidies are available for the generation of electricity using peat (€103.4million in 2017/18): this has negative consequences for both emission and biodiversity (CER, 2017[9]). However, the national peatlands strategy represents a significant step forward. Recognising, the environmental and ecosystem service benefits of peatland area, phasing out electricity generation by 2028 and the decision by Bord na móna to decarbonise through increase electricity generation from renewables to 75% by 2020 and reduce peat production from a peak of 6.5mt (2013) to 2mt (2020), are all positive steps that will benefit the peatland areas. This also represents significantly improved coordination of nexus goals as they relate to peat.

Institutions have also been established to ensure horizontal co-ordination at the sub-national level in some countries, including Mexico and Indonesia. For example, the Mexican State of Chiapas has an Inter-institutional Co-ordination Commission on Climate Change (CCICCCH) (World Bank, CIAT and CATIE, 2014[10]). In Indonesia, each provincial level government has a dedicated local development agency (BAPPENDA), which is responsible for developing provincial level development plans and ensure that it is in line with national policy norms and goals. Regarding climate change, the (federal) RAN-GRK secretariat provides technical assistance to provincial and district level governments to facilitate the mainstreaming of mitigation plans into their development plans. However, like the national context, there is a lack of overarching subnational co-ordination of nexus policies, beyond the BAPPENDA. Consequently, sub-national nexus policies are not always consistent or co-ordinated.

Improving horizontal co-ordination can also involve modifying the mandates of different national ministries. At present, these can be quite specific, or much broader – which could – at least in theory – facilitate policy coherence. For example, in Indonesia, the Ministry of Agriculture (MoA) is responsible for policy that governs the production of food and other agricultural products. The MoA issues permits and creates norms which govern the use of land that falls outside the national forest estate. The Irish Department of Agriculture, Food and the Marine has a slightly broader mandate, and that for the Mexican Ministry dealing with agriculture is broader still – including rural development and food security (Ministry of Agriculture, Livestock, Rural Development, Fisheries and Food, SAGARPA). In France, the Ministry for an ecological and solidarity transition (MTES) has a very broad remit to oversee sustainable development, the environment and climate - as well as the French Agency for Biodiversity (AFB) and the French Environment and Energy Management Agency (ADEME). The issue of agriculture and food is under the remit of a separate ministry (Ministry of Agriculture and Food, MAA), but environmental concerns have a high profile – maybe in part due to the joint responsibility of MAA and MTES in addressing synergies and trade-offs (highlighted above).

Influence of multilateral agreements or actions on institutions

International concerns also impact policies, institutions and policy coherence in the nexus. This includes supra-national agreements and actions, such as those related to the SDGs. Indeed, several countries have established inter-ministerial committees to help develop and implement policies that progress the SDGs in a coherent manner (outlined in Table 4.1). For example, Mexico has established a "National Council for the 2030 Agenda" to co-ordinate implementation of the Sustainable Development Goals (SDGs). This body is led by the Office of the President to "co-ordinate the design, execution, follow-up and evaluation" of actions relating to the SDGs – including by connecting federal government representatives with the legislative branch, as well as with local governments and other relevant stakeholders.

International initiatives such as more focused "supply-side" programmes and associated institutions, such as the REDD+ framework established under the UNFCCC have also spurred on new institutional arrangements to foster co-operation.[2] Consequently, some countries have set up national or sub-national institutions. For example, Brazil has established a national commission for REDD+, and supporting thematic advisory panels and technical groups (Government of Brazil, 2017[11]). Mexico for example, developed partnerships between different national-level institutions with the specific aim of improving co-ordination and collaboration. Thus, in 2011, SAGARPA signed a co-operation agreement with the National Forestry Commission to establish co-ordination mechanisms i.e. in areas including both agricultural activities and forests (Government of Mexico, 2015[12]). Further, Mexico has explicitly mentioned the issue of biodiversity in its "general law on climate change" (PECC), which entered into force in 2012.

International pressure has also led to "demand-side" programmes and associated institutions. These include internationally-recognised schemes, such as the "Forestry Stewardship Council" (FSC, which to date has certified more than 200 million hectares of responsibly-managed forests globally) (FSC, 2017[13]). It also includes national schemes, such as the Indonesian Forestry Certification Corporation. The governance of such schemes is often led by non-government stakeholders.

Table 4.1. National institutional arrangements for co-ordination of a country's SDG response

	Brazil	France	Indonesia	Ireland	Mexico	New Zealand
Lead co-ordination	National Commission for SDGs (CNODS)	High-level, multi-stakeholder steering committee (including representatives of all government departments)	"National Co-ordination team", led by Ministry of National Development (BAPPENAS)	Senior Officials Group (representatives of all government departments)	National Council for the 2030 Agenda	NA (no co-ordination body for SDGs)
Oversight	Office of the President	Inter-ministerial delegate for sustainable development (as mandated by the Prime Minister)	Office of the President	Cabinet	Office of the President	NA
Is each SDG assigned to a specific ministry		Yes	Yes	Yes	Yes	NA
Sub-national entity representation?	Yes	Yes	Included in the underlying working groups	No	Yes	NA
CSO/private sector representation?	Yes	Yes		No – but plans to include interaction with stakeholders (including agriculture) subsequently	Yes	NA

Source: UNDESA (2017[14]) Compendium of National Institutional Arrangements for implementing the 2030 Agenda for Sustainable Development, https://sustainabledevelopment.un.org/content/documents/22008UNPAN99132.pdf; Government of Ireland (2018[14]), The Sustainable Development Goals National Implementation Plan 2018-2020, https://www.dccae.gov.ie/documents/DCCAE-National-Implement-Plan.pdf; UNDP (2017[15]), Institutional and Coordination Mechanisms - Guidance Note on Facilitating Integration and Coherence for SDG implementation, https://www.undp.org/content/undp/en/home/librarypage/sustainable-development-goals/institutional-and-coordination-mechanisms---guidance-note.html

National parliaments can also be involved in policy co-ordination relevant to the land-use nexus. This is useful to ensure coherence between the executive and legislative branches of government. For example, Brazil's Chamber of Deputies has a special parliamentary grouping relating to the SDGs (UNECLAC, 2017[16]), and Mexico also has a Senate Working Group for Monitoring the Legislative Implementation of the SDGs (Government of Mexico, 2018[17]).

Level of vertical co-ordination in domestic policy development

Vertical policy co-ordination is important to ensure that sub-national policies and land-use practices are consistent with national objectives and policy norms. At the national level, the need for vertical policy co-ordination very much depends on the level of decentralisation in a country, as well as mandates for national and sub-national entities. In several countries, sub-national governments are either required to (e.g. France) or can (e.g. Brazil) develop sub-national climate policies. Thus, in France, the sub national regions are required to include climate policies in their regional plan for territorial planning. This requirement to develop a policy document that includes several different topics was specifically aimed at removing policy contradictions that came about from developing more focused sets of objectives (e.g. on biomass energy) (Government of France, 2010[18]). In Brazil, both Brazilian states and cities can set their own climate plan, and 14 states (out of 27) have done so (Barbi and da Costa Ferreira, 2017[19]). The Brazilian national environment system (Sisnama) "aims to establish a co-ordinated … set of actions for environmental management" and includes representation from national, State and municipalities (Government of Brazil, 2016[20]).

Sub-national biodiversity strategies are also increasingly being developed, including in some sub-national jurisdictions of Brazil, France, Ireland, Mexico and New Zealand (CDB, 2017[21]). In Mexico, the National Commission for the Knowledge and Use of Biodiversity (CONABIO) encourages States to develop sub-national biodiversity plans, and eight Mexican states have done so (Government of Michoacan, 2007[22]). Developing such strategies has sometimes involved consultation with a wide group of stakeholders. For example, the biodiversity strategy of the Mexican state of Michoacán was developed in consultation with all sectors, and via workshops and public consultation, and will be followed by a state-wide action plan to implement the strategy (Government of Michoacan, 2007[22]).

Governance of biodiversity-related issues can differ from those focused on land use. For example, local authorities in New Zealand are responsible for managing several important aspects of biodiversity on private land (Schneider and Samkin, 2012[23]). Indeed, a number of NZ local authorities have developed specific local plans to manage the pressures on biodiversity.

In France, vertical integration of regional plans that includes climate policies, with national priorities is ensured by requiring that these are jointly developed between a sub-national government (region) and the federal government (Government of France, 2010[18]). The aim of a of a regional climate plan is to fix short (to 2020) and long -term (to 2050) objectives relating to i.a. GHG mitigation and carbon sequestration.

Vertical co-ordination can also help promote policy coherence between national policies and supra-national frameworks. Vertical co-ordination for EU member states also includes co-ordination between national and EU policies. For example, the European Commission initiated the "Multi-annual Implementation Plan of the new EU Forest Strategy" which aims to co-ordinate "forest policies and initiatives relevant to forests and to the forest-based sector" (EC, 2015[24]). This implementation plan includes specific mention of increasing the use of forests for mitigation; protecting forests and enhancing ecosystem services; and "working together to coherently manage ... forests" (EC, 2015[24]).

In general, while the national government sets the over-arching framework for land-use decisions, it is the sub-national governments that are in charge of the final land-use and development decisions. Consequently, the differing priorities of sub-national governments can lead to differences in how national level norms are interpreted and applied at local levels. For example, while land-use decisions are made largely by individual land owners in New Zealand, their options are limited by national standards – such as the Resource Management Act. Nevertheless, there can be significant intra-country variation in the management of specific issues. For example, inconsistencies between regional plans between different regions of New Zealand have led to inconsistencies in managing the impacts of farming activities on freshwater (Baker-Galloway, 2013[25]). In Mexico, community-level (*ejidos* and *comunidades*) governance of forestry plays an important role in land management, but the state nevertheless has the power to "impose measures that it deems necessary to safeguard the conservation of natural resources" (Government of Mexico, 2017[26]) .

The degree of centralisation or decentralisation of policy-making in the nexus raises different challenges for the coordination of institutions. Decentralisation poses challenges for the vertical coordination of land-use policy. Ensuring that both national level policy norms are translated into local land-use decisions and that local land-use issues are accurately reflected in the national policy making process requires a continuous flow of information between national and sub-national institutions. One way of achieving this is through the sub-national representation of national level institutions, an approach common to both Indonesia and Mexico. In Mexico, the Secretariat of Agriculture, Livestock, Rural Development, Fisheries and Food (SAGARPA) is represented in each Mexican State, as well as in many hundreds of Rural Development Districts (Government of Mexico, 2018[27]). A review of REDD+ readiness in Indonesia has also highlighted the importance of sub-national institutions to support relevant activities at sub-national levels – for example, the province-level working group on REDD+ meets monthly (FCPF, 2015[28]).This decentralised presence of ministries, agencies or committees helps to provide information and promote co-ordination between agricultural producers and sub-national governments.

Despite these challenges, decentralisation provides an opportunity for innovative context-specific solutions and institutions (especially in large heterogeneous countries). For example, counties in Brazil with the highest deforestation rates have had bans imposed for loans for agricultural activities, and their ranchers embargoed from selling their cattle to slaughterhouses (Le Tourneau, 2016[29]). If decentralisation leads to greater influence of the local community over land, and the benefits that can be generated from it, this can incentivise actions that are more sustainable in the longer-term. For example, there is some evidence in Mexico that forests that are managed by communities may be done so more sustainably (e.g. storing more carbon) than other types of management (CCMSS; Rights and Resources Initiative, 2010[30]).

International trade and co-ordination with non-state actors

Given the transboundary realm of activity of the institutions involved in international trade, in addition to the cross-engagement of trade- and land use-relevant government institutions, the coordination of public and private institutions is also important. In several of the case study countries, multi-stakeholder partnerships involving both public and private actors at national and sub-national scale have been an effective mechanism to influence land-use nexus implications of global supply chains. A challenge for government institutions is how to effectively engage and coordinate with these initiatives to leverage maximum effectiveness and alignment with national policy.

The Brazilian Soy Moratorium (SoyM, discussed in chapter 5), is an example of an industry-led initiative of this kind in the Brazilian Amazon biome. Only after its creation by private actors was it joined by the Brazilian authorities. A similar initiative in the Cerrado has become known as the "Cerrado manifesto". This manifesto, published by a coalition of NGOs, foundations and scientific institutions in September 2017 and signed by over a hundred local and international firms and investors, contains a pledge to dissociate supply chains and activities from recently converted areas, deforestation and native vegetation loss in the Cerrado biome (The Consumer Goods Forum, 2019[31]). Another initiative, the Mato Grosso's "Produce – Conserve – Include" Strategy, is a multi-stakeholder partnership counting 40 members, including government institutions, NGOs and private companies (Government of Mato Grosso, 2019[32]). Also, the Brazilian coalition on Climate, Forests and Agriculture counts more than 190 member institutions and promotes the direct engagement between the government and private companies throughout the country (Brazilian Coalition on Climate, Forests and Agriculture, 2019[33]).

Similar institutions and multi-sector partnerships aim to ease pressures on land in other case study countries. In Indonesia, an initiative aiming to establish partnerships and to coordinate the palm oil sector and existing sustainability initiatives at the national level is the Indonesian palm oil platform (InPOP). Launched in 2014 by the Ministry of Agriculture, by February 2019 InPOP counted 56 members comprising national and sub-national government institutions, development partners, and members from the private sector and civil society (Indonesian Palm Oil Platform (InPOP), 2019[34]). In Ireland, a voluntary food and drink sustainability programme ("Origin Green", see also Box 5.1) brings together 321 farmers and food businesses (Bord Bia, n.d.[35]).

References

Baker-Galloway, M. (2013), *The Inconsistent Regional Management of Farming Effects on Waterways*, New Zealand Agricultural and Resource Economics Society, Christchurch, New Zealand, https://econpapers.repec.org/paper/agsnzar13/160192.htm (accessed on 4 February 2019). [25]

Barbi, F. and L. da Costa Ferreira (2017), "Governing Climate Change Risks: Subnational Climate Policies in Brazil", *Chinese Political Science Review*, Vol. 2/2, pp. 237–252, https://doi.org/10.1007/s41111-017-0061-3. [19]

Bord Bia (n.d.), *Origin Green: Ireland's food and drink sustainability programme*, https://www.origingreen.ie/ (accessed on 25 February 2019). [35]

Bord na Móna (2018), *Bord na Móna - Naturally Driven*, https://www.bordnamona.ie/ (accessed on August 31 2018). [8]

Brazilian Coalition on Climate, Forests and Agriculture (2019), *The Coalition*, http://www.coalizaobr.com.br/home/index.php/en/ (accessed on 25 February 2019). [33]

BRG (2016), *Wapres JK Larang BRG Pakai APBN untuk Restorasi*, https://brg.go.id/wapres-jk-larang-brg-pakai-apbn-untuk-restorasi. [7]

CCMSS; Rights and Resources Initiative (2010), *Sustainable Forest Management as a strategy to combat Climate Change: lessons from Mexican communities*, https://theredddesk.org/sites/default/files/resources/pdf/2010/forests_imprenta.pdf (accessed on 2018 August 2018). [30]

CDB (2017), *Subnational Biodiversity Strategies and Action Plans (SBSAPs)*, https://www.cbd.int/nbsap/related-info/sbsap/ (accessed on 31 August 2018). [21]

CER (2017), *Public Service Obligation Levy 2017/18*, Commission for Energy Regulation. [9]

CIM (2007), *Decreto n° 6.263, de 21 de Novembro 2007, Institui o Comitê Interministerial sobre Mudança do Clima - CIM, orienta a elaboração do Plano Nacional sobre Mudança do Clima, e dá outras providências*, FAOLEX, http://extwprlegs1.fao.org/docs/pdf/bra77881.pdf. [2]

EC (2015), *Commissions Staff Working Document - Multi-annual Implementation Plan of the new EU Forest Strategy*, https://ec.europa.eu/transparency/regdoc/rep/10102/2015/EN/10102-2015-164-EN-F1-1.PDF (accessed on 31 August 2018). [24]

FCPF (2015), *REDD+ Annual Country Progress Reporting (with semi-annual update)*, https://www.forestcarbonpartnership.org/sites/fcp/files/2016/Oct/230916_Final%20NS_FCPF%20%20Country%20Progress%20Report.pdf (accessed on 31 August 2018). [28]

FSC (2017), *FSC Certification: Delivering business benefits by guaranteeing environmental and social responsibility*, https://ic.fsc.org/en (accessed on 31 August 2018). [13]

Government of Brazil (2017), *Implementation of the Brazil's National Strategy for REDD+*, http://r/images/conaredd/implementaoredd-resumoexecutivo-EN-Nov17-COP23.pdf (accessed on 31 August 2018). [11]

Government of Brazil (2016), *National Biodiversity Strategy and Action Plan*, https://www.cbd.int/doc/world/br/br-nbsap-v3-en.pdf (accessed on August 31 2018). [20]

Government of France (2010), *Schéma régional du climat, de l'air et de l'énergie*, http://outil2amenagement.cerema.fr/IMG/pdf/schema_regional_du_climat_de_l_air_et_de_l_energie_cle77bbb5_cle71c139.pdf (accessed on 31 August 2018). [18]

Government of Indonesia (2016), *Indonesian Biodiversity Strategy and Action Plan 2015-2020*, The Ministry of the National Development Planning, https://www.cbd.int/doc/world/id/id-nbsap-v3-en.pdf. [4]

Government of Ireland (2018), *Climate Action Plan 2019: To tackle climate breakdown*, https://www.dccae.gov.ie/en-ie/climate-action/publications/Documents/16/Climate_Action_Plan_2019.pdf (accessed on 4 October 2019). [5]

Government of Mato Grosso (2019), *Produzir, Conservar e Incluir - Estratégia de MT para mitigar Mudanças Climáticas*, http://pci.mt.gov.br/#apresentacao (accessed on 25 February 2019). [32]

Government of Mexico (2018), *Secretaría de Agricultura, Ganadería, Desarrollo Rural, Pesca y Alimentación: Delegaciones Estatales*, https://www.gob.mx/sagarpa/acciones-y-programas/delegaciones-estatales-90613 (accessed on 31 August 2018). [27]

Government of Mexico (2018), *Voluntary National Review for the High-Level Political Forum on Sustainable Development*, https://sustainabledevelopment.un.org/content/documents/20122VOLUNTARY_NATIONAL_REPORT_060718.pdf (accessed on 31 August 2018). [17]

Government of Mexico (2017), *Estrategia National para el REDD+ 2017-2030*, http://www.enaredd.gob.mx/wp-content/uploads/2017/09/Estrategia-Nacional-REDD+-2017-2030.pdf (accessed on 31 August 2018). [26]

Government of Mexico (2015), *Mid-Term Progress Report of Mexico*, https://www.forestcarbonpartnership.org/sites/fcp/files/2015/May/MTR%20Mexico_Eng%20with%20GRM.pdf. [12]

Government of Michoacan (2007), *Estrategia para la conservacion y uso sustenable de la diversitad biologica del Estado de Michoacan*, https://www.cbd.int/doc/nbsap/sbsap/mx-sbsap-michoacan-es.pdf. [22]

Indonesian Palm Oil Platform (InPOP) (2019), *About Us - Indonesia Palm Oil Platform*, http://foksbi.id/en/about-inpop (accessed on 25 February 2019). [34]

Le Tourneau, F. (2016), "Is Brazil now in control of deforestation in the Amazon?", *Cybergeo*, http://dx.doi.org/10.4000/cybergeo.27484. [29]

MfE (2015), *Natural Resources Sector Diagram*, http://nrs.mfe.govt.nz/sites/default/files/NRS%20Goal%20and%20Focus%20Areas%20Diagram.pdf. [3]

Schneider, A. and G. Samkin (2012), "A biodiversity jigsaw: A review of current New Zealand legislation and initiatives", *e-Journal of Social & Behavioural Research in Business*, Vol. 3/2, pp. 10-26, https://researchcommons.waikato.ac.nz/handle/10289/7743 (accessed on 4 February 2019). [23]

The Consumer Goods Forum (2019), *Business for the Cerrado - Supporting the Cerrado Manifesto*, https://www.theconsumergoodsforum.com/initiatives/environmental-sustainability/key-projects/deforestation/soy/business-for-the-cerrado/ (accessed on 1 March 2019). [31]

UNDESA (2017), *Compendium of National Institutional Arrangements for implementing the 2030 Agenda for Sustainable Development*, http://workspace.unpan.org/sites/Internet/Documents/UNPAN97468.pdf (accessed on 31 August 2018). [14]

UNDP (2017), *Institutional and Coordination Mechanisms - Guidance Note on Facilitating Integration and Coherence for SDG implementation*, https://sustainabledevelopment.un.org/content/documents/2478Institutional_Coordination_Mechanisms_GuidanceNote.pdf (accessed on 31 August 2018). [15]

UNECLAC (2017), *Annual report on regional progress and challenges in relation to the 2030 Agenda for Sustainable Development n Latin America and the Caribbean*, https://repositorio.cepal.org/bitstream/handle/11362/41189/S1700474_en.pdf?sequence=7&isAllowed=y (accessed on 31 August 2018). [16]

UNEP; GEF; Global Environment Centre; Wetlands International (2008), *Assessment on Peatlands, Biodiversity and Climate change*, International Mire Conservation Group (IMCG), http://www.imcg.net/media/download_gallery/books/assessment_peatland.pdf (accessed on 31 August 2018). [6]

Wardojo, W. and N. Masripatin (2002), *Trends in Indonesian Forest Policy*, https://pdfs.semanticscholar.org/2476/e43a3e5dab1ee62ce15d915ca33a84c542c3.pdf. [1]

World Bank, CIAT and CATIE (2014), *Climate-Smart Agriculture in Chiapas, Mexico*, The World Bank Group. [10]

Notes

[1] This is a grouping of central government agencies responsible for the management and stewardship of New Zealand's natural resources composed of the DOC, the Ministry for the Environment; the Ministry for Primary Industries; the Ministry of Business, Innovation and Employment; Land Information New Zealand; Te Puni Kōkiri; and the Department of Internal Affairs.

[2] REDD+ refers to reducing emissions from deforestation and forest degradation in developing countries. This was recognised under the UNFCCC framework as a potentially-important means of reducing GHG emissions, and UNFCCC decisions invites countries to designate a national focal point who can *iter alia* receive results-based payments.

5 Policy instruments relevant to sustainable land use

Policy instruments ultimately guide the behaviour of actors in land-use systems, so understanding the interactions between policy instruments and how this impacts land use is key for managing outcomes in the land-use, biodiversity, climate and food nexus. The chapter highlights the need for secure and clear land tenure as a prerequisite for effective policymaking. It then analyses some important regulatory, economic, information and voluntary instruments currently in use across the case studies (Brazil, France, Indonesia, Ireland, Mexico and New Zealand), including where and how these instruments have been effective. The chapter also explores how to address food loss and waste, which can play an important role in reducing emissions from agriculture and pressure on land-use systems.

The need for coherent policy frameworks and instruments

Achieving the intended international and national commitments across the land-use nexus will require policies that are ambitious and coherent, as well as cost-effective and equitable. This Chapter examines some of the key regulatory (command and control), economic and information instruments in place across the six case study countries (Brazil, France, Indonesia, Ireland, Mexico and New Zealand) and provides initial analysis on areas of alignment and misalignment. Examples of policy instruments relevant to the land-use nexus are provided in Table 5.1.

A key determinant of the relative efficiency of a policy instruments is the degree of uncertainty about costs and environmental damage or benefit avoided and induced (Newell and Pizer, 2003[1]). For land-based activities (often substantial) uncertainties about relevant variables complicate the choice between multiple policy instruments aiming to address nexus impacts. For instance, methods to estimate GHG emissions from land use and agriculture are generally less accurate than for other sectors, and typically result in wider ranges of uncertainty. In the case of Ireland for example, more than 88% of the uncertainty of total GHG emissions reported under the UNFCCC was related to agriculture in 2015 (Environmental Protection Agency, 2018[2]). Similarly, imperfect knowledge of biodiversity and the rarely sufficient application of ecosystem service valuation approaches (see below) can hinder the selection of efficient policy instruments. Therefore, improving our understanding of land-based externalities should be an important element of efforts to achieve policy alignment in the land-use nexus.

Coherent policy approaches in the land-use nexus are needed to avoid the "leakage" of adverse land-use nexus impacts (such as GHG emissions (Blanco et al., 2014[3]) or adverse impacts on biodiversity (Maestre Andrés et al., 2012[4]; Lambin and Meyfroidt, 2011[5])). Leakage can occur when production shifts (within or between countries) in response to a certain policy instrument. For example, if protecting a specific area of land from deforestation shifts deforestation pressures to neighbouring areas. International trade in agricultural and forest goods means that international leakage will occur if country A protects its domestic forest but allows for imports of forestry or agricultural products from country B, where deforestation takes place. Coherent policy approaches minimise and prevent misalignments that lead to the occurrence of leakage.

The environmental trends in the case study countries are generally towards increasing absolute GHG emissions and ecosystem degradation (see Chapter 2), albeit with significant intra-country variation. Many of the policies in place have had a positive impact on land-use systems, but the trends highlighted in Chapter 2 suggest there are opportunities to strengthen the scope and implementation of policy instruments. A clear national vision for land use, supplemented with relevant quantitative sectoral targets could help ensure the policy instruments in place are sufficient to address any nexus issues associated with land use.

Clearly-defined land tenure is an important cross-cutting prerequisite for effective policy

An important underlying prerequisite for effective policies for nexus issues, is clear and secure land tenure. Land tenure is defined by Robinson et al. (2013[6]) as the set of property rights associated with land and the institutions that uphold these rights and the security of land tenure as the assurance that land-based property rights will be upheld by society. Land tenure has a variety of forms in the case-study countries, varying from more common forms, such as public or private ownership, to communal forms of tenure such as *Eijdos* and *Comunidades* in Mexico, *Quilombos* in Brazil and *Hutan Desa* (village forest) in Indonesia. Whether or not tenure systems indicate ownership or simply the rights to manage a certain area of land is also highly variable, but in general communal forms of ownership are more common in tropical countries, particularly in forested areas (Robinson, Holland and Naughton-Treves, 2013[6]).

If the tenure of a given area is not clear, it is difficult to identify the land manager, posing challenges for incentivising environmentally-sustainable activities. Correspondingly, in unclear tenure situations, identifying whether or not a particular activity is legal is challenging. When land tenure is not secure, this can incentivise activities that maximise value in the short term and activities to increase the security of tenure, which in many tropical forest areas leads to land clearing. These challenges are highlighted by the situation in Indonesia where overlapping land claims (Gaveau et al., 2017[7]) and highly fragmented land use institutions (discussed in chapter 4 and (Sahide and Giessen, 2015[8])), have resulted in widespread illegal logging, illegal mining and illegal agriculture. Historically, up to 80% of Indonesian timber exports originated from illegally-sourced wood (Observatory of Public Sector Innovation (OECD-OSPI), 2013[9]), and 2.3 million hectares of deforestation over 1991-2014 and USD 6.5 – 9 billion lost tax revenues over 2003-2014 have been attributed to illegal logging (Chitra and Cetera, 2018[10]; Corruption Eradication Comission (KPK), 2015[11]). While illegal logging may have declined in recent years, it remains a non-negligible factor in Indonesian land use change trends. Not only due to exports of illegally-logged wood products, but also because illegal logging is often a prelude to the establishment of (largely export-oriented) oil palm or timber plantations (OECD, 2019[12]).

Similar to the Indonesian case, illegal logging is also an issue in Mexico and Brazil. In Brazil, unclear land tenure exacerbated the issue of illegal logging in the Amazon as the easiest way to obtain land rights was through conversion (OECD, 2015[13]). While more recent efforts to clarify the situation have resulted in reduced deforestation, a lack of enforcement (Azevedo et al., 2017[14]) and weakening environmental governance (Rochedo et al., 2018[15]), mean the problem is still ongoing. In Mexico, illegal deforestation and forest degradation as a response to increasing demand for agricultural products, such as avocados (Hansen, 2018[16]), is an ongoing issue, which threatens ecosystem service provision (such as carbon sequestration) and critical habitat for the monarch butterfly (Leverkus et al., 2017[17]). Up to 70% of domestically consumed timber is estimated to be harvested illegally (Chapela y Mendoza, 2018[18]), and important quantities of Mexican wood imports originate from illegal logging activities in third countries like Peru (Urrunaga, Johnson and Orbegozo Sánchez, 2018[19]).

Illegal land-use activity is of critical importance to the nexus as it can cause widespread environmental degradation and significant GHG emissions, undermining a country's ability to achieve national and international targets. Furthermore, illegal activity is by definition not regulated by policy instruments aimed at incentivising environmentally sustainable land management. Reducing illegal activity, like establishing secure land tenure, is therefore a prerequisite for environmentally effective policy in the land-use nexus.

Table 5.1. Policy instruments to address climate change and ecosystem degradation in the agriculture and forestry sectors

Regulatory (command-and-control) approaches	Economic instruments	Information and other voluntary instruments	Other
Land use / spatial planning tools and requirements (e.g. environmental impact assessments [EIAs] and strategic environmental assessments [SEA])	Price-based instruments: Taxes (e.g. on carbon, groundwater extraction, pesticide and fertiliser use) Charges/fees Subsidies to promote biodiversity (e.g., target public investments in green technology)	Ecolabelling and certification (e.g. organic agriculture labelling schemes; sustainable forest/timber certification)	Trade measures, such as lowering tariffs on climate-friendly and/or biodiversity-friendly products, reduce export subsidies
Rules and standards for water, soil quality and land management	Reform of environmentally harmful subsidies (e.g., decouple farm support from commodity production levels and prices)	Green public procurement (e.g. ensuring government procurement is from sustainable sources)	R&D e.g. to decouple GHG emissions and food production, biomass energy carbon capture and storage
Standards and controls on overuse of agrochemicals and fertilisers in production	Payment for ecosystem services (including REDD+) and agri-environment measures (e.g. retirement of degraded cropland or subsidization of conservation-friendly production practices)	Voluntary approaches (e.g. negotiated agreements between businesses and government for nature protection or voluntary offset schemes)	Inclusive national planning, incorporating climate and biodiversity concerns, national and local governments, non-party stakeholders
Restrictions or prohibitions on use such as moratoria on deforestation (e.g. as used successfully by Brazil to slow deforestation); protected areas; CITES.	Biodiversity offsets/ biobanking (e.g. payment-in-lieu or project based offsetting)	Fiscal transfer schemes (e.g. transfer of resources between different governments in the same country)	Development assistance (e.g. coherent consideration of nexus areas in Natural Resource Management, forestry and biodiversity projects)
Concessions for sustainable forest management	Tradable permits (e.g. carbon emissions, water rights)		Capacity building (including education and training)
	Property rights and secure and tenure Liability instruments Non-compliance fines		

Source: Authors, adapted from OECD (OECD, 2013[20]) *Scaling Up Finance Mechanisms for Biodiversity*, https://dx.doi.org/10.1787/9789264193833-en and OECD (2011[21]) *Food and Agriculture*, https://dx.doi.org/10.1787/9789264107250-en.

Ecosystem service valuation approaches can inform land-use decisions

Ecosystem services provide significant benefits to society that are regularly un-priced or under-valued by markets (OECD, 2019[22]). The loss of these services due to environmental degradation, therefore, leads to significant cost if these services (e.g. water purification) have to be replaced - and can result in welfare and distributional impacts. For example, in Indonesia the loss of forest is associated with an increase both in childhood disease among rural communities and in local ambient temperatures (Herrera et al., 2017[23]; Wolff et al., 2018[24]).

Economic instruments to address the loss of ecosystem services are used across several of the case study countries (discussed below). Incorporating the valuation of these services into the land-use planning mechanisms could be a useful tool to help reconcile the goals of the nexus. Quantifying the changes in ecosystem services resulting from different policy options, and the value of these changes to society, is a key step to better management of nexus areas. However, despite several ongoing programmes targeting a better understanding of ES mapping and valuation, none of the case study countries has consistently integrated this approach into land-use planning systems.

The EU Mapping and Assessment of Ecosystems and their Services (MAES), aims to create a conceptual model linking pressures to ecosystem conditions and define a broad range of indicators to track ecosystem condition and service delivery across the EU. As part of this initiative, the EFESE (*L'évaluation française des écosystèmes et des services écosystématiques*) in France aims to assess the extent, quality and value of ecosystems. EFESE has already produced six assessments of different ecosystems.[1] Despite some success in using the results of EFESE to aid policy design, a recent EU assessment suggests the outputs are not, as yet, sufficient to effectively incorporate ES values into decision making (Ling et al., 2018[25]).

Beyond the EU, the natural capital approach has been used by both Indonesia and Mexico to try and incorporate the value of ecosystem services into decision making. Indonesia has been tracking forest resources for more than 30 years through the pioneering System of Integrated Environmental and Economic Accounting (SISNERLING). There is also a legal mandate in Indonesia requiring all government departments to develop and inventory of natural resources.[2] Development of the SISNERLING is ongoing with the support of the World Bank WAVES (Wealth Accounting and the Value of Ecosystem Services) partnership, which includes improved accounting, the development of land accounts for land-use and land-cover change and a pilot water account for the Citarum River basin (WAVES, 2017[26]).

Despite the considerable progress under the initiatives described above, sufficient data to underpin policymaking is lacking and capacity gaps remain in the case study countries. Consequently, the success of this approach for balancing nexus goals is largely untested. Accelerating the development of and strengthening existing natural capital accounting and ecosystem service valuation approaches is an important opportunity to improve the ability of land-use planning mechanisms to manage trade-offs between the different areas of the nexus.

Regulatory (command-and-control) instruments

Land-use planning

An important regulatory instrument for the nexus areas is land-use planning. Land-use planning is defined by Metternicht (2017[27]) as:

> *"the systematic assessment of land and water potential, alternatives for land use and economic, and social conditions in order to select and adopt the best land use options. Its purpose is to select and put into practice those land uses that will best meet the needs of the people while safeguarding resources for the future."*

Land-use planning thus includes issues relating to spatial planning, the zoning of land for specific purposes, and rights to manage land in both urban and rural areas. Approaches to land-use planning are variable within the case study countries, reflecting the different national contexts of development and land tenure.

However, there are some common approaches to land-use planning across the case study countries, with decentralised responsibility and spatial planning approaches being widely used. In most case study countries, decentralised responsibility for land-use planning involves national governments setting overarching framework legislation, providing guidelines and standards for how to adopt the most appropriate land use options. In most cases, land-use planning authority is further split between state-, region- or provincial-level governments and municipalities, and carried out through the development of spatial plans, the designation of protected areas, the issuance of permits, and the implementation of national-level policies.

This decentralisation of land-use planning to sub-national governments is unsurprising given the role of planning and development in generating revenues at a local level through taxes. Decentralisation of land-use planning also allows sub-national governments to tailor development to suit the local socio-enviro-economic circumstances, and use the most appropriate solutions to manage nexus goals, within the frameworks and guidelines laid out at a national level. Local public budgets rely on certain types of revenue-yielding land use. But ecosystem service provision is not generally revenue yielding. Some of the case study countries, such as Brazil and France, operate schemes under which local authorities are compensated financially for allocating land to ecosystem service provision. These schemes are known as inter-governmental fiscal transfers (discussed below) can allow local authorities to favour less intrusive land uses over the development of land.

In terms of decentralised land-use planning, there is, however, a key implementation gap between theory and practice. In Indonesia and Brazil, for example, poor regional-level implementation of national-level spatial planning guidelines has led to significant environmental degradation and is hampering the ability of these countries to balance nexus goals. In Indonesia, the lack of clear land tenure and the differential maps used by different nexus-relevant ministries (e.g. Ministry of Agriculture and the Ministry of the Environment and Forests) have contributed land conflicts (Abram et al., 2017[28]) and opportunities for illegal logging, mining and agriculture (Gaveau et al., 2017[7]; Carlson et al., 2012[29]). It is essential that the underlying spatial data used to create plans is consistent across all the nexus-relevant ministries. Indonesia is attempting to harmonise the use of spatial data via the *One Map* policy, which will contain 85 thematic layers, including concession boundaries, and will be used to underpin land-use decisions. Since its inception in 2011, progress has been hampered by capacity constraints, inter-ministerial conflict and lack of stakeholder enthusiasm (Shahab, 2016[30]). But, 83 of the 85 layers were completed by 2019, and the data was made accessible to the public in 2018 (OECD, 2019[12]). Once complete, the *One Map* should provide a basis for resolving land tenure and permitting issues.

In Brazil, weakening environmental governance threatens to further undermine land-use planning systems (Rochedo et al., 2018[15]). "Security suspension" ("*suspensão de segurança*") is often used to circumvent planning laws and allow infrastructure development, such as hydropower dams, inside ecological-sensitive areas (Fearnside, 2015[31]). The ease with which government can circumvent environmental protections allows the national government to prioritise large infrastructure development over the needs of local (particularly indigenous) populations and undermines the ability of Brazil to balance nexus goals. The significant gap between land-use planning in theory and practice in Brazil and Indonesia creates issues within the nexus. Thus both countries would benefit if the national level planning norms and guidelines were applied and enforced consistently at a municipal level. Achieving sufficient vertical coordination of national norms and guidelines, however, is challenging and will require dedicated institutional mechanisms (chapter 4) and a mix of incentives (such as intergovernmental fiscal transfers) and deterrents, such as credit blacklisting (e.g. in Brazil).

Urban expansion poses a threat to cropland globally, and is expected to result in the loss of 1.8-2.4% of cropland by 2030 (Bren d'Amour et al., 2016[32]). Low-density urban areas are also associated with higher road transport emissions and habitat fragmentation (OECD, 2018[33]). Consequently, provisions limiting urban sprawl and encouraging densification reduce the potential additional pressure on global crop and wild lands, representing a significant nexus alignment. Both France and Ireland have specific measures to encourage densification in their spatial-planning systems. Since 2018, France has utilised the principle of "no net land artificialisation", which means that agricultural and other non-urban areas should be spared from development. In Ireland, the national planning framework (Project Ireland 2040) includes the control of urban sprawl as a specific objective , with a target of 40% of all new housing to be built within existing built-up areas (Government of Ireland, 2018[34]). Finally, both Ireland and France also include references to biodiversity, either as a specific objective to enhance biodiversity (as in Ireland) or to ensure ecological coherence though the creation of Green and Blue belt networks (*trames verts et bleus)*. Biodiversity-specific planning measures and efforts to limit urban sprawl are well aligned with nexus goals and should be utilised more broadly.

Protected areas

Protected areas (PA)[3] are the cornerstone intervention for conserving biodiversity. Within the case study countries, the coverage of PAs has been growing, though there is still large variation in extent across countries, ranging from 12.2% (Indonesia) to 32.7% (New Zealand) of total land area in 2019 (see Figure 5.1). PAs however, represent a range of approaches from strict protection to more general national and international land-use designations, where countries can control or restrict the type of land-use management is allowed within a certain area.

The types of PAs employed by countries are influenced by national land contexts, particularly in relation to land tenure and unmanaged areas. In countries with secure land tenure and small extents of unmanaged land (Ireland and France), land-use restrictions tend be controlled through PA designation that overlap or are entirely within private land. In Ireland and France, for example, sites are designated as Natura 2000 under EU law. Other designations with differing objectives are also used, such as National Parks. Natura 2000 sites are intended to protect high quality habitat or regional nature parks, and aim to reconcile certain types of land management with biodiversity. In Ireland Natural 2000 sites often overlap with private land, and impose restrictions on activities allowed in order to maintain the quality of the site. The situation is similar in France which is subject the same EU regulations as Ireland. This approach, however, if not well managed with sufficient stakeholder engagement, can lead to conflicts between agricultural and environmental stakeholders, who often perceive each other to have conflicting goals (even if their agendas are aligned) such as in Ireland (Woodworth, 2018[35]; Visser et al., 2007[36]). A more decentralised approach, with extensive stakeholder consultation and site specific management plans, such as employed in France, can reduce the potential for conflict (OECD, 2016[37]).

In New Zealand, as well as state owned and managed PAs, "conservation covenants" are an important mechanism for protecting important ecosystems. Under a covenant, landowners enter into legally binding contracts with the Government to protect natural features or areas of natural habitat on their land. In many cases, covenanting land may make economic sense through improvements in water regulation and quality, provision of amenity value to the property, exclusion of stock from areas of land that are difficult to access or manage, and financial transfers to the farmers (QEII National Trust, 2018[38]).

Figure 5.1. Protected area as a share of total domestic land area

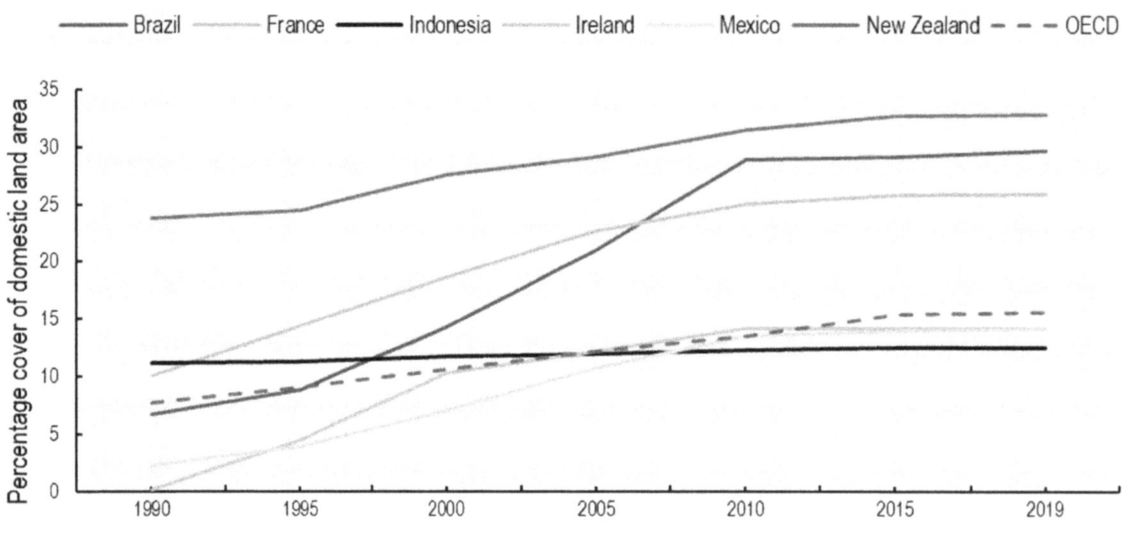

Source: OECD (2019[39]), Protected Area Statistics, http://dx.doi.org/10.1787/5fa661ce-en.
Note: Graph displays an aggregate of all PA reported to the IUCN which includes categories I-VI and No Category. For full methodology see source.

In countries with large areas of unmanaged land, PAs play a key role in preventing the conversion of forests (and other ecosystems) and conserving wilderness areas. While not completely effective, protected areas have reduced deforestation in Brazil (Nolte et al., 2013[40]), Mexico (Pfaff, Santiago-Ávila and Joppa, 2016[41]) and Indonesia (Gaveau, Wandono and Setiabudi, 2007[42]; Gaveau et al., 2012[43]). In Mexico, Brazil and Indonesia, current and historic funding shortfalls have hampered their effectiveness. By controlling land conversion, PAs can contribute to reducing emissions from land use change. In the Brazilian Amazon, an effective PA system could save 8GtCO_2e (emissions from LULUCF in Brazil were 1.17GtCO_2e in 2016 (SEEG, 2018[44])) between 2010 and 2050 (Soares-Filho et al., 2010[45]) as well as providing biodiversity benefits. Conversely, ineffectively managed PAs can become a significant source of emissions, for example deforestation in PAs in Indonesia contributed 139.4MtCO_2e a year between 2000 and 2012 (Collins and Mitchard, 2017[46]).[4] Finally, simply excluding activity from a certain area through a PA can displace that activity to another region, either within or outside the same country reducing their ability to balance nexus goals. For a system of PAs to reduce ecosystem degradation and emission from land-use change effectively, these leakage impacts must be considered.

In Brazil, 80% of the current PA system was gazetted after 2000 and now covers 29.1% of the total land area (OECD, 2019[39]). As well as the more traditional PAs, Brazil also makes extensive use of indigenous territories, which now cover 21% of the Amazon region (Le Tourneau, 2015[47]) in addition to the 22.6% already within other PA (de Marques, Schneider and Peres, 2016[48]). This approach has proved to be successful at reducing deforestation up to 2015 (although recent trends may be different). While the biodiversity benefits are less clear, the clarity of tenure associated with this approach to PAs is of benefit to nexus as it prevents conversion if sufficiently enforced. Indigenous reserves (and other forms of community managed PA) could be used more broadly to control land-use change and have the added co-benefit of addressing significant human rights issues.

Moratoriums and other land use restrictions

Moratoriums on certain land-use activities or the use of products from certain areas and other targeted land-use restrictions can work to help effectively balance nexus goals, especially in cases when effective land-use rules in one ecosystem should not be applied in other areas. For example, the high carbon value of peatlands and the emissions from soil oxidation after drainage can undermine climate change targets and therefore they may not be suitable sites for afforestation (Miettinen et al., 2017[49]; DAHG, 2015[50]). Indonesia, for example, has had a moratorium on the issuing of new operating permits in primary forest and peatland areas since 2011,[5] and more recently a regulation banning the clearance of all peat areas until after a zoning process (ongoing as of end 2018) has been completed.[6] Ireland has also restricted the use of ecologically sensitive and carbon dense peatland areas through regulation (DAHG, 2015[50]).

In isolation, a moratorium will not effectively control land use, particularly in challenging governance environments, where enforcement of other regulations may be lacking. Instead, it should form one part of a broader toolkit of policy instruments that includes a range of reforms, incentives and dis-incentives aimed at altering land use. In 2006, pressure from downstream consumers (including McDonalds and Wal-Mart) and consequently commodity traders (e.g. Cargill) to avoid buying soy grown on deforested areas in the Amazon, led to the soy moratorium in Brazil. The moratorium has been credited with helping achieve a 70% reduction in annual extent of deforestation in the Amazon by 2013 (although recent trends suggest this might be reversing) (Gibbs et al., 2015[51]). Importantly, the enacting of the soy moratorium coincided with parallel efforts by the Brazilian government to reduce the rate of deforestation through land registration (under the CAR), improve monitoring, increase enforcement and expand the PA network (Gibbs et al., 2015[51]; Nepstad et al., 2014[52]). This means that the moratorium itself was just one component of a larger strategy to control land-use change. Contrastingly, in Indonesia, where efforts to improve environmental enforcement, monitoring and reform land tenure are less well developed, the moratoriums on new concession licences have been less successful at reducing deforestation (although deforestation has reduced since 2015) (Hansen et al., 2013[53]; Busch et al., 2014[54]).

Restricting land use within a single biome or ecosystem can shift environmentally destructive behaviour elsewhere (a process known as leakage, see above), undermining the potential nexus benefits of these approaches. To some extent, this is true with the soy moratorium in Brazil, which only covers the Amazon biome, and has shifted the expansion of soy production to the neighbouring, non-forest, Cerrado biome.

In the Cerrado rates of habitat loss were consistently 2.5 times that of the Amazon from 2002 to 2011 (Strassburg et al., 2017[55]). Failing to consider the possible leakage of activities restricted by moratoria can lead to significant misalignments between nexus goals in other areas. Hence, targeted restrictions should be consistent with other national and local land-use policies and should consider the potential leakage impacts.

Standards and restrictions

Regulatory standards can have important nexus impacts, either by directly defining which activities are and are not legal in a given area or by officially mandating the use of resources. Such standards can be used in several different aspects of the nexus, such as land cover or use, type and level of agrochemical inputs (e.g. fertilisers and pesticides), mandates for water quality and the control of pollution. Standards and restrictions can be applied in a variety of ways (e.g. through zoning and permits) at local, national and international levels (e.g. EU water framework directive).

In Ireland, the number of cattle has increased by 740 000 animals (10.3%) from 2010 to 2018, predominately driven by a 38% increase in the dairy herd (Central Statistics Office, 2019[56]). This growth has also corresponded with a 10% growth in fertiliser sales in both 2017 and 2018 as dairy farming has intensified. To address the environmental consequences of this increased intensity of farming, Ireland has a nitrates derogation programme that requires intensive livestock farms (defined at above 170kg of livestock manure nitrogen/ha) to adhere to derogation measures designed to reduced pollution. These measure are predominated aimed at breaking the nutrient transport pathway (such as controlling when and how fertilisers are applied) (DAFM, 2019[57]). These derogation measures, in principle, facilitate the sustainable intensification of agriculture, so the value of sector can grow while the environmental impact is minimised, and are, therefore, well aligned with the nexus goals. However, the increasing intensification of dairy farming has corresponded to an ongoing decline in water quality in Ireland (3% decline between 2013-2015). A decline suggesting that this approach may not be sufficient to fully ameliorate the environmental impacts of intensive agriculture (EPA, 2018[58]). Supplementing these kind of derogation measures with other economic incentives, such as taxes (see below), could help improve their effectiveness. This approach was recently suggested in New Zealand, where similar environmental issues from the intensification of dairy farming exist (The Tax Working Group, 2019[59]).

National-level biofuel blending targets are a good example of a standard that can be misaligned with nexus goals. For example, in Indonesia, biofuel blending targets are likely to be driving ecosystem degradation, emissions from land-use change, undermining food production goals by occupying land for food crops, and encouraging the expansion of oil palm plantations. This particular policy was created in response to concerns about reliance on oil imports rather than any nexus-related goals, which likely led to the misaligned (Wright, Rahmanulloh and Abdi, 2017[60]).

While both Brazil and Indonesia directly regulate land cover, their approaches are contrasting. Under the forest code (CAR), Brazil mandates the minimum level of forest cover on farms, which varies between biomes (80% in the Amazon and 20% in Cerrado). Enforcement has been challenging, with one study finding only 6% of properties which had deforested illegally taking steps to reforest (Azevedo et al., 2017[14]). The legal requirement for forest cover targets will likely lead to biodiversity and ecosystem benefits. However, revisions to the CAR in 2012 (upheld but the supreme court in 2018), could reduce its environmental impacts. The revisions allow for a reduced forest cover requirement on private land (from 80% to 50%) in states in the Amazon, if the state has more than 65% of its area covered by conservation units and indigenous territories, potentially allowing the conversion of up to 15 million ha of forest (Freitas et al., 2018[61]). Indonesia takes the opposite approach to Brazil, by legally requiring the conversion of all land[7] (e.g. from forest to plantation) within a plantation concession within six years of the concession licence being issued.[8] Companies failing to do so risk having non-converted areas transferred to other companies, a policy that has already conflicted with international sustainability standards, such as the Round Table on Sustainable Palm Oil (RSPO) (discussed in section on certification below).

Regulatory standards can also regulate the legal status of certain types of import products and trade practices, and can be important instruments for ensuring forest product legality. Bi- or multilateral, product-specific memoranda of understanding or trade agreement provisions can be an effective approach for preventing the occurrence of export-driven illegal logging, promoting sustainable production standards and addressing leakage impacts.[9] One example are the voluntary partnership agreements (VPAs) that the EU has concluded with Indonesia and a number of other countries. VPAs regulate trade in tropical timber and to enforce certain production standards, including through the Forest Law Enforcement, Governance and Trade (FLEGT) scheme. The EU prohibits placing illegally harvested timber and derived products on the EU market, and requires importers to perform 'due diligence' checks on timber and timber products.[10] By exempting timber with FLEGT licenses issued by the Indonesian government under the VPA from these checks, the EU provides a powerful incentive for timber legality and sustainable production standards in Indonesia. Mexico, too, adopted a new forestry law governing trade in forest products in 2018,[11] but critics note the persistence of loopholes for illegally harvested timber to enter the country (Ortiz Tapia, 2018[62]). The impact of the law on curbing trade in illegal forest products will, therefore, be important to observe.

Environmental provisions in trade agreements and other trade policy measures

Requirements for and support to sustainable land-use practices in mutual agreements governing trade relations between trading partners (e.g. Regional Trade Agreements) is a potential way to improve the land-use nexus performance. General environment-related provisions are included in the vast majority of regional trade agreements (RTAs), although approximately one third of RTAs that make reference to the environment do so in the preamble only (Monteiro, 2016[63]). Provisions specific to a particular issue such as land use, on the other hand, are less frequent. One such example is the Comprehensive Economic Partnership Agreement between Indonesia and the European Free Trade Association (EFTA) states (Government of Indonesia and European Free Trade Association, 2018[64]), which was signed at the end of 2018. The agreement includes a chapter on sustainable development and trade, with sub-sections dedicated to specific sectors or sub-sectors. The strict enforcement and monitoring of adherence to the principles set out in this chapter will be essential to ensure a positive impact on land-use outcomes. An environment chapter or provisions on co-operation and participation in environmental matters however remain the exception among the trade agreements that Indonesia is a party to (OECD, 2019[12]).

Variations of land-use references are also included in trade agreements relevant to other case study countries. In Mexico, for instance, the North American Agreement on Environmental Cooperation (NAAEC), a side treaty of NAFTA, governs environmental aspects of trade with Canada and the US, Mexico's main trading partner. While the land-use impacts of NAFTA seem mixed (see chapter 1, (Mayrand, Paquin and Gagnon-Turcotte, 2008[65]) and (Aguilar et al., 2011[66])), in 2018, a successor to NAFTA was signed with the United States – Mexico – Canada Agreement (USMCA). USMCA contains a chapter on the environment, which includes specific articles relating to trade and biodiversity, trade and conservation, and trade and sustainable forestry management (including a reference to carbon storage) (Governments of the United States; Mexico and Canada, 2018[67]). The environmental provisions contained in the USMCA are furthermore expanded and detailed in the accompanying Environmental Cooperation Agreement (Commission for Environmental Cooperation (CEC), 2018[68]), which also provides for co-operation between the three countries on issues such as biodiversity protection, natural resource management and environmental governance.

A key determinant of the success of environmental provisions in trade agreements to positively influence trade-land use interactions is the extent of their actual implementation and enforcement. In general, information on the implementation of environmental provisions of the case study countries' existing trade agreements is limited. OECD analysis has found evidence that certain institutional arrangements and governance mechanisms, such as those aiming at increased public involvement in the verification of the implementation of environmental provisions, can benefit the concrete implementation of such provisions (George and Yamaguchi, 2018[69]).

Unilateral trade policy measures can also be an important determinant of land-use outcomes. Demand-side examples of this type of policy measure include preferential tariffs for climate- and/or biodiversity-friendly products ("environmental goods and services"), such as efficient waste management equipment. A supply-side example is the reduction of export subsidies or credits for certain land-intensive agricultural goods, such as most animal products. Another such example is the imposition of charges on exports of goods with substantial associated nexus impacts. Depending on international prices, the Indonesian government for instance imposes both an export levy (ranging between USD 0 and USD 50, (Ministry of Finance, 2018[70]) and an export tax (ranging between 0% and 22.5% (FAO, 2017[71])) on exports of palm oil and its derivatives. Revenues from the export levy, moreover, are in part used to support domestic palm biodiesel production. On the demand-side, import restrictions on nexus-relevant goods such as on corn and rice have been applied by the Indonesian government to meet domestic self-sufficiency targets (FAO, 2017[71]).

Environmental Impact Assessments (EIA) and Strategic Environmental Assessments (SEA)

EIA are used globally to control the impacts of development. Generally, EIA are applied on a project basis and involve and expert of assessment of the expected impacts of the project in predefined environmental domains such as biodiversity, water pollution and climate change. The results of the EIA can then be used by the relevant planning authority to recommend changes (which may be legally binding) to the proposed plan to limit the environmental impacts. Best practice for EIA are summarised briefly in Box 5.1. For large strategic development plans that involve multiple projects, the environmental impact of each project may not be large, but the aggregate impact of all the projects in the plan can be significant. In these cases individual EIAs of the individual projects would not be sufficient control the impacts of the whole development plan SEA can be used as to assess the whole plan as well.

EIA

The use of EIA to assess and limit the adverse impacts of development projects is a common tool throughout all the case study countries. EIA can help to ensure consistency between nexus areas. However, to function effectively, EIA must be transparent, and broad enough to consider all the impacts of development. In Ireland, EIA must assess the habitats and species impacted by the development, with a particular attention to habitats and species protected under the EU habitats and bird directives, the potential GHG emission from the project and its vulnerability to climate change (EPA, 2017[72]). EIA in Ireland also extends to agricultural activity, where certain types of potentially negative land-use change[12] must be assessed.

Contrastingly EIA in Indonesia, often do not function effectively to control the impacts of development. Capacity constraints at the local and provincial level to effectively review EIA and lack of independence (assessors are often appointed by the developer) means EIAs are often manipulated by project developers, consequently EIAs in Indonesia are considered a procedural formality (Nugraha, 2015[73]). As a result many project are approved with inadequate EIAs or no EIAs at all. Efforts, however are being made to strengthen the EIA process, for example, in 2016 criminal sanctions were introduced for officials who approve projects without a EIAs and organisations who are operating without the correct permits (OECD, 2019[12]). Continuing efforts to strengthen the EIA process and bring it in line with international best practice (Box 5.1) are encouraged.

SEA

SEAs are used to assess the impacts of larger scale plans and programmes and can be an important tool for ensuring the consistency of development plans with nexus objectives. In Ireland and France, EU law requires that SEAs are conducted for major strategic programmes and development plans taking place in 11 sectors.[13] Under Indonesian Law,[14] all major development plans are required to produce SEAs as part of the planning process. This includes medium and long-term national and regional development plans. However, capacity constraints at both a national and regional level have hampered its implementation and reduced their ability to influence development policy in Indonesia (Van Der Sluys, 2018[74]). More consistent use of SEAs and improving capacity for their creation would improve the consistency of national strategies and plans (discussed in chapter 3) with nexus goals.

Box 5.1. Principles for Effective Assessments

To effectively fulfil their function, assessments such as EIA and SEA must adhere to certain standards that ensure process integrity, efficiency and overall quality. The European Commission (European Commission, 2016[75]) defines eight guiding principles that should govern EIA, many of which should similarly apply to SEA:

1. Participation – appropriate/timely access for interested parties
2. Transparency – open and accessible assessment decisions
3. Certainty – process/timing agreed in advance
4. Accountability – decision makers responsible for their actions and decisions
5. Credibility – undertaken with professionalism/objectivity
6. Cost effectiveness – environmental protection at the least cost to society
7. Flexibility – adaptable to deal efficiently with any proposal and decision situation
8. Practicality – information/outputs readily usable in decision making and planning

Economic instruments

Economic instruments relevant to the land use nexus are widely used across the six case study countries, though these are most commonly in the form of subsidies. Economic instruments set the incentive framework for land-use and aim to influence the decisions of individual actors by increasing or decreasing the costs of particular actions. There are a wide range of different economic instruments in place across the case study countries (covered in more detail below), which create a complicated interacting set of incentives for land-use actors.

While the individual impacts of each policy instrument are often difficult to discern, on average the incentives in place have led to ongoing environmental degradation (chapter 2). Despite this there are examples where economic instruments have had positive impacts (see Brazil's ABC policy or the Burren programme and payments for ecosystem services in Indonesia, Mexico and Brazil), showing the potential role economic instruments can play in making land-use systems more sustainable. However, in general the environmental externalities associated with land-use remain largely unpriced and ecosystem services under- or un-valued. Meanwhile the majority of support for land use goes towards agriculture, with over USD 50 billion in subsidy payments in 2016 alone.[15] While much of this support is contingent on environmental constraints, a large proportion is not, and often where there are environmental constraints they are not sufficiently rigorous to ensure the sustainability of land use.

The value of native forest for biodiversity is well known and the importance of forestry for climate mitigation is recognised by all the case study countries. Some case study countries (Ireland, New Zealand and France) have set ambitious targets for emissions removal and forestry expansion. But in many cases the economic support for forestry still falls short of incentives available for agriculture, calling into question the ability of these countries to achieve their forestry targets. There is a clear need to consider the incentive structures created by economic instruments for different land-uses (agriculture, forestry, urban development) holistically to better understand how they influence the land-use system at national and local levels.

Environmentally-relevant taxes

Environmentally-relevant taxes can be used to provide a price signal to reduce activities with damaging environmental impacts such as pollution, GHG emissions and water abstraction. Taxes also have the potential to mobilise revenue, which can fund other interventions in the nexus. In general, environmentally-relevant taxes raise the price of an environmentally harmful activity or good, thereby reducing demand and associated environmental impacts. Taxes can reduce the impact of an activity cost effectively, by allowing the polluters to adjust their input variables in a way that suits them. Taxes can also be dynamically efficient by creating a continuing incentive to find new and innovative ways to reduce impacts. However, the cost-effectiveness, and ultimately the environmental effectiveness, of environmentally-relevant taxes vis-à-vis other policy instruments depends on a variety of factors, including the elasticity of demand for environmentally harmful inputs and the level of sensitivity of environmental outcomes to specific activities (Hardelin and Lankoski, 2018[76]).

Pesticide and Fertiliser Taxes

While mineral fertilisers and pesticides are important for the production of food, excess inputs lead to diffuse pollution, which affects water quality, air quality, GHG emissions and ecosystem degradation (Sutton et al., 2011[77]). Controlling their use to ensure optimum inputs taking into account these environmental externalities is essential for achieving consistency across the nexus areas. Despite the considerable environmental impacts of agrichemicals in the case-study countries, only France and Mexico tax the externalities associated with pesticide use (but not chemical fertiliser use) (Table 5.2). France and Mexico use a risk-based approach to pesticide taxation, where the tax rate on individual pesticides is based on the toxicity of the active ingredient.

Risk-based approaches to pesticide taxation allow for a reduction in environmental impacts without harming aggregate agricultural incomes or food production, by shifting pesticide consumers away from more toxic chemicals that require less frequent application (Finger et al., 2017[78]). If the rates are not sufficiently differentiated, however, such taxes could end up incentivising a shift to more environmentally harmful chemicals which can be used at lower volumes, as would be expected in volume-based approaches (Böcker and Finger, 2016[79]). However, risk-based approaches can be costly to administer and complicated to implement, which has so far limited their uptake.

Despite the tax being in place, France has missed its ambitious goals for reducing pesticide usage, with the number of unit doses (a measure of application) increasing by 29% between 2008 and 2014 (although what would have happened in the absence of the tax has not been estimated) (OECD, 2016[37]). The generally low demand elasticity of pesticides necessitates a relatively high tax rate to influence producer behaviour (Böcker and Finger, 2017[80]). Thus, the low tax rates in both Mexico and France (in France the relative rate is around 5% of the value) will probably not incentivise more sustainable pesticide usage and provide nexus benefits (OECD, 2017[81]; Böcker and Finger, 2016[79]).

Table 5.2. Taxes on fertiliser and pesticides sales in the case study countries

	Fertilisers	Pesticides
Brazil	Subsidised	Subsidised
France	VAT	Externalities taxed
Indonesia	Subsidised	VAT
Ireland	Subsidised	VAT
Mexico	Subsidised	Externalities taxed[1]

Note: 'Subsidised' means some form of tax exemptions are available, 'VAT' means the sale is subject to VAT or GST of some form and 'externalities taxed' means some form of progressive tax, based on environmental impact, is applied.
[1]In Mexico, pesticides are generally exempt from VAT/GST but progressively taxed based on toxicity.
Source: Authors

Pesticide taxes have been successful in raising revenue. In France, the pesticide tax was expected to generate around EUR 150 million by 2016, and in Mexico USD 109 million (MXN 2133.32 million) between February 2014 and September 2017 (OECD, 2017[82]). The revenue raised in France is split, with EUR 71 million funds allocated to the Ecophyto plan II (a pesticide reduction certificate scheme) and the remainder to Water Agencies (OECD, 2017[81]). Both these schemes provide environmental benefits, showing environmentally-relevant taxes can still have positive impacts even when they have limited impacts on behaviour.

The taxing of excessive fertiliser inputs could reduce the impacts of diffuse pollution, benefitting ecosystems and climate without substantial impacts on aggregate food production. Quantifying what constitutes an excessive input of fertiliser is challenging, as a number of factors such as crop, soil type, hydrology and farming practices have to be accounted for. Consequently, models of nutrient losses from agricultural land need to be developed, allowing the implementation of targeted nutrient restrictions, such as the Waikato Regional council's nitrogen reference points.[16] Because of these technical challenges and political economy issues, fertiliser taxation is not widely used globally and none of the case study countries currently tax excess mineral fertiliser inputs. However, the recent report for the Tax Working Group in New Zealand has recommended the implementation of some form of tax on fertilisers to address the impacts of agriculture on the environment (The Tax Working Group, 2019[59]). Beyond, price-based instruments such as taxes, quantitative restrictions of nitrogen and phosphorus losses from agriculture, which face similar technical challenges, are seen as an important strategy. For example, quantitative restrictions in watersheds are seen as key strategy for improving water quality for New Zealand (Muller and Neal, 2018[83]).

Conversely, several of the case study countries have reduced or zero rate VAT on fertilisers (e.g., Ireland, Indonesia and Brazil) thereby implicitly subsidising their use. Taxes are far from the only instruments available to reduce the impacts of excess fertilisers and pesticides, and all the case study countries use regulatory approaches to help address these issues already. Ireland for example has a sophisticated nitrogen derogation programme that mandates how, when and where fertilisers should be applied. However, the ongoing degradation of ecosystems in all the case study countries suggests the regulation may not be enough to address the environmental impacts of agriculture. Implementing taxes on excess fertilisers and pesticides (or at least removing implicit subsidies afforded by VAT reductions or exemptions) represents an opportunity to provide an economic incentive to enhance the impact of existing regulations and better manage nexus goals.

Carbon Taxes

Most carbon emissions from the land-use sector are not priced and while information is limited, an estimated 70% of non-road emissions are not priced or taxed at all (OECD, 2016[84]). The pricing of carbon usually occurs through the provisions of taxes and tradable emissions permits (discussed below). The effectiveness of a carbon tax is dependant of the rate of the tax (e.g. the price it assigns to carbon), which must be high enough to create incentives for taking mitigation actions. While carbon taxes on fuel can effectively price some emission from land use, there are often tax exemptions for agriculture uses (see section on Government support to land use). Carbon taxes on emissions from agricultural land use are an untested instrument for balancing nexus goals, although recent theoretical studies have suggested pricing carbon from land use would have important food security impacts (Frank et al., 2017[85]). Using carbon taxes as a tool to balance nexus goals, therefore, warrants further research.

Emissions trading schemes

Emissions trading schemes (ETS) set a cap on allowable levels of emissions. Different ETS can have different levels of coverage (e.g. geographically or in terms of gases, sectors), and different levels of stringency. Three of the case study countries have national or supra-national emissions trading schemes in place. These are the EU ETS (used in Ireland and France) and the domestic ETS in New Zealand. Currently, emissions from agriculture and forestry are not included in the EU-ETS and emissions from agriculture are excluded from the New Zealand system (although agricultural emissions have to be reported under the system). Agricultural emissions have so far been excluded from the EU ETS (except NO_2 emissions from the production of chemical fertilisers) due to concerns surrounding the accuracy of monitoring, reporting and verification, which could lead to distributional impacts through the over- or under-allocation of permits (European Commission, 2008[86]). More recent technological advances, however, have led to suggestions that its exclusion could be revisited (Grosjean et al., 2018[87]). The New Zealand Emissions Trading Scheme (NZ ETS) is the primary policy instrument underpinning New Zealand's climate change mitigation efforts and, in principle the only ETS in the world to include all sectors of the economy (OECD, 2017[88]). However, due to political constraints and concerns about economic impacts, the entry of the agricultural sector, which is the largest contributor to national emissions, has been delayed several times. Further, NZ ETS carbon prices are well below estimates of the social cost of carbon, and too low to achieve its intended influence (OECD, 2016[84]; OECD, 2017[88]).

Currently, emissions trading schemes and other carbon markets are unlikely to have a major influence on land-use decisions because they exclude the impacts of a primary driver of land-use change, ecosystem degradation and non-energy related emissions: agriculture (Grosjean et al., 2018[87]; OECD, 2016[84]). New Zealand has the only scheme in the world designed to include this sector, but so far its implementation has been slow. It remains to be seen if emissions trading can help balance climate and food goals by encouraging innovation and efficiency increases in the agricultural sector, and land use change between sectors (e.g. from agriculture to forestry). The further integration of agriculture in to the NZ ETS is recommended, as it would serve as a proof of concept. Despite having limited impacts on emissions, the NZ ETS has provided an incentive for afforestation. If the forest planted is native forest, it could also provide biodiversity benefits, representing a significant nexus alignment (Leining and Kerr, 2016[89]).

Besides the case-study countries' (supra) national-level ETS presented in this section, globally multiple ETS exist at sub-national scale, too. Sub-national ETS can be of relevance to land-use outcomes by including carbon credits from reduced tropical deforestation in third countries or regions (such as those issued under the System of Incentives for Environmental Services (SISA) programme in the Brazilian state of Acre, (Duchelle et al., 2014[90])). A case study country-relevant example for the potential of sub-national ETS to contribute to reducing deforestation is California's Cap-and-Trade programme. CARB, the scheme's governing body, has endorsed a tropical forest standard. This standard will facilitate the future allowance of tropical forest offsets into the ETS (CARB, 2018[91]), as envisioned by a Memorandum of Understanding between the States of California (United States), Chiapas (Mexico) and Acre (Brazil) signed in 2010 (State Governments of Acre, Chiapas, 2010[92]).

ETS have the potential to play a role in balancing nexus goals at both national and sub-national levels. Importantly though, without careful guidelines on what activities qualify for emissions credits, ETS could lead to carbon sequestering actives with negative biodiversity consequences, or even negative climate impacts, if activities such as forestry on peat areas are incentivised.

Biodiversity offsets

Biodiversity offsets are "measurable conservation outcomes resulting from actions designed to compensate for significant residual adverse biodiversity impacts arising from project development after appropriate prevention and mitigation measures have been taken" (BBOP, 2009[93]). Biodiversity offsets tend to work via the mitigation hierarchy (avoid, mitigate, offset).[17] The fundamental principle that underpins biodiversity offsets is that the impact of development activities can be offset if a sufficient quantity of high quality similar habitat can be created or restored. Thus, well-designed biodiversity offset policies can, in theory, allow for development while achieving a baseline goal of no-net loss of biodiversity, or the more ambitious net-gain objective, through the provision of compensatory measures (OECD, 2016[94]).

Biodiversity offsets can allow development while delivering ecosystem, and in some cases, climate co-benefits (e.g. if the offsets results in the creation of new forest), and are a useful instrument for balancing nexus goals. With the exception of Ireland, all the case study countries have introduced some form of biodiversity offset programme, though these vary substantially in terms of geographic scope, sectoral coverage and design features (e.g. mandatory[18] or voluntary). While the general characteristics of these schemes are summarised in Table 5.3, not enough information is available to comprehensively compare their effectiveness.

Table 5.3. Biodiversity offset schemes in the case study countries

	Mandatory vs voluntary	Sector coverage	Year introduced	Finance transferred	Challenges
Brazil	Mandatory	Agriculture, mining, industry	2000	Yes	Weak monitoring and reporting
France	Mandatory	In theory, all sectors	2007	No	Unclear guidance and institutions before 2016 biodiversity law reforms
Indonesia	Mandatory	In theory, all sectors	2004	No	Unclear law, definitions too broad, lack of monitoring, no implementation
Mexico CUSTF[2]	Mandatory	Damage to forests from various activities (e.g. agriculture, mining, oil and gas, tourism)	2003	Yes	[see the (OECD, 2016[95]) for examples]
New Zealand	Voluntary	Any action[1]	1987	No	Not mandatory so uptake limited

Note: :[1] More commonly referred to as environmental compensation in New Zealand, this is defined as: "Any action (work, services or restrictive covenants) to avoid, remedy or mitigate adverse effects of activities on a relevant area, landscape or environment as compensation for the unavoided and unmitigated adverse effects of the activity for which consent is being sought."
[2] Programa de Compensación por Cambio de Uso de Suelo en Terrenos Forestales.
Source: Authors

A lack of clear and consistent guidelines for biodiversity offsets at a national level can reduce the uptake of offset mechanisms and undermine their ability to prevent environmental degradation. In New Zealand for example, Brower et al. (2017[96]) found only 15% of Department of Conservation concessions for commercial activity on conservation land contained compensatory provisions and that of those only 68% reached full compliance. A lack of clarity, technical capacity and enforcement has also undermined the offset schemes of Brazil (Souza and Sánchez, 2018[97]) and a now-replaced, one-off offset scheme in Mexico (OECD, 2016[95]). In France, despite the principle of avoid, reduce, offset being established in law as far back as 1976, the lack of clear guidelines undermined the implementation of effective offsets at a local level until a series of reforms in 2007 (OECD, 2016[37]). The offset process in France was further strengthen in 2013 by guidelines on applying the mitigation hierarchy. In 2016, the French biodiversity law granted the local authority powers to prevent projects where compensatory measures were not sufficient to meet the targets of no-net loss of biodiversity and formally integrated the mitigation hierarchy into the environmental code. Finally, the 2016 law also made the Ministry of Ecological and Solidarity Transition responsible for the creating a database to track biodiversity offset measures, strengthening the process.

Careful design and oversight of biodiversity offsets are essential to ensure consistency between nexus goals. Payment-in-lieu schemes, for example, allow for economies of scale, and spending can be targeted to specific at-risk ecosystems. They also allow countries to adopt a more flexible approach to compensatory mechanisms, ensuring actions can be tailored to specific socio-ecological contexts, without having to create lengthy guidelines. The Mexican CUSTF (*Programa de Compensación por Cambio de Uso de Suelo en Terrenos Forestales*), for example, aims to compensate for all development in forested areas by requiring developers to pay into the Mexican forest fund. This money is then used to carry out rehabilitation activity in forested areas. The CUSTF covers many sectors with the most common ones being mining, energy transmission, tourism, and agriculture (OECD, 2016[95]). Similarly Brazil operates a payment-in-lieu scheme that requires developers pay into a fund which manages the National System of Units of Conservation (SNUC) (OECD, 2016[94]).

However, unless actions are carried out in a spatially and ecologically balanced way (e.g. according to the Natura 2000 network), biodiversity offset approaches could facilitate the destruction of ecosystems in areas at high-risk of development which host globally important biodiversity. Further, offsets can lead to temporal imbalances if the offset actions occur some time after the habitat conversion. The Mexican CUSTF programme, for example, has experienced difficulty in allocating the resources collected to appropriate offset projects, resulting in delays between land-use change and the creation of offsets (OECD, 2016[95]). Designing offset programmes to account for spatial and temporal imbalances is, therefore, important.

Finally, by taking a more national systematic approach to offset supply countries can avoid the issues associated with project by project approaches seen in New Zealand and France (pre 2008) (Quétier, Regnery and Levrel, 2014[98]; Brower et al., 2017[96]). Biodiversity offset schemes that apply to ecosystems such as forests, or to sectoral activities such as mining, oil and gas, agriculture, are able to target pressures that are relevant to both biodiversity and climate mitigation. But better monitoring, reporting and verification efforts are required to ensure that offsets are delivering these benefits, particularly at the agricultural frontier.

Payments for ecosystem services, including REDD+

Payment for ecosystem services

Payment for ecosystem services (PES) schemes are voluntary programmes that aim to address the market failures which lead to the degradation of ecosystems, and the services they provide, by incentivising management activities to enhance the delivery of these services. PES can be used to deliver ecosystem services at both a local, national and international scale, such as habitat provisioning for biodiversity, clean water, and carbon sequestration.

All of the case study countries, bar Mexico, lack a consistent national-level legal framework to facilitate PES. As a result, the application of PES has been heterogeneous with a wide variety of approaches, a low availability of information and inconsistent monitoring and evaluation (OECD, 2015[13]).[19] In Mexico, the national PES scheme (one of the first globally) was introduced in 2003. It has two main components, both of which target forest ecosystems, PES for the conservation of biodiversity and the payments for hydrological environmental services (PSAH). The schemes had a total of 2.4 million ha enrolled in 2016 distributing around MXN 924 million (USD 48 million) to 3111 participants. PES in Mexico has achieved some success and was estimated to avoided 18 000 ha of deforestation between 2003 and 2007 (OECD, 2013[99]) and reduced forest fragmentation (Ramirez-Reyes et al., 2018[100]).

In contrast to Mexico, Brazil does not have a national framework for PES, instead allowing regional/state level governments to formulate their own guidelines and laws (OECD, 2015[13]). This piecemeal approach has led to a number of different PES approaches, but in the majority of cases they are funded by the state and there were over 70 local level schemes operational in 2012 (Guedes and Seehusen, 2012[101]). Brazil does operate two national level schemes, the *Bolsa Verde*[20] and the *Bolsa Florestral* predominantly aimed at alleviating poverty and supporting traditional, less intensive, farming and livelihood options in communities living in federal or local protected areas. Early evidence suggests the programmes has both reduced deforestation and compensated for the potential livelihood impacts of forgoing more profitable and destructive practices (Börner et al., 2013[102]; Alves-Pinto et al., 2018[103]). An estimated 9 PES programmes (including REDD+ projects) are operational in Indonesia, though they cover a relatively small area of land (Suich et al., 2017[104]) (Table 5.4).

While there are PES projects at local and federal level in Brazil, and local level in Indonesia, national level legislation facilitating the implementation and adoption of PES would benefit the land-use nexus (OECD, 2015[13]; OECD, 2016[37]). However, legislation must take into account the experiences of existing PES schemes and maintain the flexibility that has allowed PES to be successful so far. A key component of successful PES has been the effective and efficient monitoring programmes deployed in Brazil and Mexico to ensure compliance (OECD, 2013[99]). In the case of countries with no currently operational PES, these types of projects represent a potential missed opportunity as they can provide an additional tool for balancing nexus goals and provide societal co-benefits by paying land managers to adopt more environmentally- and climate-friendly approaches.

Reduced Emissions from Deforestation and Degradation and the role of conservation, sustainable management of forests and enhancement of forest carbon stocks in developing countries (REDD+)

Indonesia in particular identifies REDD+ as a key tool for meeting its ambitious AFOLU targets (The Republic of Indonesia, 2017[105]). Since 2007 there has been significant progress towards the implementation of REDD+ in Indonesia including the development of institutions, legal frameworks and governance reforms (The Republic of Indonesia, 2017[105]). There has also been significant investment and a USD 1 billion commitment by Norway in 2010, and 37 REDD+ demonstration/pilot activities in 15 provinces by 2016 (The Republic of Indonesia, 2017[105]). A lack of monitoring and enforcement capacity in Indonesia has so far hampered the implementation of REDD+, reducing Indonesia's ability to meet GHG emission reduction targets (Enrici and Hubacek, 2018[106]).

There is considerable international interest in REDD+, and in 2010 Norway pledged USD 1 billion to support REDD+ activities in Indonesia. The majority of the USD 1 billion was earmarked for performance based payments. But slow progress mean only around USD 124 million in non-performance based payments had been dispersed by 2018. However, the first payments based on deforestation avoided were made in 2019 (9 years after the fund's creation) indicating recent progress. REDD+ still represents a key opportunity to manage nexus goals, and continued effort is needed to build on recent success in Indonesia.

In Brazil, the uptake of REDD+ occurred somewhat later than in Indonesia, with the national REDD strategy (ENREDD+) being published in 2015 (May et al., 2016[107]). In contrast to Indonesia, the better monitoring systems in Brazil (e.g PRODES and DETER) allow real-time deforestation monitoring. Implementation of REDD+ has been more successful in Brazil, with over USD 422 million dispersed to 100 projects through the Brazilian Development Bank's Amazon fund by the end of 2017 (BNDES, 2018[108]). The Brazilian approach to REDD+ uses a range of interventions, incentives and disincentives (including PES). However, while evidence indicates REDD+ has been effective at reducing deforestation up to 2014 (although recent trends may be different) (Simonet et al., 2018[109]), its impacts on forest degradation are less clear, with evaluation hampered by technical issues. REDD+ could be a cost effective tool for balancing climate mitigation goals by providing ecosystem co-benefits, however, more evidence for its effectiveness, particularly in relation to forest degradation, is required.

Table 5.4. PES schemes operating in Indonesia in 2017

Scheme	Province	Start Year	Seller	Buyer	Payment	Intermediary	Activity
Water							
Cidanau	Banten	2001	c. 30 farmer groups	State-owned enterprise	IDR 1.2 million per ha	Stakeholder group	Tree planting, agroforestry
Mount Rinjani Payments for Watershed Services	Lombok/Nusa Tenggara Barat	2009	25 groups in 12 villages	Water association members/users	IDR 30-80 million per group	NGO	Rehabilitation, reforestation
Aceh Payments for Watershed Services	Aceh	2009	10 farmer groups	Companies	IDR 70–90 million per contract	NGO & stakeholder group	Tree planting, prevent tree cutting & pollution
Sumberjaya	Lampung	2007	3 villages	Company	IDR 1.5-1.6 million per ha	NGO	Tree planting, river bank conservation, construction of terraces & sediment pits
Carbon							
Ketapand	West Kalimantan	2013[1]	Villages	Donors (including private foundations	IDR 100,000,000 per village per annum	NGO	Avoiding planned deforestation
Meragin	Jambo	2013[1]	Villages	Donors (including private foundations	IDR 100,000,000 per village per annum	NGO	Avoiding planned deforestation
Rimba Raya	Central Kalimantan	2008 (but not sales)[1]	Private sector (ecosystem restoration concession licence)	Private sector	Not applicable (90 million t, 30 years; 2.2 million verified carbon units)	Avoiding planned deforestation	-
Berau Forest Carbon Programme	East Kalimantan	2007	Villages	Donor (international)	USD 25,000 per village per annum	NGO	Reduced deforestation, forest rehabilitation

Note: [1] These schemes are paying for inputs (i.e. compensating participants for their activities) rather than paying for outputs
Source: (Suich et al., 2017[104]), *Payments for ecosystem services in Indonesia*, http://dx.doi.org/10.1017/s0030605316000259

Government support to land use

Agriculture is the single largest component of land use across all the case study countries and hence government support relevant to agriculture is likely to have significant impacts on land use. This support is highly variable and may include, among other things, market price support for agricultural commodities, payments based on agricultural outputs (whether current or historical), direct support for inputs such as fertiliser, fuel and water, preferential credit for the acquisition of equipment or land, support for improved agro-environmental practices, and support for technology research and development. Subsidies relating to forestry are also of key importance to the nexus, especially in light of the role forests are expected to play in climate mitigation through carbon sequestration. There are also a range of subsidies supporting the development of infrastructure and reducing the cost of transport that can play a role in altering patterns of land use and hence are relevant to the nexus.

Agricultural support

Figure 5.2. Producer support estimate as a percentage of gross farm receipts (GFR) 1996-2016

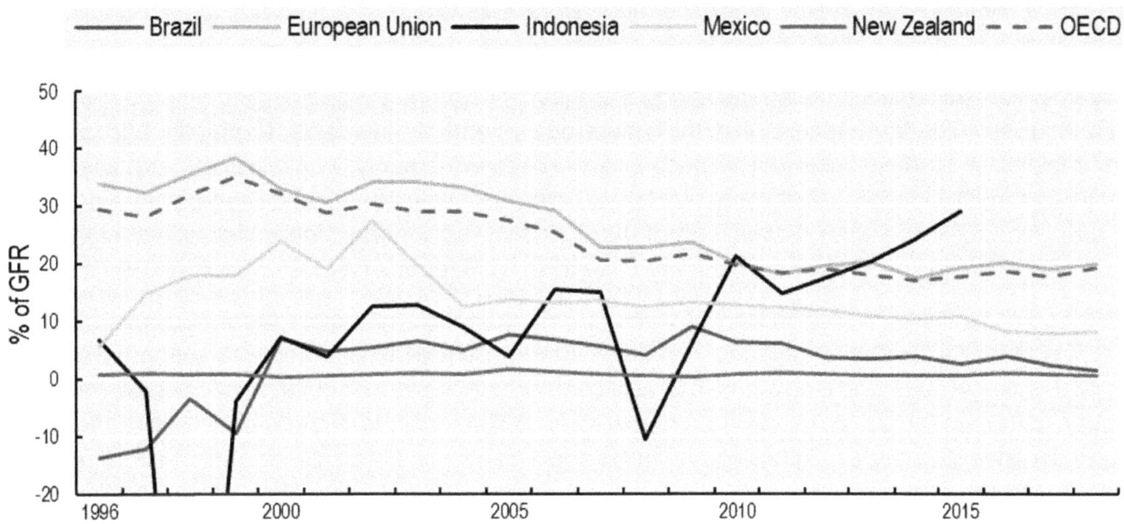

Note: Data for Indonesia only available until 2015
Source: OECD (2019[110]), Producer and consumer support estimates database, http://dx.doi.org/10.1787/6ea85c58-en

National (and international) subsidy regimes can represent significant alignments or misalignments in the nexus sector. Support, in particular for agriculture, can have large impacts on nexus areas, both positive and negative. Government support to agriculture varies substantially across the six countries (Figure 5.2). Indonesia, for example, has the highest rate of agriculture support among the case study countries, estimated to be 29.1% of gross farm receipts (GFR) in 2015 (OECD, 2019[110]).

The subsidy environment in the land-use nexus is complicated with many misalignments, synergies and opportunities to improve. Agricultural support in the case study countries can take different shapes, be that through decoupled payments[21] in the EU and Mexico or more direct producer support in Brazil and Indonesia. Agricultural support can have negative environmental impacts if it lowers the cost of finance available to farmers without constraints, if it supports unsustainable practices by lowering the costs of inputs without constraints, if it supports output directly, or if it creates a gap between domestic price of commodities and the international markets (Market Price Support – MPS) (OECD, 2016[111])(Table 5.5). Such support can help maintain unsustainable agricultural practices, maintain agriculture in marginal areas or facilitate the expansion of agriculture, leading to land-use change – such as deforestation and wetland conversion – which can reduce ecosystem services provision.

While the total amount of support relative to gross farm receipts varies considerably, MPS accounts for a large part of the total producer support in all the case study countries (Table 5.5). On the basis of their analytical frameworks, the selected environmental indicators, and the data used, Henderson and Lankoski (2019[112]) find that market price support can be among the most environmentally harmful types of producer support measures. Several countries also subsidise inputs which may lead to unsustainable practices, such as the electricity subsidy for pumping water in Mexico and a zero rate of VAT on fertilisers in Ireland and Indonesia. Further, concessional loans and insurance for agriculture, particularly working capital for commercial farmers in Brazil and the development of timber plantations in Indonesia (Mcfarland, Whitley and Kissinger, 2015[113]; OECD, 2018[114]), may encourage land use change. However, appropriate regulatory frameworks managing nexus impacts and environmental constraints on allowable activities should, in theory, limit adverse effects in some cases. Examples include, the Nitrates Directive in the EU (i.e. relevant to the France and Ireland case studies), which includes restrictions on the application of fertiliser in certain environmentally sensitive areas or the whole territory, and in Brazil environmental and climatic zoning is used to restrict access to subsidies in certain environmentally important regions (OECD, 2018[114]). Understanding where and how to reform potentially environmentally-harmful subsidies, is important for minimising the nexus impacts of agricultural support.

Reforming the most distortive and potentially environmentally harmful support is key to addressing misalignments in the nexus, but understanding the impacts of support is challenging and requires context-specific analysis. The first stage in reforming subsidy systems is, therefore, to identify and assess the nexus impacts of existing subsidies. France has undertaken a study to assess the impacts of public incentives on biodiversity (Sainteny et al., 2011[115]), and Indonesia has recently completed a peer review of its remaining fossil fuel subsidies as part of the G20 process. Greater application of national and peer reviews of subsidy regimes would help ensure incentives with negative nexus impacts are reformed.

Other forms of agricultural support can have complicated impacts on nexus areas. For example, Brazil allocates substantial funding for research and development, 30% of general services support to agriculture was spent on knowledge and innovation in Brazil, compared to 0.5% in Indonesia (Mcfarland, Whitley and Kissinger, 2015[113]; OECD, 2018[114]). This has allowed Brazil to increase the productivity of the soy crop in recent decades (Figueiredo, 2016[116]), and led to some decoupling of production growth from agricultural expansion. These improvements can allow the expansion of food production (and other agricultural products) without the need to convert areas of forest to cropland, and hence help to ensure consistency across nexus areas. However, they can also create incentives to increase cultivated area if expansion is not mediated through other instruments, such as the soy moratorium (discussed in section on regulatory instruments) and other forest conservation measures (Koch et al., 2019[117]). A lack of funding for this area, has, among other things, led to a significant yield gap in the Indonesian oil palm sector, where the average yield is (3.6t/ha) well below the theoretical maximum potential (7t/ha) (Coordinating Ministry of Economic Affairs, 2011[118]). There are also sub-optimal yields from cattle farming in some areas of Brazil, where efforts to conserve forest might lead to intensification, suggesting considerable scope to better balance nexus goals (Koch et al., 2019[117]).

There is also opportunity to improve the environmental conditionality of both coupled and decoupled support payments in Ireland and France. Payments through the European Union Common Agricultural Policy (CAP) in Ireland and France are worth approximately EUR 1.2 billion and EUR 7.1 billion in 2016 respectively, of which 99.9% in Ireland and 85% in France was de-coupled (European Commission, 2017[119]). According to OECD estimates (2019[120]) around 50% of agricultural support in the European Union is conditional on environmental constraints, which represents a considerable resource for potentially improving the environmental performance of farming within these countries. Whilst environmental cross-compliance measures are mandatory, recent reviews of the environmental and cost-effectiveness of these mechanisms suggest they lack the specificity and stringency needed to substantially reduce the environmental impacts of agriculture (OECD, 2020, forthcoming[121]).

Table 5.5. Distortive and potentially environmentally harmful support

Market price support		
Country	% of MPS in PSE (USD million 2016-18 average)	% of MPS in gross farm receipts
Brazil	48.6% (1 994)	1.3%
Indonesia[1]	91.4% (28 952)[1]	22.6%
Mexico	28.2% (1 261)	2.3%
New Zealand	83.0% (114)	0.6%
EU	19.0% (19 553)	3.8%

Other distortive and potentially environmentally harmful support				
Country	Policy	Year Active	Expenditure (2016-18 average)	Potential mechanism for impact
Brazil	Preferential interest rates on working capital loans	2008-Present	515	May support unsustainable practices on commercial farms. However, environmental and climatic zoning restrictions apply
Indonesia[1]	Subsidised fertiliser	2012-present	1 711[1]	Reduces the cost of fertiliser inputs potentially leading to excess inputs and supporting agriculture in marginal areas
Mexico	Subsidised electricity for pumping water	2001-Present	404.3	Could support unsustainable water extraction and use, leading to ecosystem impacts and increased demand for electricity
New Zealand	NA	NA	NA	NA

Note:[1] Indonesian data only available to 2015 so figures are 2013-15 average.
Source: (OECD, 2019[120]) *Agricultural Policy Monitoring and Evaluation 2019,* https://doi.org/10.1787/agr_pol-2018-en; (OECD, 2017[122]) *Agricultural Policy Monitoring and Evaluation 2017,* https://doi.org/10.1787/agr_pol-2017-en

The current CAP architecture will be replaced from 2020, and the proposed new framework aims to give more freedom to countries to design their own agri-environmental conditions (European Commission, 2018[123]). This presents an opportunity for France and Ireland to tailor direct payment mechanisms to their specific national contexts and, therefore, improve the performance of these mechanisms in managing nexus goals. Nonetheless, assessment of the environmental impacts of these measures is lacking and evidence for their environmental effectiveness remains equivocal (OECD, 2018[124]; OECD, 2020, forthcoming[121]). Greater monitoring of the environmental impacts of these measures, as proposed in Ireland under the Food Wise 2025 plan (DAFM, 2015[125]), and increased flexibility in the type of environmental constrains allowed, would help ensure decoupled payments work effectively to ensure consistency between nexus areas.

Environmentally related agricultural support

Substantial support for agriculture specifically targets environmental objectives. In theory, this kind of support ensures consistency between nexus areas by incentivising farmers to adopt certain practices that produce some kind of environmental outcome (e.g. reducing environmental pressures from agriculture, or producing ecosystem services). Frequently, this support is targeted at improving outcomes for biodiversity, reducing GHG emissions or both. In Europe, the 2016-20 CAP provides significant funding for these programmes, under Pillar II, which are called agri-environment schemes (AES). AES are voluntary programmes, which pay land managers for adopting certain environmentally friendly practices or retiring land from production.

In Ireland, AES are well funded, with approximately EUR 3.2 billion (out of a total of EUR 4.01 billion) allocated from the rural development fund to AES between 2014 and 2020 (DAFM, 2018[126]). The two largest components of this spending are the Green and Low carbon Agri-environment Scheme (GLAS)[22]

(EUR 1.1 billion) and the Areas facing Natural Constraints (ANC) scheme (EUR 1.3 billion). GLAS is a highly targeted scheme aimed at improving the sustainability in a number of priority environmental assets: vulnerable landscapes, species and watercourses. However, neither the GLAS nor ANC schemes are performance or results based[23] and while monitoring is ongoing and a systematic evaluation of GLAS in underway. The impacts of GLAS on nutrient pollution in water, emissions per ha and biodiversity (both the provision of habitat features and species) are unknown (as of 2018), but initial results show uptake of the scheme has been low with high intensity livestock farmers (DAFM, 2017[127]). Analysis of a previous scheme, the Rural Environment Protection Scheme, showed limited positive impacts on biodiversity, suggesting that these kind of broad scale programmes potentially lack the flexibility and specificity required to deliver on multiple goals (Feehan, Gillmor and Culleton, 2005[128]; McMahon et al., 2010[129]).

Performance-based and spatially focused approaches (on risk areas) have the potential to apply more appropriate solutions and have a better track record of delivering environmental gains than untargeted or practice-based approaches (DAFM and DAHG, 2014[130]; OECD, 2018[124]). A results based scheme has several advantages over other approaches; firstly, it incentivises land managers to deliver environmental benefits (OECD, 2020, forthcoming[121]). Secondly, it allows a greater flexibility in interventions by allowing a land manager to utilise their knowledge of the land to develop context specific interventions. Finally, since the payment is contingent on environmental impact, regular assessment must be a key component of the programme.

A good example of such an approach is the Burren Programme in Ireland, which is one of a number of locally led AES approaches that target specific environmental issues (other programmes target hen harrier declines or freshwater pearl mussels). Just under 50% of payments from the Burren Programme are based on environmental impact and the rest supports capital-investment projects such as improving farm buildings (DAFM and DAHG, 2014[130]). The schemes focuses of species rich limestone grasslands, and monitoring has indicated a continuing improvement in the environmental quality of enrolled fields (DAFM and DAHG, 2014[130]). While result-based approaches are potentially more cost-effective, they can be associated with higher transaction and monitoring costs, which could limit their broad appeal (DAFM, 2017[127]); however increased experience with such schemes, along with technological and institutional innovation, is expected to lower such costs over time (OECD, 2020, forthcoming[121]).

Generally, AES have the potential to improve the environmental quality of farmland, while safeguarding food production in some cases. However, when applied broadly (e.g. GLAS, BPS….) they often lack the contextual specificity to deliver on multiple fronts. Shifting to results based payments could also allow for the stacking of environmental co-benefits (e.g. water, carbon and biodiversity benefits) from land management. Stacking approaches could allow land-managers to receive payments for different ecosystems services provided by management action in the same area, thereby increasing the economic incentive for sustainable land-management (for a full discussion of stacking see (Lankoski et al., 2015[131])). If AES are to deliver multiple nexus goals, more consistent evaluation and monitoring of environmental impacts is required, as current efforts do not allow effective analysis of success, which can be used to inform future iterations of AES. Finally, AES design needs to specify clear, measurable objectives, so that policy performance is able to be evaluated (OECD, 2020, forthcoming[121]).

A different approach to environmentally conditional support is to increase the availability of credit for implementing actions to improve one or more aspects of land management. Brazil operates one such scheme, the low-carbon agriculture (ABC) programme, launched in 2010 as part of the national climate change policy (discussed in chapter 3). ABC operates as a concessional credit line facilitating investment in management practices which are good for the environment and reduce GHG emissions. These management actions include no-till agriculture, the restoration of degraded lands and facilities to treat animal waste (OECD, 2015[13]). By 2015 ABC had facilitated 25 189 loans with a value EUR 4 billion (Mello, 2015[132]), however since then uptake has slowed and 45% fewer loans were issues in 2016 than 2015 (Newton et al., 2016[133]). Between 2010 and 2018 the ABC programme is estimated to have avoided approximately 100-154 $MtCO_2e$ (Ministério da Agricultura, Pecuária e abastecimento, 2018[134]), representing a significant nexus alignment, and highlighting the ability of concessional credit schemes to help ensure consistency between nexus areas.

Forestry support

Ireland, France, New Zealand and Indonesia all identify forestry and land use as a key component of meeting their NDC commitments. Ireland, France and New Zealand hope to use an expanded forestry sector to sequester carbon and enhance removals by the land sector (DCCAE, 2017[135]; MPI, 2018[136]; MAA, 2016[137]). In contrast, Indonesia, which has one of the highest levels of GHG emission from land use change globally, aims to reduce emissions from land use change through the reduction of deforestation rates, the better management of existing forested areas and the expansion of plantation timber (Republic of Indonesia, 2016[138]). Forestry programmes have the potential to provide ecosystem and climate co-benefits though the expansion of biodiversity rich native ecosystems and the sequestering of carbon.

Ireland has set an ambitious target to increase forest cover from 11% to 18% by 2050. To achieve these targets an annual increase of 8 290 ha of forest is needed by 2020 (up from 7 140 in 2017) (DAFM, 2015[139]). Areas suitable for afforestation have been identified through an Indicative Forest Statement for Ireland which is based on spatially-explicit data. The platform for afforestation applications, an online GIS system (iFORIS), is used to communicate these data to relevant stakeholders. Areas within Natura 2000 sites may not be accepted in some cases and referred to the NPWS or other relevant state bodies.

The Irish Forestry programme is expected to cost EUR 263 million between 2015-2020, of which the majority, EUR 199.5 million (i.e. 76%), is allocated to afforestation schemes, most of which will be commercial timber plantations (DAFM, 2015[139]). There are also significant provisions for biodiversity within the programme, with requirements for natural woodland buffers around water courses (20m wide), at least 30% of the planting annually must be broadleaf species and the native woodland establishment scheme targeting import areas for biodiversity. Lastly, there is also support (albeit modest) for agroforestry, which is included for the first time. The Irish forestry programme is, therefore, well aligned with the goals of the nexus and having the appropriate safeguards to avoid the potential negative biodiversity consequences of previous programmes, where plantation forestry replaced species rich grass lands in agriculturally marginal areas (ADAS, 2014[140]).

The situation in France is similar to that of Ireland, with forests and woodlands expected to play a key role in sequestering carbon (INRA; IGN, 2017[141]). National Forests and Woodlands programme 2016-2026, highlights the need to increase the utilisation of forests in France though sustainable management practices, maintain the recreational value of forest for French citizens, and enhance their value to climate change mitigation adaptation (MAA, 2016[137]). Progress towards these goals is measured against 49 different indicators with assessments planned in 2020 and 2026. Beyond this programme there is also a national strategy to expand the use of agroforestry, with the aim of improving the contribution of agricultural land to climate change mitigation.

New Zealand had a range of funding mechanisms to encourage the planting of production and permanent forests, which work alongside the emissions trading scheme to provide additional incentives in some places or to offer alternative financing options to make afforestation more attractive to farmers. These included the Afforestation Grant Scheme, the Erosion Control Funding Programme and the Permanent Forest Sink Initiative. Together these instruments have meant that 55% of new forests planted since 2008 have received government grants (MfE, 2013[142]). As of 2019, these funds have been discontinued (or are currently being wound down) and replaced by the One Billion trees programme, with USD 153 million (NZD 234 million) in grant funding over ten years (2018-2027) (Te Uru Rākau, 2018[143]).

Afforestation programmes in New Zealand are well aligned with the countries stated climate goals. For example, providing biodiversity benefits is recognised as a core goal of the One billion trees fund, with higher payment rates available for native species and additional top up funding for meeting additional ecological restoration criteria (Te Uru Rākau, 2018[143]). This was also true historically, with the permanent

Forest Sink Initiative giving land owners the opportunity to earn emissions reduction units for carbon sequestered since 2008 through permanent forests that were planted on their land on or after the 1st of January 1990. As of 2013, more than 18 000 hectares of land had been registered under the initiative, roughly three quarters of which was reforested in native species (MfE, 2013[142]).

In contrast to France and Ireland, which have very little primary forest remaining, Brazil, Indonesia and Mexico still have large (albeit decreasing) areas of intact primary forest. In Brazil and Indonesia, historically high rates of deforestation and forest degradation have led to high levels of GHG emissions from land use (Hansen et al., 2013[53]; Ministry of Environment and Forestry, 2018[144]) and consequently forestry programmes are aimed at improving the management of remaining forest areas rather than increasing total forest extent. In Mexico there are both programmes encouraging the management of forests and promoting the expansion of commercial forestry plantation

All the forestry programmes in Mexico were consolidated, in 2013, under the umbrella programme PRONAFOR, which includes the national PES programme (discussed earlier) and the national reforestation and forest restoration scheme. The programme coordinates a range of actions aimed at reforesting and restoring, including the rehabilitation of soil, the distribution of seedlings, and the maintenance of already reforested areas. Since 2007, around 2.8 million ha have been reforested in Mexico under the scheme, although how much actual forest this equates to is unclear as this figure may not account for differential survival rates (OECD, 2013[99]; OECD, 2017[82]). In general, the reforestation actions supported are for the establishment of commercial timber species, so while they are providing climate and other ecosystem benefits, the biodiversity benefits are unclear, indicating partial alignment with nexus areas.

Indonesia also has extensive government support for reforestation, through the Reforestation fund, which comes from a levy imposed by the government on harvested timber (Barr et al., 2010[145]). However, this fund has failed to achieve significant reforestation due to chronic financial mismanagement, corruption and capacity constraints at a local level (Barr et al., 2010[145]). Finally the structure of intergovernmental fiscal transfers (discussed later), results in the reforestation fund in Indonesia actually incentivising deforestation (Nurfatriani et al., 2015[146]). As a result the reforestation fund, along with other more general producer support to agriculture (discussed above) actually become a significant nexus misalignment leading to increased emissions and significant degradation of ecosystems.

The forestry programmes of Ireland, France and New Zealand and the reforestation programme of Mexico will likely provide both biodiversity and climate benefits but in the absence of further technical progress, this may come at the expense of food production. A large proportion of the potential biodiversity benefits are lost due to the promotion of commercial forestry over natural woodland restoration. Evidence suggests that the trade-off between forestry and food production are likely to become more difficult to manage as the supply of marginal land to convert to forestry dwindles, potentially limiting the effectiveness of afforestation.

Table 5.6. Annual producer support for agriculture and forestry support in selected countries

	Estimated support for forestry (% support as proportion of forestry output)	Agricultural support (%PSE as a proportion of gross farm receipts 2016-18)
Ireland	12%	19.7%[1]
France	1.5%	19.7%[1]
New Zealand	15%	0.8%

Note:[1] EU average, as disaggregated country figures not available

Source: Forestry programmes: France: (MAA, 2016[137])Programme National de la Forêt et du Bois 2016-2026, https://agriculture.gouv.fr/le-programme-national-de-la-foret-et-du-bois-2016-2026; Ireland: (DAFM, 2015[139]), Forestry Programme 2014-2020: Ireland , https://www.agriculture.gov.ie/forestservice/forestryprogrammes2014-2020/; New Zealand: (Te Uru Rākau, 2018[143]), One billion trees fund : report on policy and design recommendations, https://www.mpi.govt.nz/dmsdocument/32908-3-appendix1-report-on-policy-and-design-recommendations-oia ; Forestry statistics for Ireland and France taken from (Eurostat, 2018[147]) Agriculture Forestry and Fisheries Statistics: 2018 edition; New Zealand (NZIER, 2017[148]) Plantation Forestry Statistics: Contribution of forestry to New Zealand.

Agricultural support: France, Ireland and New Zealand: (OECD, 2019[120]) Producer and consumer support estimates (database), https://doi.org/10.1787/agr_pol-2018-en

Notably the support for forestry in France and Ireland is smaller than support to agriculture in relative terms and considerably smaller in absolute terms, but data on producer support to agriculture below EU aggregate level is not readily available (Table 5.6). An equal balance of funding between forestry and agriculture is not desirable, given the relative economic and societal importance of the different sectors. However, the current imbalance between agriculture and forestry means the incentives for forestry are likely not sufficient to encourage reforestation and afforestation on agricultural land. Conversion of agricultural land to forestry is required in countries with ambitious targets for emissions removals from land use (e.g. in Ireland). In New Zealand, the relative support to forestry (in terms of the size of the industry) is larger than agriculture, but the extent of plantation forest has been relatively stable since 2000, suggesting other economic and social factors mean forestry is a less competitive option than agriculture. For example, farmers may be unwilling to sacrifice good-quality pasture for forestry given the quasi-permanent nature of the change, associated lifestyle changes and the lack of compensation for reduced land values (Farrelly and Gallagher, 2015[149]; Gawith and Hodge, 2018[150]).

While, reassessing the balance of public incentives between forestry and agriculture at national and local levels is a good first step to ensure forestry programmes can contribute to climate and ecosystem goals, more research is needed to understand how to make forestry more competitive with agriculture as a land-use option. Finally, without careful regulation afforestation can also be negative for biodiversity and climate if plantation forests replace ecosystems of high biodiversity value, or if it is on peat areas, as the emissions from peat oxidation could exceed the sequestration from tree growth (Miettinen et al., 2017[49]; Buscardo et al., 2008[151])

Biofuels and other

Beyond agriculture and forestry, several other types of subsidy can be significantly misaligned with nexus goals. Subsidised energy inputs in the form of fuel for transport (Brazil, Indonesia), fuel for agriculture (Ireland, France, Mexico), and electricity, often in the form of reduced taxes can lead to both increased GHG emissions and supports inefficient resource use (such as water in Mexico), impacting ecosystems. The value of these subsidies and their impacts on land-use within the case study countries are difficult to estimate, but global support to fossil fuels is estimated at USD 373 billion in 2015. Despite reform efforts (particularly in Indonesia), they represent a significant impediment to harmonising outcomes in the nexus (OECD, 2018[152]).

In several cases, subsidies promoting strategies to reduce emissions through the development of biofuel capacity can have negative impacts on other aspects of the nexus. In Brazil, for example, import duty on foreign-produced biofuel incentivises domestic production from soy (which is 70% of the biofuel feedstock in 2016) (USDA, 2017[153]) which could have negative ecosystem consequences from the further expansion of agriculture. The situation is similar in Indonesia, where large subsidies for domestically-produced biofuel, primarily from palm oil, incentivise the expansion of plantations, increasing the pressure on natural ecosystems (Mcfarland, Whitley and Kissinger, 2015[113]). In Indonesia, the biofuel policy may even have negative climate impacts when the emissions of the whole lifecycle of production are accounted for, especially if it encourages the expansion of oil palm in high carbon value areas such as peatlands (Tilman et al., 2009[154]).

In Ireland, the Public Service Obligation (PSO) is levied on all users of electricity in Ireland and represent both an alignment and misalignment. The PSO has two important nexus implications, firstly it supports the development of biomass electricity generation, which is primarily sourced from plantation forestry in Ireland. Secondly the PSO subsidises the generation of electricity using peat (€103.4million in 2017/18), one of the most carbon intensive solid fuel on the planet, which has negative consequences for both emission and biodiversity (CER, 2017[155]).

In some cases the subsidies causing misalignments in the land use, nexus were implemented for reasons entirely separate from concerns in these areas. For example, the biofuel subsidies in Indonesia are intended to reduce dependence on oil imports (Mcfarland, Whitley and Kissinger, 2015[113]) and peat subsidies in Ireland have been used since the 1950s to support isolated upland communities (DAHG, 2015[50]). However, irrespective of their original motivation, if the land-use consequences are not considered, negative nexus impacts are possible. Some trade-offs are likely to be unavoidable, but countries should try to address these misalignments by assessing subsidy regimes from a climate, land use, ecosystems and food perspective and eliminating the most pressing issues.

Beyond the subsidies that directly incentivise land use change, support to biofuels in all case study countries can have significant impacts on the nexus. Subsidising biofuel production from palm oil in Indonesia and soy in Brazil is likely to lead to increased emissions, the degradation of ecosystems from agricultural expansion and displacing the production of food crops (Mcfarland, Whitley and Kissinger, 2015[113]; Tilman et al., 2009[154]). The same is also true for other countries where biofuel or biomass subsidies might lead to increased demand, which is met with imports. Trade-offs in different nexus relevant goals are inevitable, and understanding these trade-offs in a national context can help to avoid creating perverse incentives to deforest (as in Indonesia). Removing or reforming these types of harmful subsidy would contribute significantly to changing nexus misalignments.

Land reform

As highlighted earlier, secure land tenure is essential for effective policies in the land-use nexus. In France, Ireland and New Zealand, land tenure is mostly clear and secure, but to achieve clarity and security of tenure in Indonesia and Brazil, significant reform is required. Land reform in Indonesia has two major components relevant to the forestry sector; the first is the promotion and expansion of community forestry and the second is agrarian reform. Indonesia has aims to have a total of 12.7 million ha of forest under community management, 4.5 million ha of which is to be allocated by the end of 2019 (Ministry of Environment and Forestry, 2018[144]). Under these programmes, the rights to manage and access land are transferred from the Indonesian state to a local community group. The Indonesian Ministry of Environment and Forestry identifies these schemes as an inclusive pathway to climate change reduction and poverty alleviation by providing access to and the ability to profit from forest resources for local communities (Ministry of Environment and Forestry, 2018[144]). However, the actual amount of land transferred to community management totalled 1.7 million ha by 2018, and while the rate of land reform is increasing, further efforts are needed to strengthen and streamline the process of land reform (Ministry of Environment and Forestry, 2018[144]). Several factors have caused this delay, notably budget cuts to the MoEF and complicated lengthy certification process. However, social forestry schemes still represent a promising pathway for land tenure reform. Efforts to streamline the application process for community forestry are underway, and it has been reduced from 2-3 years to approximately 1 year. But the process is still complicated and capacity building is required to improve community access and the environmental performance of social forestry schemes.

The second component of land reform in Indonesia is agrarian reform. Under the programme of agrarian reform (known as TORA), 9 million ha of land for agriculture will be redistributed to rural communities in order to reduce poverty and inequality. Of this, 4.1 million ha will come from the national forest estate (Ministry of Environment and Forestry, 2018[144]). While this programme targets social goals, it could potentially have negative biodiversity and climate impacts, if the redistributed land contains biodiversity rich ecosystems (e.g. primary forest) or is on peat land areas (Miettinen et al., 2017[49]).

In Brazil, land reform is at a more advanced stage and the approach has been different. The Forest Code has prioritised the mapping and identification of individual land holdings in forested areas and enrolling them in the national CAR (*Cadastro Ambiental Rural*) system. As of August 2016, 3.7 million properties covering 387 million ha, were enrolled in the CAR (Azevedo et al., 2017[14]). Through this system, enforcement efforts, such as credit black-listing, are used to target land holders who have deforested illegally. While there are issues surrounding the actual enforcement of the Forest Code, with Azevedo *et al.* (2017[14]) finding only 6% of registered properties took steps restore illegally cleared land, the registration of properties alone reduced deforestation by 10% (Alix-Garcia et al., 2018[156]). Land reform was thus a key component of Brazil's successful efforts (until 2015) to reduce deforestation in the Amazon.[24]

The current approaches to reforming land tenure in Brazil and Indonesia are well aligned with nexus goals. Evidence from Brazil suggests that just by the act of registering a property, the rate of deforestation decreases, bringing with it ecosystem and climate benefits (Alix-Garcia et al., 2018[156]). The situation in Indonesia is somewhat more complicated with overlapping institutional jurisdictions and conflicting maps leading to illegal land-use. As such, despite the mixed results of community forestry so far (Santika et al., 2017[157]), continuing efforts to extend community management are essential for removing misalignments in the nexus.

Intergovernmental Fiscal transfers

Every country has multiple governments (barring small city states) and intergovernmental fiscal transfers (IFT)[25] are the mechanism through which they carry out fiscal decentralisation. As a result, IFT are the most important feature of sub-national finance in most countries. In general, IFT are used to ensure that the revenue available for sub-national governments is well matched to the needs of the population. IFT can incentivise and advance national, provincial or municipal level goals and objectives such as equality, public service delivery and poverty eradication. As such, IFT are important to the nexus and are of particular importance to large, decentralised countries such as Brazil and Indonesia.

In Indonesia, the revenue a district can earn from the shared revenue fund is directly proportional to the value of the forestry revenues earned, and there is currently no penalty for over-exploiting forested areas. Under the current IFT structure about 40% of the revenues from forestry activity are returned to the producing district. Consequently, district governments have an incentive to maximise forestry revenues through logging and conversion of forests to timber plantations (Nurfatriani et al., 2015[146]). Palm oil plantations also generate revenue which is returned to the producing district, and while the proportion of the revenue returned is much lower, the higher profitability of oil palm results in higher revenue for the producing district in real terms (Irawan, Tacconi and Ring, 2013[158]). This revenue transfer incentivises district governments to maximise their revenue by facilitating the development of plantations in forested areas.

In Brazil the 'Ecological Value-Added Tax' (ICMS-E) is a mechanism whereby tax revenues from one state/municipality are transferred to another, in return for providing some form of environmental protection. Since its inception in Paraná in 1991 the ICMS-E has been adopted in 17 states by 2018. ICMS-E was first implemented to reward municipalities for hosting PAs and 16 of 17 states now include specific protected area indicators (Droste et al., 2017[159]). The value of the ICMS-E differs from state to state, but can be up to 8% of municipal value-added tax revenue, and it has been shown to encourage the creation of PA, however analysis of its ecological impacts is lacking (Droste et al., 2017[159]).

France operates a similar system of fiscal transfer to Indonesia, the DGF, where municipalities are paid according to their area and population size. Since 2007 the DGF has also included an ecological component, which awards extra money to municipalities if they are in the core area of a national park, to compensate for the reduced development opportunities (Borie et al., 2014[160]). However, of the 36 783 municipalities in French territory only 150 were eligible for the ecological allocation (in 2014) which represented on 0.02% of the EUR 13.6 billion distributed by the DGF (Borie et al., 2014[160]).

By basing revenue redistribution on environmental performance, IFT could provide a powerful incentive to prioritise nexus goals at a local level, and be used to compensate local governments for providing large shares of national level goods such as biodiversity or climate mitigation. However, by prioritising agriculture, the Indonesian approach potentially creates misalignment between nexus areas. In contrast, Brazil and France utilise specific environmental criteria, but the proportion of revenue allocated under these mechanisms is relative small, limiting their impact. Increasing the revenue available under IFT for achieving specific well-aligned nexus goals would encourage local authorities to manage, sometimes conflicting, nexus areas while allowing them the flexibility to implement locally appropriate measures.

Information, voluntary and other approaches

The inefficiencies in current land-use systems will have significant impacts for society through the climate change and the loss of the ecosystem services (see chapter 2), and have will negative consequences for large parts of the economy (OECD, 2019[22]). Therefore empowering stakeholders, both public and private sector, to make decisions that are both economically profitable and sustainable in the long term is key for effectively balancing the nexus goals. Scientific research, improved access to and use of data and enhancing the transfer of knowledge to the stakeholders that need it most, are all essential for improving land-use decisions. National and subnational governments play a key role in both supporting scientific research and facilitating the flow of information to stakeholders, such as farmers through extension services.

More broadly, governments in the case study countries have begun to use big and open data approaches to try and enhance the sustainability and transparency of land-use. In Ireland, for example, the Origin Green programme (Box 5.3) includes a large data collection effort, which is used to create adaptive management plans. Mexico, since 2013, has considered open government data a policy priority and now makes a wide variety of information on programmes such as biodiversity offsets and PES publically available (OECD, 2018[161]). The role of open access spatial data in democratising land-use is also recognised in the case study countries, with online special data platforms available through Indonesia's One Map programme, the Department of Conservation in New Zealand and National Commission for the Knowledge and use of Biodiversity (CONABIO) in Mexico.

Several emerging technologies are already playing a key role in increasing the sustainability of land-use. Remote sensing technologies, for example, are already well established for monitoring deforestation in Brazil (through the PRODES and DETER systems), and Indonesia is investing in similar systems to monitor forest fires and land cover change, to supplement existing global systems. Continuing development of these technologies, to refine the detection of non-compliance with environmental regulations, is important for improving the sustainability of land-use. Genomic research is being used to improve the efficiency of milk and beef production in Ireland and New Zealand. Finally, artificial intelligence is increasingly being used to increase the precision and efficiency of farming (CGIAR, 2018[162]) and blockchain is seen as a promising approach for ensuring end-to-end sustainability of consumption (Deloitte, 2017[163]). Governments could play a key role in facilitating research into and dissemination of new technologies when and if they are proven to be effective. Especially, when the stakeholders who need them lack sufficient resources to fully take advantage of these new opportunities (e.g. smallholders in developing countries).

Life cycle assessment approaches

Product life cycle assessment (LCA) approaches employ quantitative methods to assess environmental impacts resulting from the entire life a product, from production to consumption. In LCA, all the impacts associated with the production of a good (e.g. GHG emissions) are considered embodied in the final good at the point of consumption. Therefore, LCA impacts are location independent, and LCA could help quantify leakage under pricing mechanisms such as ETS. LCA can also help to quantify adverse nexus impacts of traded land products more generally. The application, upscaling and further development of LCA approaches in different sectors is an important demand-side measure to prevent the adverse impacts of trade on nexus areas. In the case study countries there are several different initiatives promoting the use of LCA and other approaches to quantify and limiting negative upstream or downstream impacts of domestic production and consumption of goods and services.

The National Strategy to Combat Imported Deforestation (SNDI) (Ministère de la transition écologique et solidaire, 2018[164]), will include a number of demand-side measures to better assess and ultimately reduce deforestation in the supply chain of French goods and services. For example, the introduction of a "zero deforestation" reporting category in private sector CSR reports (measure 11.1) and in reports of non-financial information required from financial institutions and investors (measure 12.1) are both proposed under the SNDI. Moreover, the SNDI recommends a potential widening of the scope of a law prescribing the "duty of care" of French companies for social and environmental risks associated with their supply chains to explicitly include deforestation risks (measure 11.2).

The sustainability criteria for biofuels – as used by France and Ireland under EU regulations – is a good example of the application of LCA in policy. Under EU law, biofuels have to meet certain sustainability criteria requiring life cycle (cultivation, processing, transport) GHG emissions savings of at least 35% compared to fossil fuels.[26] The application of LCA in this case was implemented after the initial law was passed, in response to concerns about the risks of indirect land-use change from agricultural expansion in response to increasing demand for oil crops (Frank et al., 2013[165]) . In December 2018 the Renewable Energy Directive II[27] introduced a new approach to ILUC by setting a gradually decreasing limit on the countable use of biofuels with high ILUC-risk. As of February 2019, no definition of what feedstock counts as high ILUC-risk biomass has been adopted.

Sustainability criteria in national (or supra-national, such as EU) regulations also impact nexus issues and policy coherence in countries of biofuel or feedstock origin like Indonesia and Brazil. Indonesia, for instance, supplied 49% of the EU's palm oil in 2017 (European External Action Service, 2018[166]), and around 40% of the EU's palm oil imports are used for biofuel production (Deutsche Welle, 2018[167]). Oil palm is among the most efficient oilseed crops in terms of yield. As a consequence, if the adverse local production impacts and transport emissions are effectively reduced and managed, palm oil-based biofuels could in theory constitute an example of synergistic trade-land use interactions (Mekhilef, Siga and Saidur, 2011[168]). However, so far managing the impacts of palm oil production has proven challenging (OECD, 2019[12]). While there remains large scope to more effectively manage these trade-offs (Moreno-Peñaranda et al., 2018[169]) and to reduce the land-use impacts of the wider Indonesian palm oil production system (OECD, 2019[12])[28], the introduction of the EU sustainability criteria for biofuels has indeed led to changes in Indonesian land-use regulations and practice (Hia and Kusumawardani, 2016[170]). Partly as a response to the criteria, Indonesian palm oil producers were required to follow certain production standards summarised under the Indonesian Sustainable Palm Oil (ISPO) regulation by 2014 (Ministry of Agriculture, 2011[171]).

The involvement of the widest possible range of actors on the supply- and demand-side is important if value chain and life cycle assessment approaches are to exert substantial positive influence on land-use outcomes. For example, the rapid increase in Chinese demand of several key commodity groups since the 2000s accounts for a substantial share of land-use nexus impacts attributable to exports in the case study countries. In 2016 82% of Brazilian soy exports were destined for China, and China constitutes the second-biggest export markets for both Indonesian palm oil and rubber, and the biggest for its forest products (Ministry of Agriculture; Fisheries and Food Supply, 2017[172]; BPS Statistics Indonesia, 2017[173]). Similarly, recent increases in Irish dairy and French roundwood exports are largely attributable to demand from China (Department of Agriculture; Food and the Marine, 2018[174]; Fédération nationale du bois, 2018[175]). Therefore, the involvement of China and other emerging economies in initiatives limiting land-use impacts beyond their own jurisdictional boundaries is essential.

Mandatory and Voluntary certification

A variety of certification schemes operate in the case study countries, both voluntary and mandatory, covering several nexus-relevant areas. One of the most common mechanisms is the certification of forest areas and forestry products. The Programme for the Endorsement of Forest Certification (PEFC) and the Forest Stewardship Council (FSC) are the two largest and most internationally recognised systems. All of the case study countries utilise these two certification mechanisms to differing extents (Figure 5.3). In general, both mechanisms aim to ensure the sustainability of timber supply chains by ensuring various management standards for forestry areas (such as biodiversity conservation and the delivery of ecosystem services) and the legality of timber for secondary products (PEFC, 2010[176]).

Figure 5.3. Percentage of forest area under PEFC and FSC certification in 2014

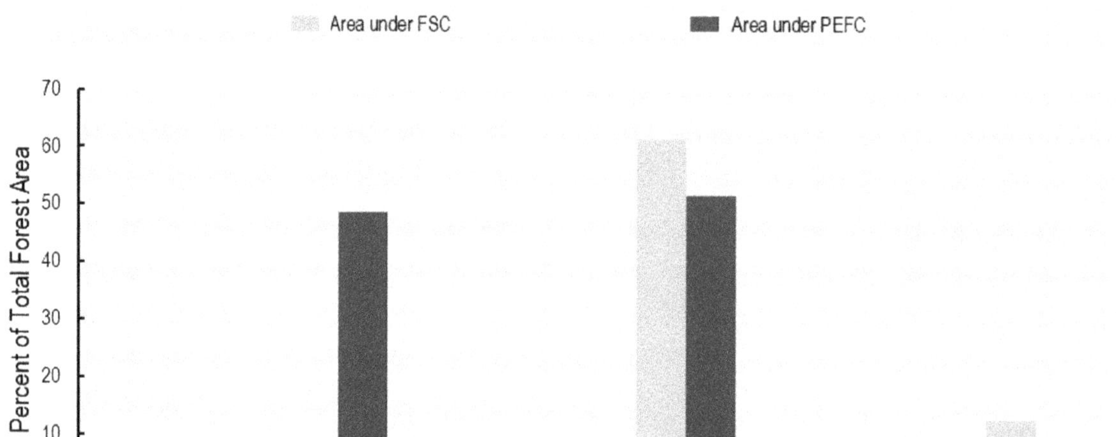

Note: PEFC national standards in Indonesia and New Zealand were officially endorsed in 2014 and 2015 respectively, hence there were no certified forests in 2014.
It must be noted that Indonesia and Brazil have much larger extents of forest so even though only a small percentage is certified, the total area certified is much larger than either Ireland or France.
Mexico does not have a PEFC endorsed national standard.
Source: FAO (2015[177]), Forest Resources Assessment 2015, http://www.fao.org/3/a-i4808e.pdf.

Large international certification systems, like FSC and PEFC, tend to have a large number of criteria for certification. As a result they do not represent a viable commercial option for smallholders or community managed forests, who often lack the capital and technical capacity required for the certification process (McDermott, Irland and Pacheco, 2015[178]). Despite offering a programme specifically tailored to these kinds of suppliers (small and low intensity managed forests programme), only 4% of forest area certified under FSC is managed by smallholders. Consequently, these programmes are not well aligned with forestry systems in tropical countries, which are typically dominated by community and smallholder managed areas. For example, in Mexico at least 70% of all forests is managed by *Ejidos* or *Comunidades* (two forms of communal tenure) which supply around 85% of all commercial roundwood (García-Montiel et al., 2017[179]). This lack of penetration into community and smallholder forest limits their utility for influencing nexus outcomes in the tropics, which is particularly important given small holder forestry generated an estimated USD 1.29 trillion in value in 2017 (Verdone, 2018[180]).

The PEFC operates slightly differently to the FSC and effectively endorses national level certification programmes that meet certain sustainability criteria. While national level forestry certification exists in all the case study countries, Mexico is the only case study country that does not have a PEFC endorsed standard.[29] Instead, the state developed Mexico Forest Certification (MFC), has fewer and less rigorous standards, making it more attractive to smallholder and community managed forest. This is reflected in the uptake of certification schemes where smallholders favour the MFC and commercial operation the more rigorous FSC (García-Montiel et al., 2017[179]).

Beyond certification for timber management, there are a range of other state, non-state, national and international certification standards covering a wide variety of agricultural supply chains. Gruère (2013[181]) analysed 544 environmental labelling schemes and found around 63% of them were aimed at nexus relevant areas (chemical control, biodiversity conservation, natural resource management and climate change). There has also been a rapid increase in the use of certification and labelling, with a fivefold increase in systems from 1988 to 2007 (Gruère, 2013[181]).

In theory at least, certification standards can be used to balance goals, however, in some cases they can conflict with national legislation. The Round Table on Sustainable Palm Oil (RSPO) provides a good example of these legislative issues. Under the RSPO, companies are required to assess the biodiversity value of the concession and set aside areas of high conservation value preventing conversion. The same is also true under Indonesian law[30], however the definitions of high conservation value are very different. Consequently, land set-aside under HCV can and has been excised from concessions and reallocated to non-RSPO companies for development into plantations, posing a challenge to RSPO implementation (Colchester et al., 2009[182]). Crucially, large markets have yet to adopt this standard: very little of the 10.6 Mt of palm oil imported by India and only 50 000 of the 4.8 Mt imported by China was RSPO certified (Schleifer and Sun, 2018[183]). Wider uptake would be needed to reach the goal of raising standards across the industry.

The second challenge to the effectiveness of certification as a tool to manage nexus goals is weak or poor enforcement of the standards. If not properly enforced, certification can fail to deliver environmental benefits and worse still it can be used to legitimise illegal activity. In Indonesia, the timber legality assurance system (SVLK) was set up in 2008 to ensure the legality of timber exported to the EU and issue FLEGT (Forest Law Enforcement Governance and Trade) licences to certified suppliers. However, the weak and inconsistent law enforcement in Indonesia has resulted in the laundering of illegal timber through certified companies (EIA and JPIK, 2017[184]). Weak enforcement of certification standards harms the credibility of the standard, particularly if such weak enforcement is publicly known. For many agricultural commodities and forest sector products, social and environmental production conditions are not visible to the final consumer. While certification schemes offer a way out of this situation of information asymmetry between producers and consumers, a lack of consumer trust (and consequently reduced price premiums) in turn can further limit certification effectiveness.

Certification is currently an effective tool for managing nexus goals in some areas, however, a lack of consistent price premium, capacity shortfalls (particularly among small holders), misalignments with national contexts and poor enforcement undermines its effectiveness. To improve the effectiveness of certification building capacity, particularly around community and smallholder land managers is essential, especially given the role they play in tropical agricultural systems (Verdone, 2018[180]). Finally, improving the auditing and enforcement capacity, again with a focus on more challenging governance environments in tropical systems, would help improve the effectiveness and the reliability of certification systems.

Box 5.2. Measures promoting responsible business conduct (RBC)

Policy measures promoting responsible business conduct (RBC) can ease pressures on land use originating from both the supply- and demand-side, in particular where they target global value chains. RBC can play an important role in positively influencing the impact of international trade on land-use nexus issues through the reduction of commodity-driven deforestation. As of June 2018, there are globally at least 785 public commitments by 471 producers, traders, manufacturers and retailers not to buy or sell commodities associated with deforestation have been made (Haupt et al., 2018[185]).[31] Whether a commitment leads to measurable reductions in deforestation, however, depends on a large array of factors and corporate motivation and the relative power of corporate participants in the supply chain are particularly important (Gasparri and de Waroux, 2015[186]; le Polain de Waroux et al., 2016[187]). Supportive public policies (and other forms of public-private interactions) have contributed to the effectiveness of RBC commitments in reducing deforestation. They include, for instance, the strengthening and endorsement of private RBC standards and codes of conduct, the facilitation of information-sharing for supply chain transparency, public coverage of compliance costs for small producers, or the encouragement of industry self-regulation through threats of stronger public regulation (Lambin et al., 2018[188]).

A best practice example for the achievement of nexus-compatible agricultural supply chains through public-private co-operation is presented by the guidance by (OECD/FAO, 2016[189]). The guidance provides a model enterprise policy for responsible agricultural supply chains and a sample framework for risk-based due diligence integrating environmental protection and the sustainable use of land resources with other RBC principles. It can be used by enterprises to identify measures to effectively improve the environmental and social performance of agricultural supply chains, and by governments to promote these and to align public policies. A pilot project aiming at the implementation of the guidance is currently being undertaken. Participants include companies and initiatives with major operations in the case study countries, but implementation results remain to be awaited and evaluated (OECD/FAO, 2018[190]).

Agricultural information and knowledge transfer schemes

The decisions of individual land managers have a large influence on nexus outcomes, but despite advances in agriculture and forestry management, there are considerable differences between the performance of individual holdings. Closing the yield and efficiency gaps will lessen the pressure on unmanaged land areas, by reducing the need to open up new areas to meet production targets and reducing the emissions-intensity of production by fostering the uptake of climate-smart agricultural techniques.

There is, however, a strong caveat that knowledge transfer and informational approaches focused on efficiency gains and reducing yield gaps will only have the desired effects if they are introduced with a robust legislative framework, particularly concerning land-use change. If the other mechanisms to control land-use change are ineffective, closing yield gaps and increasing farmer efficiency could have the opposite effect, leading to increased biodiversity impacts and emissions. The increased profitability of production could create a rebound effect whereby the level of investment in the sector increases with an associated expansion of production into unmanaged areas. This phenomenon is of particular importance countries with large potential for agricultural expansion (e.g. Indonesia, Brazil and Mexico) and is likely to reduce the potential impacts of productivity increases in the absence of other effective policies (Martha, Alves and Contini, 2012[191]).

Aside from schemes focused on efficiency gains and closing yield gaps, knowledge transfer and information schemes can also be focused on encouraging more sustainable farming and forestry practices. Generally, these are in the form or advisory and extension services, which aim to facilitate and incentivise the uptake of environmentally beneficial land management practices, by highlighting the benefits to land managers and providing the knowledge and skills to put them into practice. Advisory and extension services are provided by a wide range of actors and institutions in the case study countries. For example, they are a key component of agriculture support programmes in Ireland (e.g. GLAS) and New Zealand (e.g Sustainable Farming Fund). While quantitative assessments of advisory and extension services is limited, evidence suggests they play a vital role in the uptake of environmentally-beneficial management practices (OECD, 2015[192]).

The six case study countries use several different approaches to knowledge transfer. In Ireland, knowledge transfer programmes are an integral part of agricultural support programmes (e.g. GLAS) and forestry support schemes (e.g. NeighbourWood scheme and Native Woodland Conservation scheme). In addition, there are several specific schemes directly addressing knowledge transfer in both the agricultural and forestry sectors (e.g. Forest Knowledge Transfer Group Scheme). For example, the Irish Beef Data and Genomics Programme (BDGP) tracks maternal traits of suckler cows in commercial herds to create an index that ranks the efficiency of individual animals under a five star system. This index is then used to support farmer decisions regarding replacement animals with the long-term aim of improving the efficiency of the Irish cattle herd as a whole. Improvements that will deliver emissions mitigation and improved production. The BDGP also require participating farmers to go through an emissions assessment under the carbon navigator programme, further increasing the mitigation impacts. Ireland also co-ordinates the efforts of knowledge transfer schemes, such as the BDGP, though the Origin Green[32] programme (see Box 5.3).

Across the case study countries, the level of finance for knowledge transfer and innovation is highly variable. Brazil allocated 25.4% of all agricultural support to knowledge and innovation systems in 2015 (USD 1.8 billion) and Indonesia 0.5% in the same year (USD 209 million) (OECD, 2019[110]).[33] To create the co-benefits required for effective management of trade-offs and ensure demand for agricultural products can be met in the future, significant investment in knowledge transfer and innovation programmes is key.

Box 5.3. Origin Green in Ireland

Launched in 2012, Origin Green (OG) is a whole supply chain national sustainability programme for the Irish food and drink sector run by Bord Bía. OG aims to provide the food and beverage industry with an infrastructure to measure and guide sustainability and ensure the industry as a whole is aligned with the SDGs.

Its members include farmers, food and beverage manufacturers, retailers and the food service industry. Farmers are automatically enrolled into OG by signing up to Bord Bía's sustainability assurance scheme (mandatory for dairy farmers), which includes an 18 monthly audit of their production facilities and farm buildings. With food and drinks producers and other members, Origin Green now covers 90% of Ireland's food and beverage portfolio and includes several major retailers (Tesco, Lidl and Aldi). Member companies must submit sustainability plans targeting certain areas (e.g. packaging, transport, refrigeration) which are subsequently audited independently.

OG has created 1 600 sustainability targets and 92 biodiversity targets, and has achieved some successes since its inception. These include diverting 4 600 tonnes of waste from landfill, 1.1 million cubic metres of water saved, and reductions in CO_2e/kg of milk (1.21 in 2014 to 1.14 in 2016) and beef (11.79 in 2014 to 11.58 in 2016) (Bord Bía, 2017[193]). OG also represents a huge national data collection effort at all levels of the supply chain. The information gained from the data collection is then fed into adaptive management plans, allowing specific tailoring of sustainability programmes for individual members, and the flow of knowledge about best practice both within and between sectors (Bord Bía, 2017[193]).

Finally, the broad mandate of OG has allowed for significant co-ordination between various levels of the supply chain, and different aspect of nexus policy and the institutions responsible. OG has, for example, helped to co-ordinate knowledge transfer for AES and the BDGP, facilitated the development of remote habitat monitoring with Teagasc and helped develop the national pollinator plan with the National Biodiversity Data Centre.

Brazil, the country with the highest level of government investment (both relative and absolute) in agricultural knowledge and innovation systems across the six case studies, has achieved significant success in raising the yields of important agricultural products. These include soy (yield increased from just over 1,000kg/ha in 1970 to 3 200 kg/ha in 2012) (Figueiredo, 2016[116]), beef (17.61 kg c.e/head to 40.13 kg c.e/head 1975-2006) (Martha, Alves and Contini, 2012[191]) and reducing direct emissions from agriculture (Mello, 2015[132]). The Brazilian approach is highly decentralised with the national government playing a co-ordinating role through the Ministry of Agriculture, Livestock and Food Supply, but the actual knowledge transfer and research activities are carried out by state and municipal level organisations such as EMATER (Technical Assistance and Rural Co-operation) and EMBRAPA (Brazilian Agricultural Research Corporation). However, despite the success of these schemes highlighted above, ongoing land-use change in the Cerrado (Strassburg et al., 2017[55]), and Amazon (Hansen, Stehman and Potapov, 2010[194]), highlights the importance of having robust systems in place to control land use and ensure that improved efficiency of production does not also lead to increased land conversion.

Reducing food loss and waste (FLW)

The output of approximately 30% of agricultural land (1.4 billion ha) is wasted or lost every year (FAO, 2013[195]). Reducing FLW therefore has potential to reduce the demand for agricultural land and relieve the pressure to convert natural ecosystems to farmland. Addressing FLW will become increasingly important in the future as demand for agricultural products increases with rising population and levels of development. In fact, the area used to produce lost and wasted food annually is nearly double the predicted area of new cropland required to meet demand by 2060 (710 million ha) (FAO, 2013[195]; Tilman et al., 2017[196]).[34] Producing food that is lost or wasted is also associated with significant GHG emissions (4.4 $GtCO_2e$) and water consumption (240km^3) which leads to significant impacts on ecosystems. Reducing FLW could play an important role in reducing the impacts of food production on other areas of the nexus, with many different actors across governments, civil society and the private sector having important roles to play.

General approaches

The potential of FLW reduction measures to address nexus issues varies widely according to site-specific and product-specific factors. Thus, the land-use, climate and ecosystem impacts of FLW are heavily influenced by the type of food that is lost or wasted. While milk and meat only contribute 11 per cent of food waste by mass, they account for 78 per cent of the land occupation linked to FLW (FAO, 2013[195]).[35] By contrast, despite significant rates of loss, the land occupation associated with vegetables that are wasted is much lower due to their comparatively high yields. In terms of carbon emissions, cereal crops are the largest contributor (34%), largely driven by high fertiliser inputs and paddy field rice systems is Asia which are associated with significant methane emissions from decaying vegetable matter (FAO, 2013[195]). The contribution of cereals to carbon emissions is unsurprising given they constitute approximately 63% of the global food supply and around 57% of all plant-based FLW (Kummu et al., 2012[197]). Animal products on the other hand account for only 15% of total food waste by volume, but 33% of the carbon footprint of FLW (FAO, 2013[195]). Thus, focussing public policies on high impact animal based products and dietary shifts away from meat and dairy products may have a greater ability to relieve demand for agricultural land than policies to address food waste in a general sense, however it is likely both approaches will be required (Willett et al., 2019[198]).

The global food system is complex and consequently causes of FLW are complicated and multi-faceted as well. FLW occurs at every stage of the food production system[36], with the highest levels (by volume) associated with the upstream phases (agricultural production and postharvest handling and storage) (FAO, 2013[195]; Kummu et al., 2012[197]). This varies by region, however, and in general high income countries are associated with higher volumes of downstream (processing, distribution and consumption) FLW than lower income countries (FAO, 2013[195]). Since the environmental impacts accumulate along the food supply chain, the later the product is lost or wasted in the supply chain the higher the environmental cost, however the largest proportion of these impacts is associated with the production of the food in the first place (FAO, 2013[195]). It is also important to note that reducing FLW to zero is likely not possible or desirable, as it could lead to reduced food security though increased prices under some scenarios (OECD, n.d.[199]).

Table 5.7 summarises some of the most important sources of FLW in industrialised countries. Actions to address FLW are variable, however, it is possible to define a generalisable hierarchy of actions for addressing FLW, as shown in Figure 5.4. Actions to prevent FLW are given the highest priority under this hierarchy, because they avoid environmental and economic impacts that stretch the length of the food value chain (FAO, 2017[200]; Tonini, Brogaard and Astrup, 2017[201]). Waste management strategies are the least-preferred measures under this hierarchy because of the substantial impacts that food production, processing, and transport have before this point (FAO, 2017[200]). Jørgen et al. (2016[202]) further suggest that actions should focus more on addressing the loss and waste of foodstuffs with the highest environmental impacts, such as animal products and cereal products, and less on those with reasonably low environmental impacts such as certain root vegetables. The EIU (2018[203]) recommend that these hierarchies should be adopted as part of the formal mandates of authorities charged with addressing FLW.

Figure 5.4. Hierarchy of actions to address food waste based on the environmental, economic and social benefits typically associated with each class of action

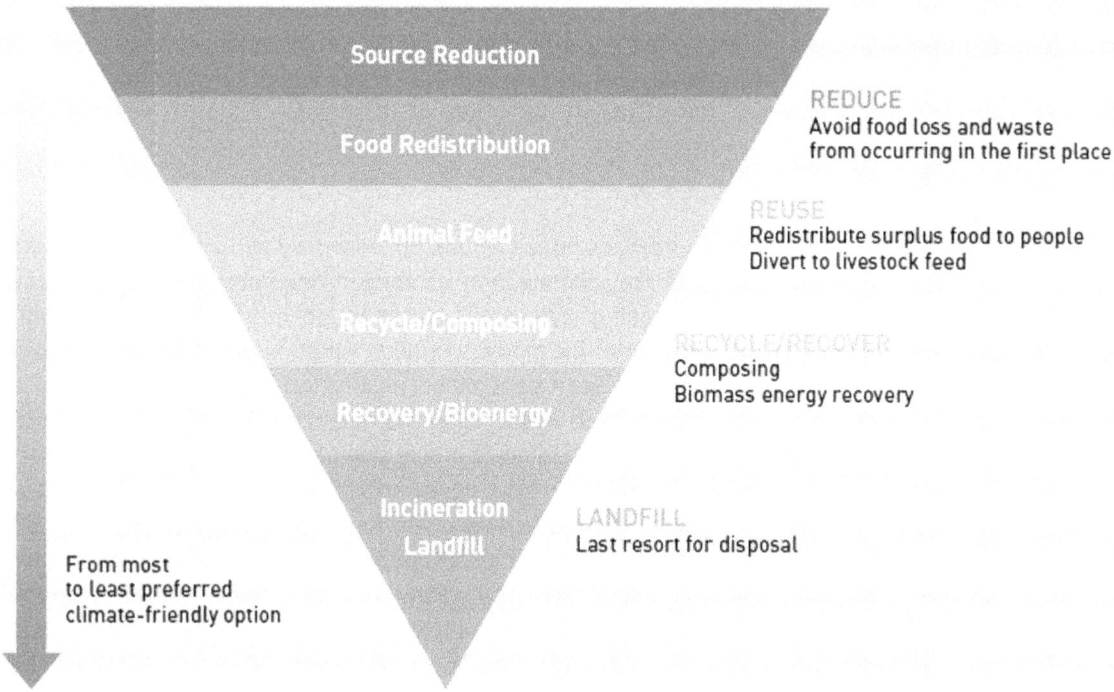

Source: FAO (2017[200]) Save Food for a Better Climate: Converting the food loss and waste challenge into climate action, http://www.fao.org/3/a-i8000e.pdf

Case study examples

There are currently no globally consistent measures of FLW that allow for a comparison of the actual volumes of FLW at different stages of the food chain system across countries (see Chapter 2). Understanding what actions are appropriate and where in the system they should be implemented is, therefore, challenging and likely to be specific to national and sub-national contexts. There are opportunities to reduce FLW at every stage of the food chain system, with downstream losses (processing, distribution and consumption) that are higher in developed countries, making interventions at the later stages of the food chain system preferable. Upstream losses, however, are relatively larger in less developed countries, so targeting these losses, through the improvement of agri-food systems is key (Kummu et al., 2012[197]).

France is a global leader in efforts to reduce FLW, and its actions far exceed the requirements set out by the European Commission, however, to date there is little evidence regarding how successful these efforts have been. France takes a holistic approach to addressing FLW including mandates for education and new business practices. Consequently, France was ranked first out of 35 countries in the EIU's (2018[203]) index of food loss and waste, which takes into account levels of food waste and the policy responses to it. The French success in passing legislation to address FLW can be attributed to broad public debate and lobbying efforts by civil society.

In 2016, France passed a range of bold measures specifically aimed at addressing FLW. These included granting tax benefits to farmers who donate food that would otherwise be lost, requiring supermarkets to sign agreements with local charities to donate unsold but still edible food, and imposing fines of up EUR 75 000 on supermarkets that discard food (Henz and Porpino, 2017[204]; EIU, 2018[203]). However, the proportion of food that must be donated is not specified by law and consequently, it is likely only a small fraction of food intended for refuse is redistributed. In addition, France has removed expiration dates from foods that do not pose time-sensitive health risks, undertaken information campaigns aimed at educating consumers about food waste prevention, and included food waste prevention within school curricula (EIU, 2018[203]). The lack of national level monitoring makes it difficult to assess the success of these programmes, but a 2017 study found around 24% of food intended for disposal had been redistributed to charities in the province of Isére (Gore-Langton, 2017[205]).

Mexico has a relatively low level of food waste when compared to the other case study countries, although measurement issues likely play a role in the favourable comparison. Measurement issues aside, Mexico does have a long-established and highly sophisticated Programme for Waste Prevention and Integrated Waste Management. This programme formalises the hierarchy of actions to address FLW (Figure 5.4) and therefore focusses efforts on waste prevention. Importantly it includes requirements to measure food waste, which places Mexico in a small grouping of (mostly highly-developed) countries to do so (Champions 12.3, 2018[206]). Furthermore, Mexico has partnered with the United States and Canada under the Commission for Environmental Cooperation (2018[207]) to form the Food Loss and Waste Measurement Expert Group in order to advance the measurement of FLW throughout the supply chain in North America. Given the international nature of food systems, transnational approaches to FLW such as this are particularly important.

Much like France, Mexico has also included FLW into agricultural policies and programmes. Specifically, under Mexico's Agricultural Sector Programme 9 Strategy 1.6, goals include improving transport networks and storage facilities, investing in cold chain technology, and improving handling capacity for perishable foodstuffs, an approach also utilised in Indonesia (González, 2017[208]; The Ministry of Agriculture, 2015[209]). In addition, the Agricultural Sector Programme 10 Strategy 1.6.8 encourages the reuse of surplus food for the benefit of food-insecure populations (González, 2017[208]), highlighting the potential of FLW reduction programmes to contribute more broadly to food security goals and the SDGs.[37]

The redistribution of surplus food to food-insecure sections of society is a common approach to addressing FLW, with programmes in operation across New Zealand, France, Mexico, Brazil and Indonesia. This approach is particularly important in countries such as Indonesia and Brazil, where food waste is relatively high, and around one third and one quarter of the population are food insecure respectively. In Brazil, more food is wasted annually than would be required to ensure food security for the entire population - making FLW a moral as well as environmental issue in the country (Henz and Porpino, 2017[204]; Embrapa, 2018[210]).

Much like other facets of the land-use nexus, the complex nature of FLW makes broad approaches difficult, especially in countries with a wide range of socio-economic contexts and differing food systems. In these cases sub-national approaches may be best suited to addressing the specific FLW issues. The city of Palembang in Indonesia, has developed one such programme, which aims to reduce the estimated 116 000 tonnes of food waste produced every year through a programmes of education and biomass utilisation for compost and biogas (Ministry of Agriculture and the Technology Assessment and Application Agency, n.d.[211]). In 2016, the Federal district in Brazil approved a law requiring supermarkets to donate rather than destroy food that is not sold. Supermarkets in breach of this law face fines of up to 3 000 USD, however as of December 2017, no such fines had been levied (Henz and Porpino, 2017[204]).

While all the case study countries have some kind of programme to address FLW the extent and scopes of these programmes is highly variable,[38] hence there is still considerable opportunity for improvement. The lack of quantitative, national level targets for reducing FLW outside of France is surprising given the economic and environmental rationale for action and the potential synergies with other key national policy agendas, such as climate change, biodiversity and food security. The absence of consistent FLW monitoring at national and sub-national levels explains to some extent why these targets are missing in many cases. The recent EU effort to define measurement standards (Directive (EU) 2018/851)[39] is an important step forward for FLW. However, greater co-ordination at an international level would increase the understanding of this complex issue and help identify key leverage points for policy interventions. While national-level approaches may prove to be too general to effectively reduce FLW in some cases, having national guidelines to define the targets, monitoring systems and basic standards for handling food waste are key for defining the scope within which more specific sub-national actions could take place. While Mexico, France and Indonesia all include some measures for reducing food waste in the agricultural plans (and to some extent Ireland through the Origin Green programme), FLW often has a relatively low profile in the ministries that could have key roles to play (e.g. Agriculture, Transport, Trade). Reducing FLW should be a key component of strategies to balance nexus goals, since it would also result in reduced demand and GHG emissions.

Table 5.7. Sources of food waste at different stages in the production cycle in industrialised countries

Agricultural production	Manufacturing	Distribution and wholesale/retail	Hospitality industry and catering	Households
Sorting out of products at farm gate due to rigorous qualitative standards set up by large-scale distributors concerning weight, size, shape and appearance	Irregular sized products trimmed to fit or rejected entirely	Lack of cold storage/interruption of the cold chain	Oversized dishes	Lack of planning/knowledge concerning food purchase and storage
Market prices that do not justify the expense of harvesting	Inconsistency of manufacturing processes leading to misshapen products or product damage	Packaging defects resulting in product damage	Offer of buffets at fixed prices encouraging people to take more than they can eat	Impulse purchases (buying items that are not currently needed)
Overproduction due to supply agreements with retail chains	Contamination in production process causing loss of quality	Overstocking due to inaccurate ordering and forecasting demand	Use of individual portion packs (e.g. for jams, cereals, juice and milk) that do not meet the customer's needs	Purchasing of new products that the consumer then 'do not like'
Crop damaged during harvesting	Food spoilage due to packaging problems	Obligation for retailers to order a wide range of products and brands from the same producer in order to get beneficial prices	Difficulties in assessing the demand (number of customers)	Inadequate package sizes (e.g. oversized ready to eat meals)
	Surplus production of supermarket's own brands that cannot be sold elsewhere	Failure to comply with minimum food safety standards (e.g. microbial contamination, pesticide residues)	EU hygiene rules, e.g. two-hour guarantee on unrefrigerated products	Poor storage management (e.g. inadequate wrapping)
	Excess stock due to 'take-back' systems and cancellation of orders	Marketing strategies like 'buy one get one free'		Confusion about date labels ('best before', 'use by')
				Lack of skills for food preparation
				Poor experience in planning meals
				Preparing oversized meals
				Lack of skills for recombining leftovers into new meals

Source: Priefer et al. (2016[212]), Food waste prevention in Europe – A cause-driven approach to identify the most relevant leverage points for action, http://dx.doi.org/10.1016/J.RESCONREC.2016.03.004

References

Abram, N. et al. (2017), "Oil palm–community conflict mapping in Indonesia: A case for better community liaison in planning for development initiatives", *Applied Geography*, Vol. 78, pp. 33-44, http://dx.doi.org/10.1016/j.apgeog.2016.10.005. [28]

ADAS (2014), *Ireland's Forestry Programme 2014-2020: Appropriate Assessment (AA), Natura Impact Statement*, ADAS UK ltd, Abingdon, UK. [140]

Aguilar, S. et al. (2011), *Environmental Assessment of NAFTA by the Commission for Environmental Cooperation: An Assessment of the Practice and Results to Date*, International Institute for Sustainable Development (IISD), Winnipeg, Canada, http://www3.cec.org/islandora/en/item/11047-environmental-assessment-nafta-commission-environmental-cooperation-en.pdf (accessed on 12 June 2019). [66]

Alix-Garcia, J. et al. (2018), "Avoided Deforestation Linked to Environmental Registration of Properties in the Brazilian Amazon", *Conservation Letters*, Vol. 11/3, p. e12414, http://dx.doi.org/10.1111/conl.12414. [156]

Alves-Pinto, H. et al. (2018), "Economic Impacts of Payments for Environmental Services on Livelihoods of Agro-extractivist Communities in the Brazilian Amazon", *Ecological Economics*, Vol. 152, pp. 378-388, http://dx.doi.org/10.1016/J.ECOLECON.2018.05.016. [103]

Azevedo, A. et al. (2017), "Limits of Brazil's Forest Code as a means to end illegal deforestation.", *Proceedings of the National Academy of Sciences of the United States of America*, Vol. 114/29, pp. 7653-7658, http://dx.doi.org/10.1073/pnas.1604768114. [14]

Barr, C. et al. (2010), *Financial governance and Indonesia's Reforestation Fund during the Soeharto and post-Soeharto periods, 1989-2009: A political economic analysis of lessons for REDD+*, CIFOR, Bogor, Indonesia, http://www.cifor.org/publications/pdf_files/OccPapers/OP-52.pdf (accessed on 12 March 2018). [145]

BBOP (2009), *Biodiversity Offset Cost-Benefit Handbook*, Business and Biodiversity Offsets Programme (BBOP) , Washington, D.C., http://www.forest-trends.org/biodiversityoffsetprogram/guidelines/. (accessed on 28 August 2018). [93]

Blanco, G. et al. (2014), "Drivers, Trends and Mitigation", in *Climate Change 2014: Mitigation of Climate Change. Contribution of Working Group III to the Fifth Assessment Report of the Intergovernmental Panel on Climate Change*, Intergovernmental Panel on Climate Change, Cambridge, UK. [3]

BNDES (2018), *Amazon Fund*, http://www.amazonfund.gov.br/en/home/ (accessed on 29 August 2018). [108]

Böcker, T. and R. Finger (2017), "A Meta-Analysis on the Elasticity of Demand for Pesticides", *Journal of Agricultural Economics*, Vol. 68/2, pp. 518-533, http://dx.doi.org/10.1111/1477-9552.12198. [80]

Böcker, T. and R. Finger (2016), "European Pesticide Tax Schemes in Comparison: An Analysis of Experiences and Developments", *Sustainability*, Vol. 8/4, p. 378, http://dx.doi.org/10.3390/su8040378. [79]

Bord Bía (2017), *Origin Green: sustainability report 2016*, Bord Bía, https://www.origingreen.com/globalassets/publications/origin-green-sustainability-report-2016.pdf. [193]

Borie, M. et al. (2014), "Exploring the Contribution of Fiscal Transfers to Protected Area Policy", *Ecology and Society*, Vol. 19/1, p. art9, http://dx.doi.org/10.5751/ES-05716-190109. [160]

Börner, J. et al. (2013), *Promoting Forest Stewardship in the Bolsa Floresta Programme: Local Livelihood Strategies and Preliminary Impacts*, Rio de Janeiro, Brazil: Center for International Forestry Research (CIFOR). Manaus, Brazil: Fundação Amazonas Sustentável(FAS). Bonn, Germany: Zentrum für Entwicklungsforschung (ZEF), University of Bonn, http://www.cifor.org/publications/pdf_files/Books/BBorner1301.pdf (accessed on 21 August 2018). [102]

BPS Statistics Indonesia (2017), *Statistical Yearbook of Indonesia 2017*, BPS, Jakarta, Indonesia, https://www.bps.go.id/publication/2017/07/26/b598fa587f5112432533a656/statistik-indonesia-2017.html. [173]

Bren d'Amour, C. et al. (2016), "Future urban land expansion and implications for global croplands", *Proceedings of the National Academy of Sciences*, p. 201606036, http://dx.doi.org/10.1073/pnas.1606036114. [32]

Brower, A. et al. (2017), "Compliance with biodiversity compensation on New Zealand's public conservation lands", http://dx.doi.org/10.20417/nzjecol.42.4. [96]

Buscardo, E. et al. (2008), "The early effects of afforestation on biodiversity of grasslands in Ireland", *Biodiversity and Conservation*, Vol. 17/5, pp. 1057-1072, http://dx.doi.org/10.1007/s10531-007-9275-2. [151]

Busch, J. et al. (2014), "Reductions in emissions from deforestation from Indonesia ' s moratorium on new oil palm , timber , and logging concessions", pp. 1-6, http://dx.doi.org/10.1073/pnas.1412514112. [54]

CARB (2018), *California Tropical Forest Standard*, California Air Resources Board, https://www.arb.ca.gov/cc/ghgsectors/tropicalforests.htm (accessed on 13 June 2019). [91]

Carlson, K. et al. (2012), "Carbon emissions from forest conversion by Kalimantan oil palm plantations", *Nature Climate Change*, Vol. 3/3, pp. 283-287, http://dx.doi.org/10.1038/nclimate1702. [29]

Central Statistics Office (2019), *Central Statistics Office*, https://www.cso.ie/en/ (accessed on 12 July 2019). [56]

CER (2017), *Public Service Obligation Levy 2017/18*, Commission for Energy Regulation, Dublin, Ireland. [155]

CGIAR (2018), *Pest and disease monitoring by using artificial intelligence | CGIAR Platform for Big Data in Agriculture*, https://bigdata.cgiar.org/pest-and-disease-monitoring-by-using-artificial-intelligence/ (accessed on 23 October 2018). [162]

Champions 12.3 (2018), *2018 Progress Report: An annual update on behalf of Champions 12.3*, http://www.champions123.org. [206]

Chapela y Mendoza, G. (2018), "Los bosques de México: Crisis del sector forestal y propuesta de política", in Leticia Merino Pérez and Alejandro Velázquez Montes (eds.), *Agenda Ambiental: Diagnóstico y propuestas*, SUSMAI, Mexico City, Mexico. [18]

Chitra, J. and K. Cetera (2018), *Indonesia Has a Carrot to End Illegal Logging; Now It Needs a Stick | World Resources Institute*, https://www.wri.org/blog/2018/01/indonesia-has-carrot-end-illegal-logging-now-it-needs-stick (accessed on 7 March 2019). [10]

Colchester, M. et al. (2009), "HCV and RSPO: results of an investigation HCV and the RSPO Report of an independent investigation into the effectiveness of the application of High Conservation Value zoning in palm oil development in Indonesia", http://www.forestpeoples.org/sites/default/files/publication/2010/08/rspoindonesiahcvstudyreportoct09eng.pdf (accessed on 30 March 2018). [182]

Collins, M. and E. Mitchard (2017), "A small subset of protected areas are a highly significant source of carbon emissions", *Scientific Reports*, Vol. 7/January 2016, p. 41902, http://dx.doi.org/10.1038/srep41902. [46]

Commission for Environmental Cooperation (2018), *CEC launches expert group to better measure food loss and waste in North America | Commission for Environmental Cooperation*, http://www.cec.org/news-and-outreach/press-releases/cec-launches-expert-group-better-measure-food-loss-and-waste-north-america (accessed on 2 November 2018). [207]

Commission for Environmental Cooperation (CEC) (2018), *Agreement on Environmental Cooperation among the Governments of the United States of America, the United Mexican States, and Canada*, CEC, Washington, D.C., https://www.epa.gov/sites/production/files/2018-11/documents/us-mxca_eca_-_final_english.2.pdf (accessed on 15 February 2019). [68]

Coordinating Ministry of Economic Affairs (2011), *Master Plan: Acceleration and Expansion of Indonesia Economic Development 2011-2025*, Republic of Indonesia, Jakarta, Indonesia. [118]

Corruption Eradication Comission (KPK) (2015), *Preventing State Losses in Indonesia's Forestry Sector: An Analysis of Non-tax Forest Revenue Collection and Timber Production Administration*, Government of Indonesia, Jakarta, Indonesia, https://acch.kpk.go.id/images/tema/litbang/pengkajian/pdf/Preventing-State-Losses-in-Indonesia-Forestry-Sector-KPK.pdf (accessed on 7 March 2019). [11]

DAFM (2019), *Public Consultation 2019 Nitrates Derogation Review*, Department of Agriculture Food and the Marine, https://www.agriculture.gov.ie/media/migration/ruralenvironment/environment/nitrates/2019/PublicConsultation2019NitratesDerogationReview290319.pdf (accessed on 18 June 2019). [57]

DAFM (2018), *Review of Expenditure under the Rural Development Programme (RDP) 2014-2020*, Department of Agriculture, Food and the Marine, https://www.agriculture.gov.ie/media/migration/ruralenvironment/ruraldevelopment/ruraldevelopmentprogramme2014-2020/ReviewRDPExpenditureJune050718.pdf (accessed on 26 July 2018). [126]

DAFM (2017), *The 2017 Evaluation on the Implementation of Ireland's Rural Development Programme 2014-2020*, Department of Agriculture, Food and the Marine, https://www.agriculture.gov.ie/media/migration/ruralenvironment/ruraldevelopment/ruraldevelopmentprogramme2014-2020/2017EvaluationofIrelandsRDP180917.pdf (accessed on 31 July 2018). [127]

DAFM (2015), *Food Wise 2025*, Department of Agriculture, Food and the Marine. [125]

DAFM (2015), *Forestry Programme 2014-2020: Ireland*, Department of Agriculture, Food and the Marine, https://www.agriculture.gov.ie/media/migration/forestry/forestryprogramme2014-2020/IRELANDForestryProgramme20142020230215.pdf (accessed on 3 August 2018). [139]

DAFM and DAHG (2014), *Burren Farming for Conservation Programme, Annual Report No. 5*, http://www.burrenprogramme.com/wp-content/uploads/2015/05/BFCP-Annual-Report-2014.pdf (accessed on 1 August 2018). [130]

DAHG (2015), *Managing Ireland's Peatlands: A national peatlands strategy 2015*, Department of Arts, Heritage and the Gaeltacht. [50]

DCCAE (2017), *National Mitigation Plan*, Department of Communications, Climate Action and Environment. [135]

de Marques, A., M. Schneider and C. Peres (2016), "Human population and socioeconomic modulators of conservation performance in 788 Amazonian and Atlantic Forest reserves", *PeerJ*, Vol. 4, p. e2206, http://dx.doi.org/10.7717/peerj.2206. [48]

Deloitte (2017), *Continuous interconnected supply chain Using Blockchain and Internet-of-Things in supply chain traceability*, https://www2.deloitte.com/content/dam/Deloitte/lu/Documents/technology/lu-blockchain-internet-things-supply-chain-traceability.pdf (accessed on 19 June 2019). [163]

Department of Agriculture; Food and the Marine (2018), *Annual Review and Outlook for Agriculture, Food and the Marine 2018*, Government of Ireland, Dublin, https://www.agriculture.gov.ie/media/migration/publications/2018/AnnualReviewandOutlook2018310818.pdf (accessed on 4 February 2019). [174]

Deutsche Welle (2018), *Can Europe defeat a palm oil 'monster' of its own making? | Environment| All topics from climate change to conservation | DW | 22.08.2018*, https://www.dw.com/en/can-europe-defeat-a-palm-oil-monster-of-its-own-making/a-45171111 (accessed on 8 March 2019). [167]

Droste, N. et al. (2017), "Municipal Responses to Ecological Fiscal Transfers in Brazil: A microeconometric panel data approach", *Environmental Policy and Governance*, Vol. 27/4, pp. 378-393, http://dx.doi.org/10.1002/eet.1760. [159]

Duchelle, A. et al. (2014), "Acre's State System of Incentives for Environmental Services (SISA), Brazil", in E.O. Sills, S. Atmadja, Sassi, C. de A.E. Duchelle, D. Kweka, I.A.P. Resosudarmo, W. (ed.), *REDD+ on the ground: A case book of subnational initiatives across the globe*, Center for International Forestry Research (CIFOR), Bogor, Indonesia, https://www.cifor.org/library/5262/ (accessed on 13 June 2019). [90]

EIA and JPIK (2017), *Still Permitting Crime*, Environmental Investigation Agency, http://jpik.or.id/info/wp-content/uploads/2017/06/Still-Permitting-Crime.pdf (accessed on 18 June 2018). [184]

EIU (2018), *Food Sustainability Index, Country Index and Data*, http://foodsustainability.eiu.com/ (accessed on 18 October 2018). [203]

Embrapa (2018), *Food loss and food waste*, https://www.embrapa.br/en/tema-perdas-e-desperdicio-de-alimentos/sobre-o-tema (accessed on 1 November 2018). [210]

Enrici, A. and K. Hubacek (2018), "Challenges for REDD+ in Indonesia: a case study of three project sites", *Ecology and Society*, Vol. 23/2, p. art7, http://dx.doi.org/10.5751/ES-09805-230207. [106]

Environmental Protection Agency (2018), *Ireland's Final Greenhouse Gas Emissions 1990-2016*, Environmental Protection Agency, Dublin, ireland, http://www.epa.ie/pubs/reports/air/airemissions/ghgemissions2016/Report_GHG%201990-2016%20April_for%20Website-v3.pdf (accessed on 11 June 2019). [2]

EPA (2018), *Water Quality in 2017: An Indicators Report*, Environmental Protection Agency, http://www.epa.ie/pubs/reports/water/waterqua/Water%20Quality%20in%202017%20-%20an%20indicators%20report.pdf (accessed on 18 June 2019). [58]

EPA (2017), *Guidelines on the Information to be Contained in Environmental Impact Assessment Reports*, Environmental Protections Agency, Ireland, http://www.epa.ie/pubs/advice/ea/EPA%20EIAR%20Guidelines.pdf (accessed on 31 July 2018). [72]

European Commission (2018), *EU Budget: The CAP after 2020*, http://dx.doi.org/10.2762/11307. [123]

European Commission (2017), *Report on the distribution of direct payments to agricultural producers (financial year 2016)*, European Commission, http://ec.europa.eu/agriculture/direct-support/direct-payments/docs/small-farmers-scheme_en.pdf (accessed on 28 September 2018). [119]

European Commission (2016), *Nature Protection and Environmental Impact Assessment*, http://ec.europa.eu/environment/legal/law/2/module_3_2.htm (accessed on 15 May 2019). [75]

European Commission (2008), *Proposal for a Directive of the European Parliament and of the Council amending Directive 2003/87/EC so as to improve and extend the greenhouse gas emission allowance trading system of the Community*, Commission of the European Communities, Brussels, https://eur-lex.europa.eu/legal-content/EN/TXT/?uri=COM:2008:0016:FIN (accessed on 28 August 2018). [86]

European External Action Service (2018), *Palm Oil Facts & Figures on Trade and Sustainability*, European Commission, Brussels, https://eeas.europa.eu/sites/eeas/files/20180920_palm_oil_fact_sheet_en.pdf (accessed on 1 March 2019). [166]

Eurostat (2018), *Agriculture, Forestry and Fisheries Statistics: 2018 edition*, European Union. [147]

FAO (2017), *Country Factsheet on Food and Agriculture Policy Trends: Indonesia*, Food and Agriculture Organization of the United Nations, Rome, Italy, http://dx.doi.org/10.1002/app5.83/full. [71]

FAO (2017), *SAVE FOOD FOR A BETTER CLIMATE converting the Food loss and waste challenge into climate action*, Food and Agriculture Organization, Rome, http://www.fao.org/3/a-i8000e.pdf (accessed on 28 February 2018). [200]

FAO (2015), *Global Forest Resources Assessment 2015*, Forest and Agriculture Organisation of the United Nations, Rome, http://www.fao.org/publications (accessed on 2 October 2018). [177]

FAO (2013), *Food wastage footprint: Impacts on natural resources - Summary report*, Food and Agriculture Organisation of the United Nations, Rome, http://www.fao.org/docrep/018/i3347e/i3347e.pdf. [195]

Farrelly, N. and G. Gallagher (2015), "The potential availability of land for afforestation in the Republic of Ireland", *Irish Forestry*, Vol. 72, pp. 120-138. [149]

Fearnside, P. (2015), "Amazon dams and waterways: Brazil's Tapajós Basin plans.", *Ambio*, Vol. 44/5, pp. 426-39, http://dx.doi.org/10.1007/s13280-015-0642-z. [31]

Fédération nationale du bois (2018), *Crise: LÉxportation croissante de chene brut ruine la filière francaise de la transformation qui en appelle au président de la république*, http://www.fnbois.com/wp-content/uploads/2018/03/DP_FNB_BoisFran%C3%A7aisEnDanger_draft9_050218.pdf (accessed on 11 February 2019). [175]

Feehan, J., D. Gillmor and N. Culleton (2005), "Effects of an agri-environment scheme on farmland biodiversity in Ireland", *Agriculture, Ecosystems & Environment*, Vol. 107/2-3, pp. 275-286, http://dx.doi.org/10.1016/J.AGEE.2004.10.024. [128]

Figueiredo, P. (2016), "New challenges for public research organisations in agricultural innovation in developing economies: Evidence from Embrapa in Brazil's soybean industry", *The Quarterly Review of Economics and Finance*, Vol. 62, pp. 21-32, http://dx.doi.org/10.1016/J.QREF.2016.07.011. [116]

Finger, R. et al. (2017), "Revisiting Pesticide Taxation Schemes", *Ecological Economics*, Vol. 134, pp. 263-266, http://dx.doi.org/10.1016/J.ECOLECON.2016.12.001. [78]

Frank, S. et al. (2013), "How effective are the sustainability criteria accompanying the European Union 2020 biofuel targets?", *GCB Bioenergy*, Vol. 5/3, pp. 306-314, http://dx.doi.org/10.1111/j.1757-1707.2012.01188.x. [165]

Frank, S. et al. (2017), "Reducing greenhouse gas emissions in agriculture without compromising food security?", *Environmental Research Letters*, Vol. 12/10, p. 105004, http://dx.doi.org/10.1088/1748-9326/aa8c83. [85]

Freitas, F. et al. (2018), "Potential increase of legal deforestation in Brazilian Amazon after Forest Act revision", *Nature Sustainability*, Vol. 1/11, pp. 665-670, http://dx.doi.org/10.1038/s41893-018-0171-4. [61]

García-Montiel, E. et al. (2017), "An Analysis of Non-State and State Approaches for Forest Certification in Mexico", http://dx.doi.org/10.3390/f8080290. [179]

Gasparri, N. and Y. de Waroux (2015), "The Coupling of South American Soybean and Cattle Production Frontiers: New Challenges for Conservation Policy and Land Change Science", *Conservation Letters*, Vol. 8/4, pp. 290-298, http://dx.doi.org/10.1111/conl.12121. [186]

Gaveau, D. et al. (2012), "Examining protected area effectiveness in Sumatra: importance of regulations governing unprotected lands", *Conservation Letters*, Vol. 5/2, pp. 142-148, http://dx.doi.org/10.1111/j.1755-263X.2011.00220.x. [43]

Gaveau, D. et al. (2017), "Overlapping Land Claims Limit the Use of Satellites to Monitor No-Deforestation Commitments and No-Burning Compliance", *Conservation Letters*, Vol. 10/2, pp. 257-264, http://dx.doi.org/10.1111/conl.12256. [7]

Gaveau, D., H. Wandono and F. Setiabudi (2007), "Three decades of deforestation in southwest Sumatra: Have protected areas halted forest loss and logging, and promoted re-growth?", *Biological Conservation*, Vol. 134/8, pp. 495-504, http://dx.doi.org/10.1016/j.biocon.2006.08.035. [42]

Gawith, D. and I. Hodge (2018), "Moving beyond description to explore the empirics of adaptation constraints", *Ecological Indicators*, Vol. 95, pp. 907-916, http://dx.doi.org/10.1016/J.ECOLIND.2018.08.022. [150]

George, C. and S. Yamaguchi (2018), "Assessing Implementation of Environmental Provisions in Regional Trade Agreements", *OECD Trade and Environment Working Papers*, No. 2018/01, OECD Publishing, Paris, https://dx.doi.org/10.1787/91aacfea-en. [69]

Gibbs, H. et al. (2015), "Brazil's Soy Moratorium", *Science*, Vol. 347/6220, pp. 377-378, http://dx.doi.org/10.1126/science.aaa0181. [51]

González, A. (2017), *Políticas públicas para la alimentación en México*, https://fr.slideshare.net/FAOoftheUN/polticas-pblicas-para-la-alimentacin-en-mxico (accessed on 2 November 2018). [208]

Gore-Langton, L. (2017), *France's food waste ban: One year on*, https://www.foodnavigator.com/Article/2017/03/24/France-s-food-waste-ban-One-year-on (accessed on 10 January 2019). [205]

Government of Indonesia and European Free Trade Association (2018), *Comprehensive economic partnership agreement between the Republic of Indonesia and the EFTA states*, https://www.efta.int/sites/default/files/documents/legal-texts/free-trade-relations/indonesia/efta-indonesia-main-agreement.pdf (accessed on 28 February 2019). [64]

Government of Ireland (2018), *Project Ireland 2040*, Government of Ireland. [34]

Governments of the United States; Mexico and Canada (2018), *UMSCA: Chapter 24 - Environment*, https://ustr.gov/sites/default/files/files/agreements/FTA/USMCA/Text/24_Environment.pdf (accessed on 15 February 2019). [67]

Grosjean, G. et al. (2018), "Options to overcome the barriers to pricing European agricultural emissions", *Climate Policy*, Vol. 18/2, pp. 151-169, http://dx.doi.org/10.1080/14693062.2016.1258630. [87]

Gruère, G. (2013), *A Characterisation of Environmental Labelling and Information Schemes*, OECD publishing, Paris, https://www.oecd-ilibrary.org/environment-and-sustainable-development/a-characterisation-of-environmental-labelling-and-information-schemes_5k3z11hpdgq2-en (accessed on 28 September 2018). [181]

Guedes, F. and S. Seehusen (2012), - *Gestão - Série Biodiversidade 42 - Pagamentos por Serviços Ambientais na Mata Atlântica - Biodiversity Series 42 - Payments for Environmental Services in the Atlantic Forest*, MMA - Ministério do Meio Ambiente, http://www.terrabrasilis.org.br/ecotecadigital/index.php/estantes/gestao/2109-serie-biodiversidade-42-pagamentos-por-servicos-ambientais-na-mata-atlantica (accessed on 28 August 2018). [101]

Hansen, M. et al. (2013), “High-resolution global maps of 21st-century forest cover change.”, *Science (New York, N.Y.)*, Vol. 342/6160, pp. 850-3, http://dx.doi.org/10.1126/science.1244693. [53]

Hansen, M., S. Stehman and P. Potapov (2010), “Quantification of global gross forest cover loss.”, *Proceedings of the National Academy of Sciences of the United States of America*, Vol. 107/19, pp. 8650-5, http://dx.doi.org/10.1073/pnas.0912668107. [194]

Hansen, O. (2018), “Deforestation Caused by Illegal Avocado Farming: A Case Study on the Effectiveness of Mexico' s Payment for Ecosystem Services Program”, *University of Miami Inter-American Law Review*, Vol. 89, https://repository.law.miami.edu/umialr/vol49/iss1/6 (accessed on 29 August 2018). [16]

Hardelin, J. and J. Lankoski (2018), “Land use and ecosystem services”, *OECD Food, Agriculture and Fisheries Papers*, No. 114, OECD Publishing, Paris, https://dx.doi.org/10.1787/c7ec938e-en. [76]

Haupt, F. et al. (2018), *Progress on Corporate Commitments and their Implementation 2 2 Progress on Corporate Commitments and their Implementation*, https://www.tfa2020.org/wp-content/uploads/2018/06/Progress-on-Corporate-Commitments-and-their-Implementation.pdf (accessed on 20 March 2019). [185]

Henderson, B. and J. Lankoski (2019), “Evaluating the environmental impact of agricultural policies”, *OECD Food, Agriculture and Fisheries Papers*, No. 130, OECD Publishing, Paris, https://dx.doi.org/10.1787/add0f27c-en. [112]

Henz, G. and G. Porpino (2017), “Food losses and waste: how Brazil is facing this global challenge?”, *Horticultura Brasileira*, http://dx.doi.org/10.1590/s0102-053620170402. [204]

Herrera, D. et al. (2017), “Upstream watershed condition predicts rural children's health across 35 developing countries”, *Nature Communications*, Vol. 8/1, p. 811, http://dx.doi.org/10.1038/s41467-017-00775-2. [23]

Hia, A. and N. Kusumawardani (2016), “Indonesian Sustainable Palm Oil (ISPO), A Way to Reach The European Union Renewable Energy Directive (EU RED) 2009 and Boosting Indonesian Palm Oil Market to European Union (EU) 2009-2014”, *AEGIS: Journal of International Relations*, Vol. 1/1, http://e-journal.president.ac.id/presunivojs/index.php/AEGIS/article/view/83. [170]

INRA; IGN (2017), *The Role of French Forests and the Forestry Sector in Climate-Change Mitigation: Summary of a study conducted by INRA and IGN for the Ministry of Agriculture and Food*, INRA and IGN, https://inventaire-forestier.ign.fr/IMG/pdf/419860-c1d9a-resource-etude-forets-bois-changement-climatique-resume-anglais.pdf (accessed on 30 August 2018). [141]

Irawan, S., L. Tacconi and I. Ring (2013), "Stakeholders' incentives for land-use change and REDD+: The case of Indonesia", *Ecological Economics*, Vol. 87, pp. 75-83, http://dx.doi.org/10.1016/j.ecolecon.2012.12.018. [158]

Jørgen, R. et al. (2016), *Food losses and food waste Extent, underlying drivers and impact assessment of prevention approaches.*, http://ifro.ku.dk/publikationer/ifro_serier/rapporter/FindotherIFROCommissionedWork. [202]

Koch, N. et al. (2019), "Agricultural Productivity and Forest Conservation: Evidence from the Brazilian Amazon", *American Journal of Agricultural Economics*, Vol. 101/3, pp. 919-940, http://dx.doi.org/10.1093/ajae/aay110. [117]

Kummu, M. et al. (2012), "Lost food, wasted resources: Global food supply chain losses and their impacts on freshwater, cropland, and fertiliser use", *Science of The Total Environment*, Vol. 438, pp. 477-489, http://dx.doi.org/10.1016/J.SCITOTENV.2012.08.092. [197]

Lambin, E. et al. (2018), "The role of supply-chain initiatives in reducing deforestation", *Nature Climate Change*, Vol. 8/2, pp. 109-116, http://dx.doi.org/10.1038/s41558-017-0061-1. [188]

Lambin, E. and P. Meyfroidt (2011), "Global land use change, economic globalization, and the looming land scarcity.", *Proceedings of the National Academy of Sciences of the United States of America*, Vol. 108/9, pp. 3465-72, http://dx.doi.org/10.1073/pnas.1100480108. [5]

Lankoski, J. et al. (2015), "Environmental Co-benefits and Stacking in Environmental Markets", *OECD Food, Agriculture and Fisheries Papers*, No. 72, OECD Publishing, Paris, https://dx.doi.org/10.1787/5js6g5khdvhj-en. [131]

le Polain de Waroux, Y. et al. (2016), "Land-use policies and corporate investments in agriculture in the Gran Chaco and Chiquitano", *Proceedings of the National Academy of Sciences*, Vol. 113/15, pp. 4021-4026, http://dx.doi.org/10.1073/pnas.1602646113. [187]

Le Tourneau, F. (2015), "The sustainability challenges of indigenous territories in Brazil's Amazonia", *Current Opinion in Environmental Sustainability*, Vol. 14, pp. 213-220, http://dx.doi.org/10.1016/J.COSUST.2015.07.017. [47]

Leining, C. and S. Kerr (2016), "Lessons Learned from the New Zealand Emissions Trading Scheme". [89]

Leverkus, A. et al. (2017), "Mexico's logging threatens butterflies.", *Science (New York, N.Y.)*, Vol. 358/6366, p. 1008, http://dx.doi.org/10.1126/science.aar3826. [17]

Ling, M. et al. (2018), *A review of ecosystem service valuation progress and approaches by the Member States of the European Union*, UNEP-WCMC, Cambridge, UK. [25]

MAA (2016), *Le programme national de la forêt et du bois 2016 - 2026*, Ministère de l'Agriculture et de l'Alimentation, https://agriculture.gouv.fr/le-programme-national-de-la-foret-et-du-bois-2016-2026 (accessed on 6 June 2019). [137]

Maestre Andrés, S. et al. (2012), "Ineffective biodiversity policy due to five rebound effects", *Ecosystem Services*, http://dx.doi.org/10.1016/j.ecoser.2012.07.003. [4]

Martha, G., E. Alves and E. Contini (2012), "Land-saving approaches and beef production growth in Brazil", *Agricultural Systems*, Vol. 110, pp. 173-177, http://dx.doi.org/10.1016/J.AGSY.2012.03.001. [191]

May, P. et al. (2016), *The context of REDD+ in Brazil: drivers, agents, and institutions - 3rd edition*, Center for International Forestry Research (CIFOR), http://dx.doi.org/10.17528/cifor/006338. [107]

Mayrand, K., M. Paquin and S. Gagnon-Turcotte (2008), "Environmental Assessment of NAFTA: Lessons Learned from CEC's Trade and Environment Symposia", *Background Paper for the Experts Roundtable JPAC Public Session, Phoenix, Arizona, April 2008*, http://www.cec.org (accessed on 12 June 2019). [65]

McDermott, C., L. Irland and P. Pacheco (2015), "Forest certification and legality initiatives in the Brazilian Amazon: Lessons for effective and equitable forest governance", *Forest Policy and Economics*, Vol. 50, pp. 134-142, http://dx.doi.org/10.1016/J.FORPOL.2014.05.011. [178]

Mcfarland, W., S. Whitley and G. Kissinger (2015), *Subsidies to key commodities driving forest loss Implications for private climate finance*, Overseas Development Institute, London, http://www.odi.org. [113]

McMahon, B. et al. (2010), "Interactions between livestock systems and biodiversity in South-East Ireland", *Agriculture, Ecosystems & Environment*, Vol. 139/1-2, pp. 232-238, http://dx.doi.org/10.1016/J.AGEE.2010.08.008. [129]

Mekhilef, S., S. Siga and R. Saidur (2011), "A review on palm oil biodiesel as a source of renewable fuel", *Renewable and Sustainable Energy Reviews*, Vol. 15/4, pp. 1937-1949, http://dx.doi.org/10.1016/J.RSER.2010.12.012. [168]

Mello, F. (2015), *ABC- National Plan for Low Carbon Emissions in Agriculture - Brazilian Experience, presentation to the OECD*, https://csa.guide/csa/brazil-s-low-carbon-agriculture-abc-plan (accessed on 29 August 2018). [132]

Metternicht, G. (2017), *GLOBAL LAND OUTLOOK WORKING PAPER: LAND USE PLANNING*, United Nations Convention to Combat Desertification, https://static1.squarespace.com/static/5694c48bd82d5e9597570999/t/593a42d7197aea88458703df/1496990441721/Land+Use+Planning+__G_Metternicht.pdf (accessed on 31 August 2018). [27]

MfE (2013), *New Zealand's Sixth National Communication under the United Nations Framework Convention on Climate Change and Kyoto Protocol*. [142]

Miettinen, J. et al. (2017), "From carbon sink to carbon source: extensive peat oxidation in insular Southeast Asia since 1990", *Environmental Research Letters*, Vol. 12/2, p. 024014, http://dx.doi.org/10.1088/1748-9326/aa5b6f. [49]

Ministère de la transition écologique et solidaire (2018), *Strategie nationale de lutte contre la deforestation importee 2018-2030*, Government of France, Paris, https://www.ecologique-solidaire.gouv.fr/sites/default/files/2018.11.14_SNDI_0.pdf (accessed on 4 February 2019). [164]

Ministério da Agricultura, Pecuária e abastecimento (2018), *Adoção e mitigação de Gases de Efeitos Estufa pelas tecnologias do Plano Setorial de Mitigação e Adaptação às Mudanças Climáticas (Plano ABC)*, Government of Brazil, Brasilia, http://www.agricultura.gov.br/assuntos/sustentabilidade/plano-abc/plano-abc-em-numeros/arquivos/ResumodaadooemitigaodegasesdeefeitosestufapelastecnologiasdoPlanoABCPerodo2010a2018nov.pdf (accessed on 3 June 2019). [134]

Ministry for the Environment (2010), *The New Zealand Waste Strategy: Reducing harm, improving efficiency | Ministry for the Environment*, http://www.mfe.govt.nz/publications/waste/new-zealand-waste-strategy-reducing-harm-improving-efficiency (accessed on 24 October 2018). [214]

Ministry of Agriculture (2011), *Pedoman Perkebunan Kelapa Sawit Berkelanjutan Indonesia (Indonesian Sustainable Palm Oil/ ISPO)*, Government of Indonesia, Jakarta, http://perundangan.pertanian.go.id/admin/file/Permentan%2011-2015%20ISPO.pdf. [171]

Ministry of Agriculture and the Technology Assessment and Application Agency (n.d.), *Biomass Town Plan: Palembang City, Indonesia*, http://www.scielo.org.co/pdf/esju/v17n1/v17n1a01.pdf. [211]

Ministry of Agriculture; Fisheries and Food Supply (2017), *Intercâmbio comercial do agronegócio principais mercados de destino*, Government of Brazil, Brasilia, http://www.agricultura.gov.br/assuntos/relacoes-internacionais/documentos/intercambio-comercial-do-agronegocio-10a-edicao/IntercambioComercial2017_web.pdf/view. [172]

Ministry of Environment and Forestry (2018), *The State of Indonesia's Forests 2018*, The Ministry of Environment and Forestry, Republic of Indonesia. [144]

Ministry of Finance (2018), *Amendment to the regulation of the Minister of Finance number 81 / PMK.05 / 2018 concerning the tariff service agency's general service to the palm plantation funding management agency at the Ministry of Finance*, http://www.bpdp.or.id/wp-content/uploads/2018/12/PMK-15-2018-Pungutan-Ekspor-Sawit.pdf. [70]

Monteiro, J. (2016), "Typology of Environment-related Provisions in Regional Trade Agreements", *WTO Working Paper*, No. ERSD-2016-13, World Trade Organization, Geneva, Switzerland, https://www.wto.org/english/res_e/reser_e/ersd201613_e.pdf (accessed on 11 June 2019). [63]

Moreno-Peñaranda, R. et al. (2018), "Stakeholder Perceptions of the Ecosystem Services and Human Well-Being Impacts of Palm Oil Biofuels in Indonesia and Malaysia", Springer, Tokyo, http://dx.doi.org/10.1007/978-4-431-54895-9_10. [169]

MPI (2018), *Planting one billion trees | MPI - Ministry for Primary Industries. A New Zealand Government Department.*, https://www.mpi.govt.nz/funding-and-programmes/forestry/planting-one-billion-trees/ (accessed on 9 November 2018). [136]

Muller, C. and M. Neal (2018), "The impact of nutrient regulations on dairy farm land values in Southland", *New Zealand Journal of Agricultural Research*, pp. 1-19, http://dx.doi.org/10.1080/00288233.2018.1509876. [83]

Nepstad, D. et al. (2014), "Slowing Amazon deforestation through public policy and interventions in beef and soy supply chains.", *Science (New York, N.Y.)*, Vol. 344/6188, pp. 1118-23, http://dx.doi.org/10.1126/science.1248525. [52]

Newell, R. and W. Pizer (2003), "Regulating stock externalities under uncertainty", *Journal of Environmental Economics and Management*, Vol. 45/2, pp. 416-432, http://dx.doi.org/10.1016/S0095-0696(02)00016-5. [1]

Newton, P. et al. (2016), "Overcoming barriers to low carbon agriculture and forest restoration in Brazil: The Rural SustentÃ¡vel project", http://dx.doi.org/10.1016/j.wdp.2016.11.011. [133]

Nolte, C. et al. (2013), "Governance regime and location influence avoided deforestation success of protected areas in the Brazilian Amazon", *Proceedings of the National Academy of Sciences of the United States of America*, Vol. 110/13, pp. 4956-4961, http://dx.doi.org/10.1073/pnas.1214786110. [40]

Nugraha, I. (2015), *Faulty impact assessments plague Indonesian mines: Komnas HAM*, Mongabay, https://news.mongabay.com/2015/04/faulty-impact-assessments-plague-indonesian-mines-komnas-ham/ (accessed on 26 July 2018). [73]

Nurfatriani, F. et al. (2015), "Redesigning Indonesian forest fiscal policy to support forest conservation", *Forest Policy and Economics*, http://dx.doi.org/10.1016/j.forpol.2015.07.006. [146]

NZIER (2017), *Plantation Forestry Statistics: Contribution of forestry to New Zealand*, New Zealand Institute of Economic Research, https://nzier.org.nz/static/media/filer_public/c6/a5/c6a55bbf-8f36-484e-82a0-91bb59211880/plantation_forestry_statistics.pdf. [148]

Observatory of Public Sector Innovation (OECD-OSPI) (2013), *The Indonesian Timber Legality Assurance System (SVLK) - Observatory of Public Sector Innovation Observatory of Public Sector Innovation*, https://oecd-opsi.org/innovations/the-indonesian-timber-legality-assurance-system-svlk/ (accessed on 6 March 2019). [9]

OECD (2019), *Agricultural Policy Monitoring and Evaluation 2019*, OECD Publishing, Paris, https://dx.doi.org/10.1787/39bfe6f3-en. [120]

OECD (2019), *Agricultural support* (indicator), http://dx.doi.org/10.1787/6ea85c58-en (accessed on 22 August 2019). [110]

OECD (2019), "Biodiverisity: Protected areas", *OECD Environment Statistics* (database), http://dx.doi.org/10.1787/5fa661ce-en (accessed on 15 May 2019). [39]

OECD (2019), *Biodiversity: Finance and the Economic and Business Case for Action*, http://www.oecd.org/environment/resources/biodiversity/G7-report-Biodiversity-Finance-and-the-Economic-and-Business-Case-for-Action.pdf (accessed on 22 May 2019). [22]

OECD (2019), *Green Growth Policy Review of Indonesia*, Organisaiton for Economic Co-operation and Development. [12]

OECD (2018), *Agricultural Policy Monitoring and Evaluation 2018*, OECD Publishing, Paris, http://dx.doi.org/10.1787/agr_pol-2018-en. [114]

OECD (2018), *Deepening the Sustainable Productivity Framework*, Organisation for Economic Co-operation and Development, Paris, France. [124]

OECD (2018), *OECD Companion to the Inventory of Support Measures for Fossil Fuels 2018 - en - OECD*, OECD publishing, https://www.oecd.org/tax/oecd-companion-to-the-inventory-of-support-measures-for-fossil-fuels-2018-9789264286061-en.htm (accessed on 29 August 2018). [152]

OECD (2018), *Open Government Data in Mexico: The Way Forward*, OECD Digital Government Studies, OECD Publishing, Paris, https://dx.doi.org/10.1787/9789264297944-en. [161]

OECD (2018), *Rethinking Urban Sprawl: Moving Towards Sustainable Cities*, OECD Publishing, Paris, http://dx.doi.org/10.1787/9789264189881-en. [33]

OECD (2017), *Agricultural Policy Monitoring and Evaluation 2017*, OECD Publishing, Paris, https://dx.doi.org/10.1787/agr_pol-2017-en. [122]

OECD (2017), *Environmental Performance Reviews Mid-term progress report: Mexico*, https://one.oecd.org/document/ENV/EPOC/WPEP(2018)5/en/pdf (accessed on 13 March 2018). [82]

OECD (2017), *OECD Environmental Performance Reviews: New Zealand 2017*, OECD Environmental Performance Reviews, OECD Publishing, Paris, http://dx.doi.org/10.1787/9789264268203-en. [88]

OECD (2017), *The Political Economy of Biodiversity Policy Reform*, OECD Publishing, Paris, http://dx.doi.org/10.1787/9789264269545-en. [81]

OECD (2016), *Biodiversity Offsets: Effective Design and Implementation*, OECD Publishing, Paris, http://dx.doi.org/10.1787/9789264222519-en. [94]

OECD (2016), *Effective Carbon Rates: Pricing CO2 through Taxes and Emissions Trading Systems*, OECD Publishing, Paris, http://dx.doi.org/10.1787/9789264260115-en. [84]

OECD (2016), "Mexican Environmental Compensation Scheme for Land-Use Change in Forested Areas", in *Biodiversity Offsets: Effective Design and Implementation*, OECD Publishing, Paris, http://dx.doi.org/10.1787/9789264222519-10-en. [95]

OECD (2016), *OECD Environmental Performance Reviews: France 2016*, OECD Environmental Performance Reviews, OECD Publishing, Paris, http://dx.doi.org/10.1787/9789264252714-en. [37]

OECD (2016), *The PSE Manual*, OECD Publishing, Paris, http://www.oecd.org/agriculture/topics/agricultural-policy-monitoring-and-evaluation/documents/producer-support-estimates-manual.pdf. [111]

OECD (2015), *Fostering Green Growth in Agriculture: The Role of Training, Advisory Services and Extension Initiatives*, OECD Green Growth Studies, OECD Publishing, Paris, https://dx.doi.org/10.1787/9789264232198-en. [192]

OECD (2015), *OECD Environmental Performance Reviews: Brazil 2015*, OECD Environmental Performance Reviews, OECD Publishing, Paris, http://dx.doi.org/10.1787/9789264240094-en. [13]

OECD (2013), *OECD Environmental Performance Reviews: Mexico 2013*, OECD Environmental Performance Reviews, OECD Publishing, Paris, http://dx.doi.org/10.1787/9789264180109-en. [99]

OECD (2013), *Scaling up finance mechanisms for biodiversity*, OECD Publishing, Paris, http://www.oecd.org/env/resources/OECD%20Finance%20for%20Biodiversity%20%5Bf%5D%20%5Blr%5D%20WEB%20SM.pdf. [20]

OECD (2011), *Food and Agriculture*, OECD Green Growth Studies, OECD Publishing, Paris, http://dx.doi.org/10.1787/9789264107250-en. [21]

OECD (2006), "Decoupling: A Conceptual Overview", *OECD Papers*, Vol. 5/11, https://dx.doi.org/10.1787/oecd_papers-v5-art37-en. [213]

OECD (2020, forthcoming), *Economic and Environmental Sustainability Performance of Environmental Policies in Agriculture: A Literature Review*, Organisation of Economic Co-operation and Development. [121]

OECD (n.d.), *Options for climate change mitigation in the agricultural sector: A partial equilibrium analysis*, Organisation for Economic Co-operation and Development, Paris. [199]

OECD/FAO (2018), *OECD-FAO Pilot project on the implementation of the OECD-FAO Guidance for Responsible Agricultural Supply Chains : Baseline Report*, http://www.oecd.org/about/publishing/corrigenda.htm. (accessed on 20 March 2019). [190]

OECD/FAO (2016), *OECD-FAO Guidance for Responsible Agricultural Supply Chains*, OECD Publishing, Paris, https://dx.doi.org/10.1787/9789264251052-en. [189]

Ortiz Tapia, E. (2018), *The black hole in Mexico's Forestry Law - Investigación | Ojo Público*, OjoPúblico.com, https://ojo-publico.com/902/black-hole-mexicos-forestry-law (accessed on 7 March 2019). [62]

PEFC (2010), *PEFC International Standard: Requirements for certification schemes*, PEFC Council, Geneva, https://www.scribd.com/document/44967214/Sustainable-Forest-Management-PEFC-ST-1003-2010#download&from_embed (accessed on 18 September 2018). [176]

Pfaff, A., F. Santiago-Ávila and L. Joppa (2016), "Evolving Protected-Area Impacts in Mexico: Political Shifts as Suggested by Impact Evaluations", *Forests*, Vol. 8/1, p. 17, http://dx.doi.org/10.3390/f8010017. [41]

Priefer, C., J. Jörissen and K. Bräutigam (2016), "Food waste prevention in Europe – A cause-driven approach to identify the most relevant leverage points for action", *Resources, Conservation and Recycling*, Vol. 109, pp. 155-165, http://dx.doi.org/10.1016/J.RESCONREC.2016.03.004. [212]

QEII National Trust (2018), *FAQs: About Covenanting*, http://www.openspace.org.nz/Site/About_covenanting/FAQs.aspx. [38]

Quétier, F., B. Regnery and H. Levrel (2014), "No net loss of biodiversity or paper offsets? A critical review of the French no net loss policy", *Environmental Science and Policy*, Vol. 38, pp. 120-131, http://dx.doi.org/10.1016/j.envsci.2013.11.009. [98]

Ramirez-Reyes, C. et al. (2018), "Payments for ecosystem services in Mexico reduce forest fragmentation", *Ecological Applications*, http://dx.doi.org/10.1002/eap.1753. [100]

Republic of Indonesia (2016), "First Nationally Determined Contribution", http://www4.unfccc.int/ndcregistry/PublishedDocuments/Indonesia%20First/First%20NDC%20Indonesia_submitted%20to%20UNFCCC%20Set_November%20%202016.pdf (accessed on 12 June 2018). [138]

Robinson, B., M. Holland and L. Naughton-Treves (2013), "Does secure land tenure save forests? A meta-analysis of the relationship between land tenure and tropical deforestation", *Global Environmental Change*, http://dx.doi.org/10.1016/j.gloenvcha.2013.05.012. [6]

Rochedo, P. et al. (2018), "The threat of political bargaining to climate mitigation in Brazil", *Nature Climate Change*, p. 1, http://dx.doi.org/10.1038/s41558-018-0213-y. [15]

Sahide, M. and L. Giessen (2015), "The fragmented land use administration in Indonesia - Analysing bureaucratic responsibilities influencing tropical rainforest transformation systems", *Land Use Policy*, http://dx.doi.org/10.1016/j.landusepol.2014.11.005. [8]

Sainteny, G. et al. (2011), *Les aides publiques dommageables à la biodiversité*, Centre d'analyse stratégique, http://archives.gouvernement.fr/fillon_version2/sites/default/files/fichiers_joints/Aides_dommageables_a_la_biodiversite_Rapport_CAS_Octobre2011.pdf (accessed on 3 June 2019). [115]

Santika, T. et al. (2017), "Community forest management in Indonesia: Avoided deforestation in the context of anthropogenic and climate complexities", *Global Environmental Change*, Vol. 46/August, pp. 60-71, http://dx.doi.org/10.1016/j.gloenvcha.2017.08.002. [157]

Schleifer, P. and Y. Sun (2018), "Emerging markets and private governance: the political economy of sustainable palm oil in China and India", *Review of International Political Economy*, pp. 1-25, http://dx.doi.org/10.1080/09692290.2017.1418759. [183]

SEEG (2018), *Emissions By Sector - Mudança de Uso da Terra e Floresta|*, http://plataforma.seeg.eco.br/sectors/mudanca-de-uso-da-terra-e-floresta (accessed on 12 November 2018). [44]

Shahab, N. (2016), *Indonesia: One Map Policy*, Open Government Partnership, https://www.opengovpartnership.org/sites/default/files/case-study_Indonesia_One-Map-Policy.pdf (accessed on 26 March 2018). [30]

Simonet, G. et al. (2018), "Effectiveness of a REDD+ Project in Reducing Deforestation in the Brazilian Amazon*", *American Journal of Agricultural Economics*, http://dx.doi.org/10.1093/ajae/aay028. [109]

Soares-Filho, B. et al. (2010), "Role of Brazilian Amazon protected areas in climate change mitigation.", *Proceedings of the National Academy of Sciences of the United States of America*, Vol. 107/24, pp. 10821-6, http://dx.doi.org/10.1073/pnas.0913048107. [45]

Souza, B. and L. Sánchez (2018), "Biodiversity offsets in limestone quarries: Investigation of practices in Brazil", *Resources Policy*, Vol. 57, pp. 213-223, http://dx.doi.org/10.1016/J.RESOURPOL.2018.03.007. [97]

State Governments of Acre, Chiapas, A. (2010), *Memorandum of Understanding on Environmental Cooperation Between the State of Acre of the Federative Republic of Brazil, the State of Chiapas of the United Mexican States, and the State of California of the United States of America*, Authors, https://www.arb.ca.gov/cc/capandtrade/sectorbasedoffsets/2010%20MOU%20Acre-California-Chiapas.pdf (accessed on 13 June 2019). [92]

Strassburg, B. et al. (2017), "Moment of truth for the Cerrado hotspot", *Nature Ecology & Evolution*, Vol. 1/4, p. 0099, http://dx.doi.org/10.1038/s41559-017-0099. [55]

Suich, H. et al. (2017), "Payments for ecosystem services in Indonesia", *Oryx*, Vol. 51/3, pp. 489-497, http://dx.doi.org/10.1017/s0030605316000259. [104]

Sutton, M. et al. (2011), *The European nitrogen assessment : sources, effects, and policy perspectives*, Cambridge University Press, Cambridge (UK), https://inis.iaea.org/search/search.aspx?orig_q=RN:42079361 (accessed on 28 August 2018). [77]

Te Uru Rākau (2018), *One Billion Trees Fund: Report on Policy and Design Recommendations*, Forestry New Zealand, https://www.mpi.govt.nz/dmsdocument/32908-3-appendix1-report-on-policy-and-design-recommendations-oia (accessed on 17 May 2019). [143]

The Ministry of Agriculture (2015), *Rencana Strategis Kementerian Pertanian Tahun 2015-2019*, The Ministry of Agriculture, Jakarta, Indonesia. [209]

The Republic of Indonesia (2017), *Third National Communication Under the United Nations Framework Convention on Climate Change*, UNFCCC. [105]

The Tax Working Group (2019), *Future of Tax: Final Report Volume I - Recommendations*, https://taxworkinggroup.govt.nz/resources/future-tax-final-report-vol-i-html (accessed on 22 May 2019). [59]

Tilman, D. et al. (2017), "Future threats to biodiversity and pathways to their prevention", *Nature*, Vol. 546/7656, pp. 73-81, http://dx.doi.org/10.1038/nature22900. [196]

Tilman, D. et al. (2009), "Beneficial Biofuels—The Food, Energy, and Environment Trilemma", *Science*, Vol. 325/5938, pp. 4-5, http://dx.doi.org/10.1126/science.1177970. [154]

Tonini, D., K. Brogaard and T. Astrup (2017), *Food waste prevention in Denmark Identification of hotspots and potentials with Life Cycle Assessment*. [201]

Urrunaga, J., A. Johnson and I. Orbegozo Sánchez (2018), *Moment of Truth: promise or peril for the Amazon as Peru confronts its illegal timber trade*, Environmental Investigation Agency, Washington, D.C., http://www.eia-global.org/momentoftruth (accessed on 7 March 2019). [19]

USDA (2017), *Brazil Biofuels Annual*, United States Department of Agriculture, https://gain.fas.usda.gov/Recent%20GAIN%20Publications/Biofuels%20Annual_Sao%20Paulo%20ATO_Brazil_9-15-2017.pdf (accessed on 29 August 2018). [153]

Van Der Sluys, C. (2018), *The Evolution of Strategic Environmental Assessment in Indonesia*, Environmental Support Programme - Indonesia, Jakarta, Indonesia, http://www.esp3.org/images/Library/PapersReports/SEA-Review-Eng.pdf (accessed on 26 July 2018). [74]

Verdone, M. (2018), *The world's largest private sector? Recognising the cumulative economic value of small-scale forest and farm producers*, IUCN, International Union for Conservation of Nature, http://dx.doi.org/10.2305/IUCN.CH.2018.13.en. [180]

Visser, M. et al. (2007), "The Irish agri-environment: How turlough users and non-users view converging EU agendas of Natura 2000 and CAP", *Land Use Policy*, Vol. 24/2, pp. 362-373, http://dx.doi.org/10.1016/J.LANDUSEPOL.2006.04.004. [36]

WAVES (2017), *Indonesia Country Report 2017*, Wealth Accounting and Valuation of Ecosystem Services, http://www.wavespartnership.org (accessed on 22 October 2018). [26]

Willett, W. et al. (2019), "Food in the Anthropocene: the EAT-Lancet Commission on healthy diets from sustainable food systems.", *Lancet (London, England)*, Vol. 0/0, http://dx.doi.org/10.1016/S0140-6736(18)31788-4. [198]

Wolff, N. et al. (2018), "Impacts of tropical deforestation on local temperature and human well-being perceptions", *Global Environmental Change*, Vol. 52, pp. 181-189, http://dx.doi.org/10.1016/J.GLOENVCHA.2018.07.004. [24]

Woodworth, P. (2018), *The farmer and the ecologist should be friends*, Irish Times, https://www.irishtimes.com/opinion/the-farmer-and-the-ecologist-should-be-friends-1.2143105 (accessed on 25 July 2018). [35]

Wright, T., A. Rahmanulloh and A. Abdi (2017), *Indonesia Biofuels Annual Report 2017 Biofuels Annual Indonesia*, USDA, Foreign Agricultural Service, https://gain.fas.usda.gov/Recent%20GAIN%20Publications/Biofuels%20Annual_Jakarta_Indonesia_6-20-2017.pdf (accessed on 18 June 2018). [60]

Notes

[1] i) Forests ecosystems; ii) Marine and coastal environments; iii) Urban ecosystems; iv) Rocky and high mountain ecosystems; v) Agricultural ecosystems; vi) Continental wetlands

[2] Law No. 32/2009 on Environmental Protection and Management

[3] As defined by the IUCN: A protected area is a clearly defined geographical space, recognised, dedicated and managed, through legal or other effective means, to achieve the long term conservation of nature with associated ecosystem services and cultural values. (https://www.iucn.org/theme/protected-areas/about)

[4] Author calculations based on supplementary data from Collins and Mitchard (2017[46]).

[5] Most recently extended through presidential regulation 6/2017.

[6] Government regulation 57/2016 bans the clearance of peatlands for up to 2 years if the government has not yet completed a zoning process. The zoning process essential separates peat areas into 2 zones depending on criteria laid out in the regulation.

[7] Unless the land is officially designated as protection forest (*Hutan Lindung*).

[8] Law 39/2014.

[9] An example of a multilateral agreement limiting illegal trade in other products of relevance to at least some dimensions the land-use nexus (in particular biodiversity) is the Convention on International Trade in Endangered Species of Wild Fauna and Flora (CITES), which encourages measures to curb both supply and demand of illegally traded animal and plant species.

[10] Regulation (EU) No 995/2010 of the European Parliament and of the Council of 20 October 2010

[11] Ley General de Desarrollo Forestal Sustenable, 05/06/2018

[12] (1) Restructuring of rural land holdings (2) commencing to use uncultivated land or semi-natural areas for intensive agriculture and (3) land drainage works on lands used for agriculture (excluding drainage or reclamation of wetlands).

[13] These sectors are: (i) Agriculture; (ii) Forestry; (iii) Fisheries; (iv) Energy; (v) Industry; (vi) Transport; (vii) Waste management; (viii) Water management; (ix) Telecommunications (x); Tourism, Town; and (xi) Country Planning or Land use.

[14] Government Regulation of the Republic of Indonesia No.46 Year 2016 on Procedures for Implementation of Strategic Environmental Assessment (Peraturan Pemerintah Republik Indonesia No.46 Tahun 2016 Tentang tata Cara Penyylenggaraan Kajian Lingkungan Hidup Strategis).

[15] Only approximate number based on OECD PSE database for Brazil, Indonesia, Mexico and New Zealand and figures for CAP spending from the EC in France and Ireland.

16 https://www.waikatoregion.govt.nz/council/policy-and-plans/plans-under-development/healthy-rivers-plan-for-change/infosheets/nitrogen-reference-points/

17 For more details see OECD (2016[94]) *Biodiversity Offsets: Effective Design and Implementation*.

18 Certain types of development are required by law to purchase offsets for unavoidable environmental damage in some countries (see table 5.2).

19 The European Innovation Partnership for Agriculture Productivity and Sustainability, for example, supports a broad range of projects in Ireland. These projects include some conceptually similar to PES, such as the Inishowen Upland Farmers Project, amongst other non-PES projects. For more information see https://www.nationalruralnetwork.ie/eip-agri/.

20 Often referred to as a conditional cash transfer programme.

21 For a policy measure to be deemed decoupled, that production (or trade) not differ from the level that would have occurred in the absence of the measure. For more detailed explanation see (OECD, 2006[213]).

22 Often referred to as an agri-environment-climate scheme.

23 Performance-based means the scheme is targeted at reducing agricultural pressure on the environment. Results-based means the schemes are targeting a specific environmental outcome or outcomes.

24 Since 2015, weakening environmental governance, budget cuts and political instability have led to an increase in deforestation in the Brazilian Amazon.

25 Intergovernmental fiscal transfers consist in the transfer of resources between different governments in the same country, e.g. from one state or regional government to another.

26 These include *inter alia* the requirement that biomass used for biofuel production must not originate from primary forest, protected areas or highly biodiverse grasslands. Wetlands, peatlands and other land with high carbon stock, however, can be used for biomass production under certain circumstances.

27 Directive (EU) 2018/2001

28 OECD (2019[12]), for instance states that on current trends, growing demand for Indonesian palm oil for biofuel production would be met by expansion of harvested area. While the Indonesian government is planning to increase the productivity of already harvested areas, both of these options likely imply adverse impacts on at least some dimensions of the nexus.

29 The PEFC endorsed standards as of 2018 are: Brazil Forest Certification programme (CERFLOR), PEFC France, Indonesia Forestry Certification Cooperation (IFCC), PEFC Ireland and New Zealand Forest Certification Association Inc. (NZFCA).

30 Law 39/2014

31 Commodities covered by these commitments are those accounting for the majority of land-use nexus impacts associated with international trade in the case study countries, namely palm, soy, timber and pulp, and cattle.

32 https://www.origingreen.ie

33 Full list of countries' spending on agricultural knowledge and innovation systems as a percentage of total support estimate in 2015 is as follows: Brazil 25.4% (USD 1.8 billion); European Union (disaggregated

figures for France and Ireland not available) 5.77% (USD 6.2 billion); Indonesia 0.5% (USD 209 million); Mexico 5.19% (USD 394 million); New Zealand 36.5% (USD 182.8 million).

34 The geographic distribution of land needed by 2060 and land used for wasted food is different, so they are not directly replaceable.

35 Land occupation refers to land utilised in the production of these products and in the case of livestock also includes land utilised to produce feed.

36 Agricultural production, postharvest handling and storage, processing, distribution, consumption, end of life.

37 SDG 2: Zero hunger.

38 New Zealand for example lacks national level policy measures to address food waste, and there is no mention of food waste or specific strategies to reduce organic waste in New Zealand's Waste Strategy (Ministry for the Environment, 2010[214]).

39 This directive requests the Commission to adopt legislation on food waste measurement by end-March 2019.

www.ingramcontent.com/pod-product-compliance
Ingram Content Group UK Ltd.
Pitfield, Milton Keynes, MK11 3LW, UK
UKHW051504290926
15471UKWH00008B/1400

9 789264 478015